Representation and
the Electoral College

Representation and the Electoral College

ROBERT M. ALEXANDER

OXFORD

UNIVERSITY PRESS

OXFORD

UNIVERSITY PRESS

Oxford University Press is a department of the University of Oxford. It furthers
the University's objective of excellence in research, scholarship, and education
by publishing worldwide. Oxford is a registered trade mark of Oxford University
Press in the UK and certain other countries.

Published in the United States of America by Oxford University Press
198 Madison Avenue, New York, NY 10016, United States of America.

© Oxford University Press 2019

Library of Congress Cataloging-in-Publication Data
Names: Alexander, Robert M., 1972– author.
Title: Representation and the Electoral College / Robert Alexander.
Description: New York, NY : Oxford University Press, 2019. |
Includes bibliographical references and index.
Identifiers: LCCN 2018043342 (print) | LCCN 2018054115 (ebook) |
ISBN 9780190939441 (Universal PDF) | ISBN 9780190939458 (E-pub) |
ISBN 9780190939465 (Oxford Scholarship Online) |
ISBN 9780190939434 (pbk. : alk. paper) | ISBN 9780190939427 (hardback : alk. paper)
Subjects: LCSH: Electoral college—United States. |
Representative government and representation—United States.
Classification: LCC JK529 (ebook) | LCC JK529 .A694 2019 (print) |
DDC 324.6/3—dc23
LC record available at https://lccn.loc.gov/2018043342

To my grandparents: Annabelle, William, Doc, and Carolyn.
Their smarts and hard work paved the way.

Contents

Acknowledgments

LIKE MANY GOOD ideas, this book can be traced to a conversation over a beer with a friend. I was attending the Republican National Convention in Cleveland, Ohio, as a Faculty Leader through the Washington Center program. The convention was off to an interesting start with Ohio Governor John Kasich refusing to attend the coronation of Donald Trump as the GOP's nominee. Meanwhile, Hillary Clinton was getting a lukewarm reception from supporters of Bernie Sanders in the days before the Democratic National Convention. As it would turn out, Trump and Clinton were among the most disliked presidential candidates in polling history. In the following days, I wrote an op-ed suggesting that their poor favorability ratings could translate into faithless votes in the Electoral College. Having surveyed electors in each of the past four elections, I had found an appetite among a significant number of electors to defect in each of those contests. The 2016 meeting of the Electoral College did indeed yield an historic number of faithless votes (as detailed in Chapter 7).

Given the candidacies of Trump and Clinton, I was discussing the possibility of a potential Electoral College revolt with Steve Caliendo at Mike's Bar and Grille in Berea, and he was amazed that my research on electors was not universally known. The Electoral College is often treated as a footnote among many political scientists. Although many are familiar with the importance of the institution, few scholars devote attention to it. Steve suggested that I needed to think more broadly about approaching my data on electors. After all, the Electoral College is an institution intersecting many areas of American politics—campaigns, voting behavior, federalism, and *representation*. In that "aha" moment, I decided to examine the Electoral College in the context of representation.

The purpose of the study is to help readers understand the ways in which the institution does or does not align with expectations relating to representative democracy. The Electoral College has a long history and has been the subject of controversy from its inception. The Framers struggled mightily with the problem of selecting the nation's chief executive. Many of the arguments made in 1789 persist to this day. Examining those arguments relative to norms of representation provides an opportunity to appropriately evaluate the Electoral College process.

This book represents a very long journey. As a graduate student, Lillard Richardson reminded me that presidential electors were real people and that scholars knew very little about them. Without his prompting, I never would have sought to examine them. I have benefited greatly from the tutelage of Tony Nownes. My "academic dad" has been an outstanding mentor and friend. He has provided considerable help with this research over the years. The political science honor society, Pi Sigma Alpha, awarded multiple chapter activity grants to help fund each of my surveys of presidential electors. I would like to thank Sean Twombly, Jim Lengle, Nancy McManus, and members of the Chapter Activity Grant Award Committee for their help and support over the years.

Such an effort would not have been possible without the assistance of many excellent students from Ohio Northern University. I have been fortunate to have remarkable students who are excited to learn and eager to please. I owe each of these students a deep debt of gratitude: Rebecca Boler, Lisa Bradley, Jessica Brasee, Troy Brinkman, David Brown, Zachary Bushatz, Kara Calomeni, Doug Chapel, Alexis Cobb, John Curiel, Christopher Difrancesco, Adam Downing, Elizabeth Drummond, Zac Esterline, Tiffany Ferry, Christine Frankart, Adam Gallagher, Dakotah Gray, Ross Grilliot, Anna Hoard, Jennifer Jameson, Jason Kaseman, Brittani Knisely, Maggie Koch, Steve Kochheiser, Jesse Longbrake, Tina Loughry, Melissa Mead, Robert Moorman, Kelly Morman, Matthew Oyster, Shaili Patel, Taylor Phillips, Derek Price, Robert Putnam, Dexter Ridgway, Stephen Saunier, Heather Stassen, Brad Stoll, Barbara Tate, Jamie Uppenkamp, Daniel Warren, and Benjamin Wollet.

I will forever be indebted to Jennifer Carpenter and David McBride, my editors at Oxford University Press. I am thankful for their collaboration and belief in this project. Holly Mitchell's guidance throughout the process has been a delight. I am also thankful to Rajesh Kathamuthu, Wendy Walker, Sangeetha Vishwanthan, and Seth Cotterman for their attention to detail which improved the book. This project also benefited greatly from the five anonymous reviewers during its early stages. As a first-generation college graduate whose grandparents had no more than an eighth-grade education, I am overwhelmed and overjoyed to publish with OUP.

My sincere appreciation is also due to the multitude of presidential electors who responded to the surveys over the years. Many went far beyond simply answering questions, providing additional information and insights and offering to answer any additional questions beyond those asked in their survey. I am also thankful to Derek Muller, James McCrone, and Kyle Cheney for their shared devotion to understanding the Electoral College—especially throughout the 2016 election cycle. Sometimes, it is nice to know that you are not alone. I must acknowledge that most all of this book was written with Radiohead, Weezer, Cake, or the Foo Fighters in the background. Thank God for music.

Lastly, I wish to thank my absolutely wonderful support network, from my colleagues at ONU to my friends from high school, college, and graduate school—I have been truly blessed. Obviously, one can neither obtain nor enjoy success alone. Nowhere can this be seen more than from my family. My parents, Bob and Phyllis Alexander, showed me what hard work really looks like. More important, they showed me love. I have always known that they would be there for me, regardless of the situation, and for that I am forever thankful. I have tried to serve as a similar inspiration to my children—Olivia, Anabel, and Amelia. I hope to have taught them the values of hard work, perseverance, and work/life balance. I am thankful that they have always had the ability to keep me grounded and to serve as constant reminders of what is truly important in life. Finally, my wife, Shelleigh, continues to be my biggest fan. From reminding me to eat to talking me through a thorny issue, her help and insights have been extraordinarily beneficial. I came to rely on our morning "coffee talks" to maintain my focus and my sanity. Without her selflessness, love, support, and encouragement this book would not have been possible. Thank you.

I

Introduction

THE 2016 PRESIDENTIAL election was among the most controversial and unpredictable contests in American history. Hillary Clinton (former First Lady, senator from New York, and Secretary of State) was heavily favored to win the presidency in the months, weeks, and days preceding the election. She appeared poised to become the first female president as polls across the country indicated she enjoyed comfortable margins over her foe, mogul Donald J. Trump (who had never held elected office). The day of the election Nate Silver's 538.com forecast gave Clinton a 71 percent chance to win the presidency with 302 electoral votes to Trump's 236.

Trump had run an unconventional campaign—refusing at one point to debate fellow Republicans during the primary season, spending very little campaign money throughout the election cycle, frequently claiming that the electoral process is rigged, and brazenly attacking Clinton as well as fellow Republicans. In a decidedly anti-Washington era, Trump capitalized on his lack of political experience and called on Americans to wreck the Washington establishment. On the day of the election few experts gave him a chance to win the presidency. However, as election returns started to come in, it became increasingly clear that he did indeed have a chance. Close races in Michigan, Wisconsin, and Pennsylvania indicated that it was Clinton and not Trump who was going to have a difficult path to the presidency. A few hours later, in a stunning turn of events, Trump was addressing the country as the president-elect, while Clinton was preparing a concession speech for the following day.

The surprises did not end that evening. Within days, it became clear that Clinton was likely to claim more votes across the country than Trump. When all the votes were counted, Clinton ended up with nearly 3 million more votes than Trump. The 2016 election marked the sixth time a candidate ascended to the presidency while losing the popular vote to an opponent. Trump's victory took many by surprise, and his path to the presidency was the subject of great criticism. Four years earlier, Trump famously tweeted that "the electoral college is a disaster for a democracy" and "This election is a total sham and a travesty. We are not a democracy!" (Donald J. Trump, November 7, 2012). Minutes later, he tweeted the following call for action: "Let's fight like hell and stop this great and disgusting injustice! The world is laughing at us" (Donald J. Trump, 2012). Four years later, he changed his tune. A week after his victory, he tweeted, "The Electoral College is actually genius in that it brings all states, including the smaller ones, into play. Campaigning is much different!" (Donald J. Trump, November 15, 2016).

After a brief respite, the Electoral College once again featured prominently in discussions across the United States and the world. The 2016 campaign highlighted a number of issues commonly debated regarding the Electoral College. The popular/electoral vote split was chief among the arguments in the wake of the election. Americans were quickly reminded that the presidential election consists of a state-by-state tally of votes, rather than a national popular election. Clinton received 48 percent of all votes cast to Trump's 45.9 percent. This was in near perfect alignment with Silver's final 538.com forecast—48.5 percent for Clinton and 45 percent for Trump (Silver, November 8, 2016). Yet, *where* those votes were cast was critical in determining the outcome of the election.

Trump won 30 states (and Maine's 2nd congressional district) to Clinton's 20 states and the District of Columbia. Victories in Wisconsin, Michigan, Pennsylvania, and Florida were key to Trump's gaining an Electoral College majority. His margins of victory in these states were slim: he won Wisconsin, Michigan, and Pennsylvania by less than 1 percent of all votes cast in those states and Florida by just 1.2 percent of all votes cast in the state. These four states accounted for 75 electoral votes. For some perspective, it is worth noting that about 20 percent of voters make up their minds in the final two weeks of a presidential campaign (Box and Giammo, 2009–2010, 335). These "late deciders" typically are less partisan and less knowledgeable and care less about election outcomes than those who make their decisions earlier in the campaign (Box and Giammo, 2009–2010, 340). Late deciders are notoriously capricious. In a close race, they very well could change an election from one candidate to another based on very little information, little partisan attachment, and little interest in the outcomes of the race. A change in just 1 percent in those key states would have swung the election to Clinton with 307 electoral votes to Trump's 231 (and a 3 million vote margin in the popular vote as well). Combined with the popular vote total, such an Electoral College outcome would have been precisely in line with most predictions for the race. Recall that Silver's final forecast had Clinton winning the Electoral College with 302 votes to Trump's 236, along with a 2 to 3 percent nod in the popular vote (Silver, November 8, 2016).

Of course, this is not what happened. Instead, we witnessed the largest discrepancy between the popular vote winner and the electoral vote winner in American history. In spite of Clinton winning the popular vote 48 percent to 45.9 percent, Trump won 56.5 percent of all electoral votes cast to Clinton's 42 percent. Trump was quick to note that if the election were based on the popular vote, he would have campaigned very differently. He maintained that because of the rules of the Electoral College, he ran a campaign to win electoral votes, not popular votes.

The fractious outcome led to a movement to unseat Trump in the days and weeks after the general election. Nearly 5 million people signed a Change.com petition asking presidential electors to vote for Hillary Clinton (Change.com, December 19, 2016). A related but separate campaign emerged *within* the Electoral College. Members of the Electoral College calling themselves "Hamilton Electors" engaged in a campaign to lobby fellow electors to abandon Trump in favor of a consensus Republican candidate. While the campaign was not successful, ten electors tried to exert their independence and strayed from their party's nominees. Two electors were removed and one more changed his mind and voted for his party's nominee. Ultimately, seven electors joined the ranks of so-called faithless electors. Apart from the death of a candidate during the interregnum period, this marked the largest number of rogue votes in American history. Lastly, while rare, we saw a state split its electoral votes between candidates for the second time in the last three elections. Trump was able to claim one electoral vote in Maine. Barack Obama was able to claim a single electoral vote in Nebraska in the 2008 election. While many states consider district or proportional representation schemes, these are the only two states that currently allocate their electoral votes in this fashion. This fact has a profound effect on presidential campaigns.

To be sure, the 2016 election experienced just about everything when it comes to the Electoral College. As expected, calls for its abolition, modification, and maintenance accompanied the tumultuous campaign season. Although often treated as an afterthought, the 2016 election reminded observers that the institution is at the center of presidential elections. Most arguments supporting and opposing the Electoral College come down to notions of whom it ultimately represents. This book sets out to examine the Electoral College as it relates to representation.

The Mechanics of the Electoral College

The Electoral College consists of 538 electoral votes. This number corresponds to the representation each state is afforded in the House of Representatives (435 electoral votes), which is based on the population of each state, combined with two votes each state is afforded based on its representation in the US Senate (100 electoral votes). The 23rd Amendment to the US Constitution provides that the District of Columbia receives representation in the Electoral College (three electoral votes). It indicates that while the District may have electors, it may have no more electors than the state with the fewest electors. Regardless of the District's population, it will never have more votes than the least populous state. For the foreseeable future, it would appear that the District will be relegated to three electoral votes, regardless of its population. Only a new amendment providing so would change this feature.

Electoral votes are awarded on a state-by-state basis. Essentially, 51 individual elections occur throughout the states (and the District of Columbia) to determine how electoral votes are awarded. For all states but two (Maine and Nebraska), if a ticket wins a plurality of votes in a state, it claims *all* of the state's electoral votes. To win the presidency, a ticket must earn a majority of all electoral votes in the Electoral College (270). If no ticket earns a majority, the House of Representatives is tasked with selecting the president from among the top three candidates receiving electoral votes in the Electoral College. Each state votes as a unit, and a majority of state delegations is needed to win the presidency. Interestingly, the Senate is tasked with selecting the vice president from among the top two candidates receiving Electoral College votes for vice president. This is due to the 12th Amendment.

Employing the House and Senate to determine the size and nature of the Electoral College is considered to be a means to achieve balance between more populated states and less populated states in the selection of the nation's chief executive. This is because the House apportions representation based on population and all states have equal representation in the Senate with two senators. This is a prime example of how important the notion of representation is to the Electoral College. In practice, this feature can lead to great disparities in the relative voting power of citizens across the country. For instance, in 2016, California had 55 electoral votes compared to Wyoming's 3. On first glance, this would seem to convey great voting power for the Golden State. Yet, when one translates electoral votes per person, we see that in the 2016 election, one electoral vote in California was equal to approximately 720,000 people and one electoral vote in Wyoming was equal to approximately 196,000 people. The constant two Senate votes provided to each state has the effect of increasing a less populated state's per-person voting power relative to more populated states in the Electoral College. This is a feature that many opponents of the institution often criticize as being undemocratic. Others argue that without this feature, campaigns would mainly take part in more populated states, with little attention devoted to less populated states. Much more will be said about these arguments later.

The term "Electoral College" is actually a bit confusing. It is not one "college," but 51 "colleges" where electors from each of the 50 states and the District of Columbia cast one vote for president and one vote for vice president. The term "college" simply means assemblage. Electors meet for one purpose and one purpose only—to select the president and vice president. Once they have done so, their duties are completed and each state's college is disbanded.

The Constitution indicates that state legislatures control how electors are chosen. There is no mandate that electors are chosen by the citizenry, nor are they constitutionally required to vote in accordance with the popular vote in their respective states. In the earliest presidential elections, several state legislatures selected the electors, rather than having them selected by a popular vote. With each succeeding election, more and more state legislatures devolved elector selection to the citizenry. By 1876 all states chose their electors by a popular ballot. This is important to note, as the Electoral College has been subject to many attempts to *democratize* it. This is one way in which the institution has indeed become more democratized over the years. Still, rather than directly voting for president and vice president, Americans vote for slates of electors who are committed to a specific party ticket. These electors are then entrusted with the duty of casting their votes for the party ticket when they meet about a month after the general election takes place. To this day, then, citizens continue to *indirectly* select the president and vice president when they cast their ballots in the general election.

All but two states apportion their electoral votes by means of the "winner-take-all" or unit rule. This means that whichever ticket receives the most votes in a state wins *all* of the state's electoral votes. This is true whether the margin is large or razor thin. In 2000, Al Gore received 2,912,253 votes to George W. Bush's 2,912,790 votes in Florida (a 537-vote difference out of nearly 6 million votes cast). Because of the winner-take-all feature, Gore received exactly zero votes in the Electoral College from the state. Critics charge that the winner-take-all method of awarding electoral votes often fails to accurately reflect statewide election results and has important negative implications regarding representation.

The unit rule is one of the reasons why popular vote margins can diverge from Electoral College vote margins. A candidate's margin of victory simply does not change his or her electoral vote total in winner-take-all states. Winning the state is what matters. This was the case for George W. Bush in Florida. Regardless of whether he had won the state by 500 votes or by 5 million votes, he would have earned all of Florida's 27 electoral votes. In most elections, this feature tends to magnify the winning ticket's vote margins. For instance, Bill Clinton won 43 percent of the popular vote in 1992 but 69 percent of the Electoral College vote. As noted, while Trump earned 45.9 percent of the popular vote in 2016, he claimed 56 percent of the Electoral College vote. Differences between the popular and electoral vote are mostly due to the influence of the winner-take-all feature most states employ.

As noted, Maine and Nebraska have adopted the "district plan." In this model, each congressional district is up for grabs. The ticket receiving the most votes in a congressional district wins that district. The ticket with the most votes across the state claims the two "bonus" electoral votes for that state. Many contend this is a fairer means to apportion electoral votes. It allows for interests within a state to gain some level of representation when they may otherwise have no chance to win an electoral vote if they were to use the unit rule. For instance, in 2008, John McCain overwhelmingly won Nebraska (56 percent to 41 percent). However, Obama was able to obtain one electoral vote in the state due to his strong showing in Omaha's congressional district. In 2016, Trump bested Clinton in 7 of Illinois's 18 congressional districts. However, because of Clinton's overwhelming support from urban areas, the popular vote total in the state was not even close. Therefore, Clinton was able to claim all 20 of Illinois's electoral votes, although significant pockets of support existed for Trump in the state. This is a chief reason why deviations occur between the popular and electoral vote in presidential elections.

Proponents of the district plan suggest it more accurately reflects the electorate's wishes. It can lead to more competition and it democratizes the process. Over the years, several states have considered moving to the district plan. After the 2012 election, Florida, Michigan, Ohio, Virginia, Pennsylvania, and Wisconsin considered changing their allocation of electoral votes to proportional or district plans (Liebelson, 2013). While these efforts received considerable attention, none of these states changed how they apportioned their electoral votes for the 2016 election. In the wake of the 2016 election, state representatives in Pennsylvania once again introduced legislation to award their electoral votes based on the district plan. Many of these efforts lose momentum because they are seen to weaken the power of political parties by making conditions easier for third parties or local "sons" or "daughters" to win electoral votes and potentially become spoilers in the national election.

Once electors are selected, be it by the winner-take-all method or the district plan, they are then charged with translating their state's vote into the electoral vote. That no constitutional requirement exists binding electors to the outcome of the popular vote vexes many observers of the presidential selection process. Still, almost all electors follow the will of voters in their state. Less than 1 percent of all electors have cast so-called faithless votes over the course of presidential elections. Whether faithless electors are being *faithful* to the Constitution or not was a widely debated topic in the aftermath of the 2016 election.

Ten electors attempted to cast faithless votes when the Electoral College convened in December 2016. Two of those electors were immediately replaced and their votes were not counted. Another rogue elector was asked to reconsider his vote for Bernie Sanders and on a second ballot cast it for Clinton instead. Still, seven electors cast faithless votes (five Democrats and two Republicans). These seven faithless votes represented anywhere between 1 and 2 million votes cast in the general election. Writing about his faithless vote weeks after the election, an elector who cast his vote for Ron Paul contended he was being faithful to the Constitution (Greene, January 7, 2017). He argued that the general election was more like a "straw poll" so that electors could get a feeling about what the country was thinking (Greene, 2017). For him, it was an elector's duty, not the citizenry's, to determine who should be selected as the president and vice president of the United States. I examine this claim in much greater detail in Chapters 6 and 7. I argue that most Americans do not believe they are leaving the selection of the president up to virtually anonymous electors who do not appear on ballots throughout the country. Indeed, many Americans are dismayed when they learn that electors may cast faithless votes.

Common Arguments Concerning the Electoral College

There are many arguments supporting and opposing various features of the Electoral College.[1] Writing about the institution in *Federalist 68*, Alexander

---

1. For a more complete treatment of arguments enveloping the institution, please see Bugh (2010b), Kimberling (1992), and Schumaker and Loomis (2002a).

Hamilton famously stated that the "the mode of appointment of the Chief Magistrate of the United States is almost the only part of the system, of any consequence, which has escaped without severe censure, or which has received the slightest mark of approbation from its opponents." He went further, boldly claiming that when it came to selecting the president, "if the manner of it be not perfect, it is at least excellent" (*Federalist 68*). In spite of Hamilton's enthusiasm for the Electoral College, it has been one of the most controversial institutions in all of American politics.

Advocates of the Electoral College argue that it promotes political stability by supporting the two-party system, requires candidates to generate broad voting coalitions, guards against the tyranny of more populated areas over less populated areas, maintains the federal system of representation, and curtails electoral fraud. Opponents charge that the institution violates political equality, fails to accurately translate the public's will, produces "wrong winners," discourages widespread political participation, and invites chicanery due to the potential for faithless electors. Each of these arguments is intimately related to how one operationalizes representation. It is worth discussing each of these claims in greater detail.

Arguments for the Electoral College

Support for the two-party system has a long tradition among political scientists. In 1950, the American Political Science Association released a report emphasizing the importance of a vibrant two-party system in the United States. The report concluded that an effective two-party system works to educate voters, simplify issues, effectively recruit candidates, run campaigns and helps organize legislatures to make public policy. It is argued that reliance on this system provides a relatively easy means for voters to hold the parties accountable at the ballot box. Multiparty systems and coalition governments are presumed to be more unstable and make it difficult to determine which party is to take credit or blame for public policies that are enacted.

In spite of the support of political scientists, many Americans express frustration with the two-party system. In 2015, 60 percent of Americans agreed that a third party was needed in the United States to ensure adequate representation (McCarthy, 2015). Support for third-party candidates has ebbed and flowed over time, with Ross Perot's candidacy in 1992 serving as the last major bid to win the presidency. In that election, nearly one in five Americans voted for the Texas billionaire with no governing experience, yet he failed to receive a single Electoral College vote. Institutional barriers (such as the

Electoral College) make it very difficult for third parties to be successful in the United States.

The winner-take-all process that most states employ to award their electoral votes is mostly responsible for producing two viable choices among voters. In accordance with Maurice Duverger's (1954) observations many years ago, single-member, winner-take-all systems result in two-party dominance. States are free to award their electoral votes as they see fit. Awarding them according to the unit rule most assuredly works toward the maintenance of the two-party system. As previously discussed, state legislatures sometimes consider alternative methods to award their electoral votes. Proportional representation and the district plan are the most common plans states mull. However, due to potential political fallout from a perceived power grab or the simple recognition that the unit rule helps maintain the two-party system, no state has changed its allocation of electoral votes since Maine did in 1992.

A related argument speaking to political stability is that the Electoral College forces candidates to create broad voting coalitions. This argument is closely tied to those supporting the institution as a bulwark to protect federalism. Proponents argue that without the Electoral College, campaigns would only take place in urban areas, with great attention devoted to states such as New York and California. To be sure, in my studies of presidential electors, one told me that "without the Electoral College, all we'd see is the underside of his plane on his way to New York or California—if you have a set of binoculars" (personal interview, April 16, 2004).

The constant two electoral votes afforded by the Constitution to *all states* regardless of their population gives greater voting power per capita to less populated states. Supporters argue that this feature requires candidates to visit more states and build broad-based coalitions. Thus, candidates need to appeal to both more populated and less populated states. The argument suggests that the Electoral College ensures that less populated states cannot be ignored in presidential campaigns.

In spite of such claims, candidates rarely visit sparsely populated states. Wyoming, Rhode Island, Idaho, Montana, and Alaska are routinely ignored by presidential campaigns. They do not receive campaign visits, nor are they the targets of campaign advertising. The most populated states are also eschewed by presidential campaigns. In 2016, four of the five most populated states (California, New York, Texas, and Illinois) received virtually no attention by the Trump and Clinton campaigns. Instead, the battleground states of Florida, Ohio, North Carolina, and Pennsylvania received the bulk of campaign advertising and campaign visits.

It is the Electoral College (and particularly the unit rule) that has created the occurrence of battleground or swing states. Candidates rightly focus their campaign resources in those states that are competitive. The more electoral votes nested within a closely contested state, the greater the attention among contenders for the presidency. The unit rule's requirement that the candidate receiving the most votes in a state receives all of a state's electoral votes makes these swing states especially important. If battleground states were to award their electoral votes via proportional representation, it is thought that this would most likely dampen their influence in presidential elections. Although some states have considered changing how they award their electoral votes, they recognize the benefit in maintaining the winner-take-all allocation of their electoral votes in order to be attractive to presidential campaigns.

In short, rather than campaigning across the country, typically candidates target no more than a dozen states. Yet a good argument could be made that if swing states are representative of the nation as a whole, then current electoral strategies caused by the Electoral College system create an efficient means of campaigning in a large republic. Chapter 4 takes up such arguments in greater detail.

The emphasis on the role of states in the Electoral College process is considered to be one of the bedrock principles among advocates of the institution. They contend that the Electoral College protects the principle of federalism. As we shall see in Chapter 3, the Framers were very much concerned with the relationship between the national government and the states. Proponents contend that the Electoral College represents one of many compromises to assuage those concerned with the power of a strong national sovereign. The push and pull between national and state power has been a common thread throughout American history, and the Electoral College is seen as an important fortification to protect states from the power of the national government. Any move to undo the Electoral College would be viewed as a move toward greater power at the federal level, and many Americans are uncomfortable with that proposition.

Yet many have criticized the emphasis on federalism proponents give to the Framers' intentions when it comes to the Electoral College. Jack Rakove (2000, A35) notes that rather than an endorsement of federalism, the Electoral College simply "replicated other political compromises that the Constitutional Convention had already made." Others point out that citizens should look to the composition of the legislature rather than the one nationally elected figure (the president) if they are concerned about institutional protections of federalism. Neal Peirce bluntly argues that "the vitality of federalism rests chiefly on the constitutionally mandated system of congressional representation and the will and capacity of state and local governments to address compelling problems, not on the hocus-pocus of an eighteenth-century vote count system" (quoted in Edwards, 2004, 116).

Lastly, advocates of the Electoral College often contend that it works to curtail and contain voter fraud. The Florida recount in the 2000 election is commonly invoked in support of this argument. The thought of a national recount is disconcerting to many Americans. Because electoral rather than popular votes matter most, supporters assert that voter fraud can be contained at state and local levels. Closely contested states can be placed under a microscope if allegations of fraud emerge. It is argued that tracking voter fraud across the nation would be too difficult for election officials. However, others suggest that voter fraud would be *less likely* under a national popular vote. Jamin Raskin asserts that having 51 separate elections actually incentivizes attempts to manipulate the vote as actors can be more strategic in where they seek to manipulate the vote (2008, 189). Similarly, George Edwards (2004) argues that a national vote would take a herculean effort to either suppress or inflate vote totals. Echoing this point, Matthew Streb notes that while states can be and have been decided by infinitesimal margins, close national vote margins have been measured in hundreds of thousands, rather than thousands or hundreds. He states: "A recount was needed in Florida because 537 votes separated Bush and Gore. Recounts could have occurred in Iowa, New Mexico, and Wisconsin as well, because only a few hundred votes separated the candidates. Yet, there was no need for a recount nationwide, since Gore had more than a 537,000 vote lead over Bush" (2016, 167). Rather than seeking to alter outcomes in states with hundreds of thousands of voters, conspirators would need to alter outcomes in a pot of over 100 million voters from across the country.

Arguments Against the Electoral College

In many ways, the perceived benefits of the Electoral College are seen as the root of many of its perceived problems. For instance, the desire to protect the rights of states is seen to be at odds with political equality among citizens. Political equality is among the chief concerns critics of the Electoral College have about the institution. Toward this end, opponents contend that the Electoral College violates the principle of one person, one vote; discourages participation; has the potential to produce "wrong winners"; and invites mischief from potential faithless electors.

One of the institution's greatest critics, George Edwards, observes that a "central theme of American history is in fact the democratization of the Constitution. What began as a document characterized by numerous restrictions on direct voter participation has slowly become much more democratic" (2004, 33). Examples of the movement toward greater democratization abound. Ensuring suffrage for African Americans and women is among the most obvious illustrations of this fact. The 17th Amendment's provision that senators be elected directly by the citizenry rather than indirectly by state legislatures is another significant change toward greater democratization. While not tied to the Constitution, the rise of direct democracy within the states is another means where decision making has devolved toward greater direct citizen participation.

The Electoral College is not a democratic institution, nor was it intended to be. Yet, as Robert Dahl notes, political equality is a fundamental feature of American democracy. He asserts that "every member must have an equal and effective opportunity to vote, and all votes must be counted as equal" (2003, 37). The US Supreme Court decisions *Baker v. Carr* and *Reynolds v. Sims* emphasize political equality in congressional elections. In particular, these cases require state legislatures to take into account the principle of one person, one vote when drawing congressional districts. The effect of these cases was to provide greater representation to urban areas relative to rural areas. This is consistent with concerns over how changes to the Electoral College would affect representation geographically throughout the country.

As noted, the "bonus two" electoral votes awarded for each state based on its statehood has the effect of inflating the voting power of citizens in less populated states. Voters in Wyoming currently have nearly five times the voting power of voters in Texas. Many examples of this phenomenon exist across the states. When considering the Electoral College, one person most assuredly does not equal one vote. It is argued that this feature violates the basic tenet of political equality. Yet the Senate itself also violates the practice of one person, one vote. Defenders of the institution point out that because the Electoral College incorporates the addition of two additional Senate votes, it is consistent with the same practice that provides for state equality in the Senate and therefore should not be changed.

A related criticism is that rather than working to protect the power of less populated states or preserving the power of more populated states, it is swing states that have gained undue attention from national tickets. Many recognize that candidates themselves do not treat the states equally. Daron Shaw (2006) has convincingly documented the inordinate focus candidates give to swing states in terms of campaign advertising and candidate visits. Voters in uncompetitive states seldom see the candidates and typically see few, if any, campaign advertisements. Conversely, residents in battleground states see candidates crisscrossing their states multiple times in the campaign's final stretch. Lipsitz suggests that such behavior affects participation patterns across the states. Specifically, she found evidence that voters in swing states are more likely than voters in non-swing states to go to the polls in competitive campaign cycles (2009, 203). Thus, voter participation appears to be affected in part by the Electoral College process.

Schumaker and Loomis note that "electoral rules do matter, as different procedures can produce different winners of presidential elections" (2002b, 203). One consequence of the current Electoral College system as practiced in the states is the potential that a ticket can win the presidency while losing the popular vote across the country. This "wrong winner" scenario has come to be known as a "misfire" election. Nearly 1 in 10 presidential elections has ended in a misfire. The potential for misfires has actually been more of a norm than an exception. In almost half of all presidential contests, a shift in a relatively small number of votes scattered across one or a few states would have resulted in either a different winner or a contingent election due to no candidate receiving a majority of the electoral vote. While rare, popular/electoral vote splits do happen and have come close to occurring far more often than most recognize. Proponents of the Electoral College might take umbrage with the term "misfire" and suggest that the system has actually worked as intended—given the emphasis on federalism over democracy as embodied by the Electoral College. Yet it is fair to say that issues of legitimacy arise when candidates who lose the popular vote across the country ascend to the nation's only nationally elected office. Chapter 5 examines this issue in greater detail.

A final concern opponents note is the potential for mischief among presidential electors. Most Americans are quite surprised to learn they indirectly select the president and vice president of the United States. That surprise turns to disdain when they learn that no federal mandate exists requiring electors to vote according to the popular vote in their respective states. Over time, efforts to bind electors to the popular vote have occurred in a number of states. However, the constitutionality of laws to bind electors remains unclear.

For many Americans, concern over presidential electors is not particularly pressing. Almost all electors vote as anticipated. Nonetheless, faithless electors have occurred in 10 of the last 18 presidential elections. Often outside of the public's eye, major campaigns have emerged to entice electors to change election outcomes in recent presidential contests. In the most recent misfire elections (2000 and 2016) electors faced a barrage of requests to honor the national popular vote over the Electoral College vote. Although they did not affect election outcomes, faithless electors occurred in both of those contests. Because each electoral vote represents hundreds of thousands of votes cast in the general election, large numbers of citizens are effectively disenfranchised by the actions of faithless electors. For many, the office of presidential elector is obsolete and should be abolished. This is in line with the push toward greater democratization of the Constitution discussed earlier. Remarking on the office of presidential elector in 1961, John F. Kennedy stated the following (Judson, 2016):

> The area where I do think we perhaps could get some improvements would be in providing that the electors would be bound by the results of the State elections. I think that that would be a useful step forward. The electors, after all—the people vote, they assume the votes are going to be cast in the way which reflects the judgments of a majority of the people of the State. And therefore, I think it would be useful to have that automatic, and not set up this independent group who could vote for the candidate who carried the State or not, depending on their own personal views.

The potential for mischief among presidential electors is disconcerting to politicians and laypeople alike. Elector fidelity also figures prominently in any discussion of the notion of representation and the Electoral College.

A Controversial Institution

The many arguments enveloping the Electoral College confirm that it has been one of the most controversial institutions in all of American politics. Gary Bugh concludes that there have been at least 772 electoral amendments introduced to change or abolish the Electoral College since 1789 (2010b, 84). This does not include statutes at the state level meant to impact the Electoral College process. By most accounts, no other federal institution has witnessed more attempts to amend or abolish it.

Indeed, a major flaw in the Electoral College process was detected by just the third presidential election. The Framers did not foresee the emergence of party tickets and their subsequent effects on the presidential selection process. Originally, presidential electors cast two votes for president. The candidate with the highest number of electoral votes was chosen as the president and the runner-up was selected as the vice president. As Robert Bennett (quoted in Bugh, 2010b, 187) notes: "George Washington was the consensus choice to be the nation's first president, but in the midst of his tenure it became clear that for the choice of later presidents the selection process set out in the Constitution was unlikely to proceed as anticipated." The rise of the Federalists and the Democratic-Republicans revealed a problem with the original process that came to a head in the election of 1800.

In that election, Thomas Jefferson and Aaron Burr both ran on the Democratic-Republican ticket while John Adams and Charles Pinckney ran on the Federalist ticket. Jefferson and Adams were considered to be the head of their respective party tickets. When the Electoral College met, Democratic-Republican electors cast one vote each for Jefferson and Burr. Federalist electors did the same for Adams and Pinckney. In total, Jefferson and Burr each received 73 electoral votes compared to 65 votes for Adams and 64 votes for Pinckney. The Constitution made no distinction in electoral votes between president and vice president. Instead, the top two candidates receiving votes were to become president and vice president. Because electors cast the same number of ballots for both Jefferson and Burr, no candidate had a majority of Electoral College votes. Consequently, the election was thrown into the House of Representatives. Many Federalists in the House were intent on denying Jefferson the presidency and subsequently deadlocked 35 times. On the 36th ballot and with some encouragement by Alexander Hamilton, the House selected Jefferson as president. Hamilton, no fan of Jefferson, weighed in on the situation, arguing that while he did not like Jefferson's principles, at least he had some. Conversely, he wrote that Burr was "bankrupt beyond redemption except by the plunder of his country" (Weller, Lubin, and Gould, 2016).

The legislature quickly took action and the 12th Amendment was adopted in 1804. Among other things, it required electors to cast one vote for president and one vote for vice president. The election of 1800 is also noteworthy because it dramatically changed the role of presidential electors. Instead of being chosen for their judgment, electors were to be selected for their loyalty. The emergence of party tickets transformed the office of elector from one of independence to one of servitude to the party.

In just over a decade of its existence, the Electoral College resulted in a constitutional crisis and underwent a major transformation. Continued efforts to amend or abolish the institution have occurred since. Two significant changes have occurred at the national level as a result of these efforts. The first, the Electoral Count Act of 1887, was born out of the 1876 election.

That contest has come to be seen as one of the most controversial presidential elections in American history. In that race, Samuel Tilden won the popular vote over Rutherford B. Hayes but failed to secure a majority of Electoral College votes. Tilden was just one electoral vote short of an Electoral College victory. Complicating matters, political parties in three states claimed that their ticket was the winner in those states. Additionally, an elector in Oregon was disqualified and removed from office. Altogether, this left 20 electoral votes in dispute. In what came to be known as the Compromise of 1877, Hayes was awarded all 20 of the electoral votes and the presidency. In return, Hayes was to remove federal troops from Southern states. After a decade of debate, Congress passed the Electoral Count Act of 1887. The act codified a process to determine disputed electoral votes. In short, unless both houses of Congress dispute the submission of a state's electoral vote tally, the certified vote submitted by a state's executive official is to be counted.

The second major change at the national level occurred with the passage of the 23rd Amendment, which was ratified in 1961. The amendment provides that the District of Columbia receives representation in the Electoral College but no more than the least populated state. At the time, the political effects did not appear to advantage one party over the other. However, the District has since voted overwhelmingly for Democrats and has come to be counted on as reliably in the column for Democrats.

Taken together, these changes have dramatically altered the original vision of the Electoral College, emphasizing the dominance of political parties and the will of the people. While its operation has evolved, the body has remained largely intact, even in the face of considerable opposition. Gallup surveys have dependably shown that Americans, by a two-to-one margin, would like to scrap the Electoral College in favor of a popular vote (Gallup, 2000). In 1968, at the height of the movement to abolish the institution, 81 percent of Americans favored doing so (Gallup, 2000).

In spite of the tumult of the 2016 election, support for the Electoral College actually *increased* in the days after the election. In 2011, 35 percent of Americans supported keeping the Electoral College. Less than a month after the 2016 election, that number had swollen to 47 percent, the highest amount of support for the institution that Gallup had ever registered (Gallup, 2016). This increased support for the institution was mostly due to Republican voters. That same poll found that just 19 percent of Republicans favored a national popular vote. This is in stark contrast to surveys of Republicans on the topic in the not-so-distant past. In 2004, 49 percent of Republicans favored a national popular vote and, in 2011, 54 percent preferred basing the winner on direct election (Gallup, 2016). An outcome benefitting one's own party likely has much to do with this change in support for the Electoral College process.

In his 2004 polemic *Why the Electoral College is Bad for America*, George Edwards was puzzled that Americans did not take to the streets after George W. Bush's narrow victory in 2000. He wrote that in that contest, "the election of a president of the United States hung exclusively on a totally arbitrary, largely irrational eighteenth-century counting system" (2004, ix). He concluded that the razor-thin victory, Florida recounts, reliance on election observers to count various types of chads, and the involvement of the Supreme Court would surely invite change to the process. Yet, while some protests occurred, there seemed to be little energy to change the process. He lamented that in the immediate aftermath, very few called for reform.

Another popular/electoral vote split just four elections later presented a very different outcome. With the election of Trump over Clinton, protests erupted in many cities throughout the country. In New York, Seattle, and Chicago, hundreds of thousands of protestors took to the streets to rally against both the Electoral College and the prospect of a Trump presidency (Jaffe, 2016). The election came as a tremendous surprise to most observers, as public opinion polls had pointed to a convincing Clinton victory in the Electoral College. On the campaign trail, Trump had engaged in heated rhetoric that many suggested was racist, xenophobic, and divisive. Combined with his lack of experience and his surprising victory, a great sense of unease took hold of many who protested in the days after the election (Jaffe, 2016).

In addition to civil unrest, several more systematic efforts were immediately undertaken to reform the Electoral College process. Within weeks of the election, California Senator Barbara Boxer introduced a bill to abolish the Electoral College in favor of a national popular vote (Wire, 2016). Like most bills before it, it was never considered by the legislature. At the same time, the National Popular Vote Interstate Compact (NPV) gained renewed momentum among detractors of the Electoral College. The NPV provides a means to ensure that the winner of the national popular vote also wins the Electoral College vote. In short, states accounting for at least 270 electoral votes enter into a compact with the agreement that they will award their state's electoral votes to the winner of the national popular vote. Proponents note that the arrangement does not require an amendment to the Constitution, which is very difficult to achieve, and yet it is wholly permitted through the Constitution's interstate compact clause, which enables states to enter into compacts with one another.

By the November 2016 election, eleven states representing 165 electoral votes had enacted the law. Legislation aimed to enact the NPV had passed in at least one legislative chamber in 12 additional states, representing another 96 electoral votes. Each of the states that have adopted the law have voted reliably for Democrats in recent elections. Many Republican lawmakers have expressed concern that adoption of a national popular vote would hurt their chances in presidential elections. Just as this sentiment has made constitutional amendments relating to the Electoral College difficult to enact, it also presents a significant impediment for advocates of the NPV, particularly given the number of state legislatures that Republicans have controlled in recent years. Nonetheless, the NPV has emerged as a chief means to change the Electoral College.

These reform efforts are the latest in a long line of attempts to change or abolish the institution. Bugh notes that much of the energy directed at Electoral College reform has occurred in the last 100 years. In fact, almost 90 percent of all congressional bills to reform the Electoral College (682 out of 772) were introduced from 1910 to 2010 (Bugh, 2010b, 85). The majority of these efforts occurred during the 1960s and 1970s (Bugh, 2010b, 433). It was during this time that public opposition to the Electoral College was at its peak. Recall that the passage of the 23rd Amendment granting the District of Columbia representation occurred during this period. Likewise, the 25th Amendment—detailing presidential succession—was also passed during this decade. It would seem that the time was ripe for significant change to the Electoral College. Indiana Senator Birch Bayh, chairman of the Senate Judiciary Committee and member of its subcommittee on constitutional amendments, devoted a great deal of energy to undoing the Electoral College. He found a lightning rod with the 1968 presidential campaign.

The 1968 presidential election was yet another very closely contested race. Less than 1 percent of all votes cast across the country separated Richard Nixon from Hubert Humphrey (43.4 percent to 42.7 percent). Additionally, third-party candidate George Wallace garnered nearly 10 percent of all electoral votes (46). While Humphrey lost the popular vote by a whisker, Nixon ended up with 56 percent of the Electoral College vote to just 36 percent for Humphrey. The disparity between the popular and electoral vote, combined with the strong showing by Wallace, led New York State Representative Emanuel Celler to introduce a joint resolution with Bayh to abolish the Electoral College.

The Bayh–Celler amendment called for the Electoral College to be replaced with a national popular vote. By September 1969, the amendment was passed by the House of Representatives with strong bipartisan support. President Nixon endorsed it, and in 1970 the Senate Judiciary Committee passed it, 11–6. Concern among less populated states began to grow and the bill was filibustered, never receiving a full vote by the Senate. Crezo contends this was "the beginning of the end for the best attempt in history to abolish the Electoral College" (December 6, 2016).

To recap, the institution has been a consistent target for reform, several significant changes have occurred to it over time, and Americans have historically favored a popular vote over the Electoral College process. Yet, as maligned as the institution has been over the years, it has been resistant to wholesale change. In the wake of the 2000 election, Edwards (2004, x) opined that the inertia to change the Electoral College might be attributed to Americans' being "so accustomed to a rule of law that they're strangely accepting, even when legal systems produce strange results or defy the people's will." The Electoral College has remained a venerable institution, in spite of much pressure to change it over the years. The 2016 election once again brought great attention to the body and heated debate over its merits.

Plan of the Book

Although the Electoral College is at the center of presidential elections, many observers of American politics scarcely understand the multitude of issues surrounding it. Foremost among these issues is its role regarding representation. This work focuses on the Electoral College as it relates to federalism, republicanism, legitimacy, and the evolution of the body relative to the evolution of representation in the United States. Chapter 2 investigates common theories relating to representation in a republican form of government. Detractors of the institution frequently claim the Electoral College is undemocratic—and in fact it is. Proponents note that the body is a function of a republican form of government and was not intended to be a body where the popular vote should necessarily prevail. An examination of various conceptions of representation helps our understanding of the competing goals of representation in a mass democracy. While no electoral system is perfect, various goals relating to representation will be satisfied accordingly through different means.

Chapter 3 examines the founding and evolution of the Electoral College. Detailing the origins of the institution aids our understanding of the intentions of the Framers. Many claims are made about the intentions of the Framers, and these claims are addressed in detail. It is also imperative to examine how the institution has evolved over time. Doing so enables us to get a more complete understanding of how it functions today. Acknowledging the differences between the original body and the evolved body is essential in any examination of the Electoral College. Likewise, an examination of how representation in the United States has evolved over time further helps us to evaluate the institution.

Chapter 4 investigates arguments relating to the federal nature of the institution. Presidential elections are composed of 51 individual contests across the states. The "bonus two" feature of the Electoral College adds greater electoral weight to less populated states relative to more populated states. The emphasis on federalism in the Electoral College is often a core argument in favor of the institution. Advocates claim that the Electoral College works to create broad-based support, helps to ensure that rural areas receive representation, and serves as a check against the tyranny of the majority. I examine these assertions as they relate to the original intent of the Framers and evaluate how the institution operates in contemporary presidential elections relative to these claims.

Chapter 5 analyzes the role of the Electoral College in yielding broad electoral support and legitimacy for presidents. The Electoral College violates the notion of political equality through its allocation of votes based on both population *and* statehood. Moreover, the winner-take-all feature that most states employ can skew election results in closely contested races. That the person receiving the most votes across the nation is not assured of winning the presidential election is unnerving for many citizens. Because that scenario has happened in two of the last five presidential elections, new energy has been devoted to preventing such developments in the future. Misfire elections and the legitimacy afforded by the Electoral College are examined throughout Chapter 5.

Chapter 6 evaluates the role of presidential electors in the process. Electors are a direct means of representation embodied in the Electoral College process. Citizens vote for electors, and electors vote for the president and vice president. Their dependably performing their duties is essential for the process to work as expected, yet the 2016 election showed that many electors consider themselves to be free agents. Although almost all electors remain faithful, some do stray from time to time. I examine who electors are and how they see their role in the process by relying on original research I have collected over the past five presidential election cycles.

Chapter 7 is devoted to examining the Electoral College as it relates specifically to the 2016 presidential campaign. I detail the campaign strategies of Trump and Clinton as well as the Hamilton elector movement that occurred in the wake of the election. As I mentioned at the outset of this chapter, many of the arguments that have been leveled against the Electoral College were present in this campaign. A deeper investigation of these issues helps us not only understand the events of the 2016 election, but allows us to consider what changes, if any, we may expect to the body in future elections.

Chapter 8 considers a number of reforms that have emerged over the years. The Electoral College remains largely intact despite myriad attempts to change it. I look at past and current attempts to alter or abolish the institution. I conclude by considering prospects for change in the near term. I couch these reform efforts as they relate to relevant goals of representation.

For many, the beauty of the Electoral College is in the eyes of the beholder. Those who feel disadvantaged by it see it as an ugly relic of a bygone era. Those who feel advantaged by it see it as a beautifully crafted work of genius by the Framers. Trump's tweets about the institution from 2012 and 2016 exemplify these conflicting views. This book examines the institution by laying out a framework for representation and analyzing it as it relates to this framework. Ultimately, for republican forms of government to be successful, they must be legitimate. This is perhaps the most relevant standard to use when evaluating the Electoral College.

2

Theories of Representation

THE PREMISE OF this book is to understand representation in the context of the Electoral College. At its simplest, the Electoral College is a counting mechanism to determine who is selected as the president and vice president of the United States. However, this description fails to accurately capture the many complexities associated with the institution. This is particularly the case as it relates to *how* individuals are represented through the body. There are unlimited ways leaders can be chosen, and these myriad ways may advantage or disadvantage various groups or individuals in the society in which they are used. I examine several well-developed theories on representation that are applicable to an understanding of the Electoral College. This discussion provides greater context to evaluate the institution.

Nearly sixty years ago, Eulau, Wahlke, Buchanan, and Ferguson argued that few have adequately examined how the process of selecting government officials affects how those officials represent the governed. They state that "the appropriate process of selecting public decision-makers has never been the really fundamental question for theories of representation" (1959, 743). Since then, a great deal of scholarship has been devoted to understanding issues relating to representation. McCrone and Kuklinski contend that "the proper relationship between the representative and the represented" is a central question posed by those examining theories of representation (1979, 278). The Electoral College both is a process to select the nation's leader and serves as a means to represent citizens across the nation through that process.

John Fairlie states that a "representative democracy has been defined as 'a form of government where the powers of the sovereignty are delegated to a body of men, elected from time to time, who exercise them for the benefit of the whole nation'" (1940, 456). G. Bingham Powell contends that democratic representation requires that the actions of policymakers should be responsive to the wishes of the people (2004, 273). For centuries, theorists have wrestled with the notion of who "the people" actually are. Determining their "wishes" has also been a tricky task. The Electoral College process represents a uniquely American attempt to represent the citizenry in its only nationally elected office. As such, it has attracted great debate regarding who is represented through the institution.

Political principles such as popular sovereignty, federalism, and legitimacy are among those the Electoral College seeks to accommodate. All nation-states must grapple with how they seek to represent those who are governed. Many different systems have been adopted in order to represent the populace. The Electoral College process is one that is unique to the world. No other country uses a system quite like it. I discuss several of the ways leaders are chosen in other countries. I leave authoritarian regimes aside and focus solely on democratic systems. Regardless of how leaders are chosen, electoral rules matter. They affect how candidates campaign and how voters accept the results of any given election.

This chapter examines traditional theories of representation in democratic regimes. Understanding the inherent goals relative to representation along with the problems associated with accomplishing those goals is important to understand the benefits and problems associated with the Electoral College. All electoral systems are the result of choices that seek to satisfy norms of democracies (e.g., authority, legitimacy, equality). Through this discussion, we will be able to more fully evaluate controversies enveloping the Electoral College. The remainder of this chapter is devoted to examining relevant theories of representation and how they relate to current arguments regarding the Electoral College.

Theories of Representation

There is a robust literature examining concepts related to theories of representation. Few scholars, however, have made as much of an impact on our understanding of the concept as Hannah Pitkin (1967). She examines various facets of representation and illustrates the complexities inherent in any treatment of the subject. In doing so, she provides scholars with a roadmap to evaluate the various forms of representation that may be present in any particular regime at any particular time.

Pitkin sets out to show that while sometimes difficult to ascertain, representation is a "single, highly complex concept that has not changed much in its basic meaning since the seventeenth century" (1967, 8). She argues that representation can be best understood by recognizing the *context* with which scholars, representatives, or laypeople are seeking to apply the term. By viewing representation from multiple angles, we can more fully understand what is or is not being represented at any given time. To do this, she identifies a typology of representation to get a more complete picture of the concept. For Pitkin, understanding representation requires one to look at it through different lenses, including the *formalistic, descriptive, symbolic*, and *substantive* perspectives.

Formalistic representation is conceived as the arrangements relating to modes of representation. Formalistic representation relates to the "rules of the game" that determine who is represented and how they are represented. For instance, the Electoral College is an established process to select the president and vice president of the United States. Although many Americans may not be fully aware of the details of that process, the procedure is well known to those aspiring to the presidency. The process dictates where candidates campaign, what messages they communicate, and how they deploy their resources. Campaigns rely upon an understanding of the rules of the game in order to wage an effective outcome based on those rules.

Reliance on rules enables formalistic representation to occur. Laws controlling elections are expected to reflect whatever the society's goals are relative to representation. Those rules are supposed to ensure representation based on their adherence. Yet, sometimes goals may be murky or in conflict with one another. We see this with the Electoral College process. The question of whether people across the country are being represented, states are being represented, parties are being represented, groups are being represented, or whether individuals in states are being represented leads to different conclusions regarding the goals of representation as implemented through the Electoral College process.

The Electoral College is not a democratic process, nor was it intended to be so. Pitkin notes that while representation is often tied to democracy and liberty, "through much of their history both the concept and the practice of representation have had little to do with democracy or liberty. Representation need not mean representative government" (1967, 2). Nonetheless, principles of democratic governance have come to be an expectation of republican governments. The rise of direct democracy throughout the American states (as well as Europe) and the rise of proportional representation over the unit rule underscore this point.

Pitkin suggests that formalistic representation can be broken into two subsets: authorization and accountability. Authorization relates to one's having the ability to act on behalf of others. For instance, you hold an election, you win, then you have the ability to act on behalf of others. Authority goes hand in hand with legitimacy, which is the willing acceptance that those in power have a right to their positions. The Electoral College process leads to malapportionment due to the constant two electoral votes each state receives. Smaller states are thusly overrepresented in the Electoral College. Yet, malapportionment does not automatically translate to a lack of legitimacy. Although issues relating to malapportionment *may* affect legitimacy, those issues should not affect one's authority. Similarly, misfire elections may or may not affect legitimacy but should have no bearing on one's authority. Still, the presence of legitimacy is thought to be very important in democratic nation-states.

Accountability relates to the ability of citizens to sanction their representatives for their actions. Regular, competitive elections are expected to provide a means to ensure accountability in a democratic regime. However, arguments regarding the competitiveness of presidential elections persist due to various attributes of the Electoral College. Some contend the constant two Senate vote feature favors Republicans due to their strength in rural states. Conversely, the winner-take-all feature and the strength of Democrats in many of the larger states allows them to begin any presidential election with the expectation that they can already count on large numbers of electoral votes at the outset. A third criticism splits these arguments by pointing out that it is swing states that receive most of the attention in presidential campaigns. The vast majority of states are not in contention and are thus ignored. Lack of competition and the subsequent inability to sanction representatives suggests accountability is a particularly salient issue relative to the Electoral College. This is a topic we will return to in Chapter 4.

Symbolic representation and descriptive representation relate to what Pitkin refers to as "standing for" something in a society. This is to be differentiated from representation that "acts for" something in response to the citizenry. Symbolic representation focuses on whether citizens *believe* they are being represented in government. If there is widespread acceptance of government actions, then one can be comfortably assured that citizens feel their interests are being represented. This may or may not have any bearing as to an objective view of whether or not the citizens are being represented through the actions of government leaders. But if people *feel* like they are being represented, then for all intents and purposes they are being represented.

Likewise, descriptive representation speaks to the level to which those occupying positions of power reflect the population they represent. In short, legislatures should bear a strong physical resemblance to the population at large. Advocates for greater descriptive representation may prefer proportional representation as a better means to achieve that goal over the winner-take-all system. Those working from this perspective seek to understand whether legislatures resemble their districts when it comes to their demographics, geography, opinions, and interests. Descriptive representation gets to the heart of a central argument many proponents of the Electoral College make. The emphasis the institution places upon federalism ensures that citizens living in states throughout the country have some level of representation when it comes to selecting the president. This geographic representation may come with a price, as many critics of the institution contend that the interests of minorities (which are often located in more densely populated states) are not well represented due to the institution's focus on geographic representation.

Lastly, substantive representation examines whether or not representatives take actions that are in concert with their constituency. Unlike symbolic representation, substantive representation is less concerned with whether citizens feel like they are being represented and more concerned with whether legislators are taking actions they believe are in the public's interest. This may mean they take unpopular stances on issues when they believe they are in the best interests of the citizenry. This concept is closely related to the trustee–delegate dilemma discussed below.

More recently, Jane Mainsbridge (2003) has argued that we should "rethink representation" apart from traditional visions associated with delegates and trustees. She articulates four categories of representation: *promissory, anticipatory, gyroscopic,* and *surrogate*. Promissory representation is "a model in which representatives 'promise' to do what they are authorized to do, and their failure to redeem the promissory note results in their facing sanction by being turned out of office" (Rehfelt, 2009, 220). This is akin to Pitkin's formalistic representation and its emphasis on accountability. Anticipatory representation occurs when a representative seeks to "anticipate" voters' desires prior to the next election. Doing so presumably binds representatives toward actions they believe are in concert with the wishes of their constituency, provided they seek to maintain their position in the next election. Again, as with Pitkin's observations with formalistic representation, anticipatory representation is a means to produce accountability among representatives. Their concern over maintaining their seat serves to limit their actions to those things they believe will contribute to reelection.

Whereas promissory and anticipatory representation are closely aligned with constituent interests, gyroscopic and surrogate representation focus more on representing interests (broadly defined). Each is closely connected to trustee-style representation. For instance, gyroscopic representation relies upon doing what representatives believe is in the best interests of the constituency. They are seen as professionals and as such must use their own knowledge and expertise as a guide to produce good public policy for the citizenry. Surrogate representation occurs when legislators represent interests beyond the lines of their congressional district. Mainsbridge suggests that the surrogate form of political participation is especially relevant in single-member, winner-take-all districts that provide essentially no representation for losing parties in their legislatures. She argues that representatives in such systems are mindful of this fact and their ability to represent those who have no representation in the legislature from their district is a means to ensure they have some level of representation.

Like Pitkin's observation that representation must be understood from various angles, Mainsbridge's perspectives deepen our understanding of the multiple and sometimes competing ways representatives (and the represented) see the relationship between those who govern and those who are governed. Inherent in these examinations of representation is an understanding of not simply how one is represented, but how those who represent others understand their relationship to those whom they represent. It is to this discussion that we now turn.

The Trustee–Delegate Dilemma

The classification schemes developed by Pitkin and Mainsbridge help us recognize the many dimensions of representation. However, understanding how legislators see their role determines in large measure how representation takes place in a republic. Scholars have devoted great energy to studying how legislators see their duties relative to their constituency. Fairlie points out that "etymologically, the literal meaning of represent is to 'present again,' and from this it has come to mean to appear in place of another" (1940, 236). Yet, understanding the degree to which one appears "in place of another" is open to frequent debate. Thoughts on the subject often come back to one's belief concerning how representatives view their relationship with their constituency.

Pitkin notes that "the concept of representation, particularly of human beings, representing other human beings is essentially a modern one" (1967, 2). Although much is often made of an idealized vision of Greek democracy, few Greeks were actually seen as citizens, and what they considered as democracy would hardly be recognizable by today's standards. For instance, citizenship was generally limited to a select group of males, based on heredity. Sabine and Thorson state that "what was aimed at was the selection of a body sufficiently large to form a sort of cross-section or sample of the whole body of citizens, which was permitted in a given case or for a short term to act in the name of the people" (1973, 22). Membership in the *demes* (or local townships) was hereditary. The *demes* would present candidates, who were then chosen by lot. Thus, representatives were ultimately chosen through luck! Sabine and Thorson conclude that "to the Greek understanding this mode of filling offices by lot was the distinctly democratic form of rule, since it equalized everyone's chances to hold office" (1973, 23).

The modern notion of democratic representation is most often associated with the British House of Commons and the thoughts of Edmund Burke. Burke challenged the traditional ideal that representatives were solely chosen to represent the interests of their constituency. Instead, he argued that it was the duty of legislators to use their "mature judgment" and enlightened conscience" when coming to a decision. For Burke, legislators are to be entrusted to use their experience and wisdom to act in their best judgment for the country. Doing so may come into conflict with the interests of one's constituency or the passions of the people. Burke states that for the legislator, "once elected he is responsible for the whole interest of the nation and the empire, and he owes to his constituents his best judgment freely exercised, whether it agrees with theirs or not" (Sabine and Thorson, 1973, 560). Experience and expertise along with deliberation and discernment occurring through the legislative body should be the guide for the public good. Since then, political theorists (and citizens) have continued to ponder the proper relationship between legislators and their constituency.

Eulau, Wahlke, Buchanan, and Ferguson provide a cogent review of the issues relating to delegates, trustees, and politicos. They offer the following definitions for each (1959, 749–750):

> **Delegates**—should not use their independent judgment or convictions as criteria of decision-making. But this does not mean that they feel equally committed to follow instructions, from whatever clientele. Some merely speak of consulting their constituents, though implying that such consultation will have a mandatory effect on their behavior. Others frankly acknowledge their direct dependence on instructions and accept them as a necessarily or desirable premise for their decisions.

Trustees—the representative is a free agent, he follows what he considers right or just—his convictions or principles, the dictates of his conscience. . . . He follows his own judgments based on an assessment of the facts in each case, his understanding of the problems involved, his thoughtful appraisal of the sides at issue.

Politicos—Depending on circumstances, a representative may hold the trustee orientation at one time, and the delegate orientation at another time. Or he might seek to reconcile both in terms of a third. One can think of representation as a continuum, with the Trustee and Delegate orientations as poles, and a midpoint where the orientations tend to overlap and, within a range, give rise to a third role. Within this middle range the roles may be taken simultaneously, possibly making for conflict, or they may be taken serially, one after another as conditions call for.

Rehfelt contends that according to Burke, the trustee position specifies that "national legislation ought to aim at the national good; the representative, in deliberation with other legislators, should be the ultimate judge of what constitutes that national good; and the representative should be less responsive to electoral sanctions, motivated instead by some form of civic virtue" (2009, 218). Conversely, he suggests that for the delegate, "the aims of legislation are the good of a particular electoral constituency, citizens are the source of judgement about what constitutes that good, and representatives are supposed to be highly responsive to the threat of sanction" (2009, 218).

McCrone and Kuklinksi (1979, 278) contend that the delegate style of representation occurs (1) "when legislators think of themselves as delegates" and (2) when constituencies "provide constituent cues regarding district preferences to their representatives." They conclude that "the absence of either or both conditions seriously disrupts delegated representation" (1979, 278). The saliency of particular issues has been found in large part to determine the presence of delegate-style representation. This is particularly true when citizens are mobilized *against* matters of public policy that are up for debate. This discussion becomes especially salient when considering the role of presidential electors in the Electoral College.

The Framers and Representation

Thus far, we have examined representation in broad terms. The Framers gave great thought to the issue of how the new republic would be best served through the representative process. The Electoral College reflects many concerns the Framers had about representation in the fledgling nation. Its creation would serve to placate both Federalists and Anti-Federalists at the constitutional convention. The following chapter examines the creation of the Electoral College in this context. In the meantime, it is worth examining the broad concerns the Framers voiced regarding issues related to representation.

The unease voiced by the Federalists regarding democracy is well documented. Madison observed that "if men were angels, no government would be necessary" (Rossiter, 1961, 322). The Framers did not trust the passions of the people and put a number of "auxiliary precautions" in place to counter the ambition of men. In *Federalist 10* and *51*, Madison articulated a vision to control the "mischiefs of faction" that would occur absent a more powerful national sovereign. Both he and Alexander Hamilton employed history to reveal flaws associated with human nature and self-government. In *Federalist 6*, Hamilton produces numerous examples through history revealing the nature of humanity to be "ambitious, vindictive, and rapacious" (Rossiter, 1961, 54). Madison urged a reliance on checks and balances, understanding that "enlightened statesmen will not always be at the helm" (Rossiter, 1961, 80). Rather than rely upon representatives, it is through separation of powers and checks and balances that the new constitution would best be able to protect the liberty of the people.

Not all Framers were moved by these arguments. The Anti-Federalists sought a government more closely connected to the citizenry. Lending support to the notion of popular representation, Brutus argued for the "full, fair, and equal representation of the people" in government (Ketcham, 1986, 275). Similarly, in the debate over the new constitution, Patrick Henry (June 5, 1788) offered the following:

> But we are told that we need not fear; because those in power, being our Representatives, will not abuse the power we put in their hands: I am not well versed in history, but I will submit to your recollection, whether liberty has been destroyed most often by the licentiousness of the people, or by the tyranny of rulers? I imagine, sir, you will find the balance on the side of tyranny.

Ultimately, they settled on what has come to be known as mixed government, generally seen as a government composed of monarchy, aristocracy, and democracy (Ely, 1999, 283). Ely suggests that the American break with England put greater emphasis on the role of aristocracy and democracy in the new republic. The Federalists' reliance on institutions to guard against the passions of the people reflects their partiality toward aristocracy. The Anti-Federalists' determination to ensure government's accountability to the citizenry reflects their preference toward democracy. These tensions can be loosely associated with our earlier discussion regarding the relationship of representatives to the represented as seen through the perspectives relating to delegates (i.e., democracy) and trustees (i.e., aristocracy).

Writing about the Electoral College, Gary Bugh reframes the delegate–trustee dichotomy into one examining popular representation and traditional representation. This, too, recognizes the tensions implicit in the notion of a mixed government. He states that "popular representation involves equal citizens directly electing their representatives and institutions and rights that make this possible" (2010b, 8). He adds that over time, the United States has taken steps toward greater popular representation. The direct election of senators, the rise in direct democracy, and protections to ensure voting rights are examples of ways the United States has become more "democratized" over time. Robert Dahl argues that the American Constitution is wanting in regard to democracy, concluding that "it fell far short of the requirements that later generations would find necessary and desirable in a democratic republic" (2003, 15).

Bugh suggests that traditional representation "involves indirect selection of representatives and government decision making that takes into account diverse interests" (2010b, 6). The Framers had their concerns relating to self-government. They were certainly no fans of direct democracy and took deliberate steps to guard against such a thing from occurring. Ensuring the primacy of the federal government over state governments through the Constitution's "supremacy clause" was one such step. Many others can be seen through the system of checks and balances crafted in the new constitution.

In many respects, the Constitution reflects a number of compromises to satisfy both those seeking greater federal authority and those who were wary of such authority. The Electoral College serves as an example of these compromises. The institution would function as yet another buffer between "the people" and their government. Alexander Hamilton contended that "there are few positions more demonstrable than that there should be, in every republic, some permanent body to correct the prejudices, check the intemperate passions, and regulate the fluctuations, of a popular assembly" (Ely, 1999, 283). Bugh states that "the indirect selection of members of Congress, presidential electors, the president, and even the Supreme Court would prevent any one faction from dominating the national government" (2010b, 7).

Proponents of the system today often cite the wisdom of the Framers, neglecting that many of those same Founders had their concerns about the proper relationship between the citizenry and the government. For instance, rather than having intermediaries select representatives, Thomas Jefferson argued that citizens should directly select their leaders, from their local judges to the president of the United States (Bugh, 2010b, 9).

To be sure, the Framers did not speak with a single voice relating to the new constitution. This point should give pause to those who attribute a sense of certainty to the Framers' handiwork. Fairlie points out that not only were they in conflict with each other, they were sometimes in conflict with themselves. He contends that "in the American constitutional convention of 1787, differing views were presented as to the nature and purpose of representation, not only by different members, but to some extent by the same persons" (1940, 243). For instance, James Madison at one point states that "it seems indispensable that the mass of citizens should not be without a voice in making the laws which they are to obey, in choosing the magistrates who are to administer them" (Madison, 1966). Yet, he also "observed that if the opinions of the people were to be our guide, it would be difficult to say what course we ought to take. No member of the convention could say what the opinions of his constituents were at this time" (Madison, 1966). These contradictions may echo Ernest Bruncken's observation that "one of the things we have learned . . . is that elected representatives may be very far from representing the true deliberate will of their constituents. They may represent a passing phase of popular emotion or delusion" (1914, 222).

The balance the Framers sought regarding representation of the Republic can be evidenced in Edmund Burke's famous speech to the electors of Bristol in 1774. He stated (12):

> Parliament is not a congress of ambassadors from different and hostile interests; which interests each must maintain, as an agent and advocate, against other agents and advocates; but parliament is a deliberative assembly of one nation, with one interest, that of the whole; where, not local purposes, not local prejudices ought to guide but the general good, resulting from the general reason of the whole.

It was thought that the Electoral College would be a means to represent and provide for the general good, given its role in selecting the sole representative of the nation. In fact, the original conception of presidential electors heavily relied on the Burkean view of trustee representation. It would be through each state's Electoral College that "men of discernment" would come to their own best judgment as to who should occupy the position of the nation's chief executive.

Electors—Delegates or Trustees?

Originally, presidential electors were viewed as autonomous decision makers. They were not initially selected by the citizenry, nor was there a clear mandate that they were supposed to be directly tied to the wishes of the populace in their states. Madison argued that the meetings of presidential electors would provide "that the public voice, pronounced by the representatives of the people, will be more consonant to the public good than if pronounced by the people themselves, convened for the purpose" (Rossiter, 1961, 82).

As pointed out in Chapter 1, the Hamiltonian vision of a wise elector exercising his judgment, independent of the citizenry, eroded almost immediately. The introduction of party tickets was the effective death knell for this vision. Electors came to be chosen for their loyalty, not their discernment. Yet, as we will see in Chapters 6 and 7, many electors continue to cling to the Hamiltonian vision where they are meant to use their best judgment, particularly when faced with candidates they believe are unworthy of the presidency. This conflict between the original and evolved perceptions of electors' duties remains unsettled.

In *Ray v. Blair* (1952), the Court ruled that political parties were able to demand pledges of electors to vote for their party's ticket, but the Court was silent as to whether electors had to follow through with those pledges. It is worth noting Justice Jackson's fervent argument in favor of elector independence. He states (*Ray v. Blair*, 1952) that "no one faithful to our history can deny that the plan originally contemplated what is implicit in its text—that electors would be free agents, to exercise an independent and nonpartisan judgment as to the men best qualified for the Nation's highest offices."

Few studies have examined this issue because electors are hyper-partisans who rarely defect. Few change their votes, and it is assumed they see themselves as delegates acting in the stead of the people who elected them to their positions. Yet, surveys of electors reveal that many believe they should have discretion to vote as they see fit. While most act as delegates, they believe they can act as trustees if the situation calls for it.

Fairlie provides an important point of emphasis as it relates to the responsibility of electors to consider their choices, stating that "seldom, if ever, can any person completely represent even another single person unless bound by definite instructions" (1940, 466). Likewise, Pitkin contends that a "representative is sent to the central government with explicit instruction, or to do a particular thing. He is sent with a commission; he is sent on a mission" (1967, 134). In *Ray v. Blair*, the Supreme Court indicated that electors were representatives of their states rather than the national government. For most, the mission is to follow the will of the voters in their state as well as that of their political party. This would preclude them from considering additional choices. This is one reason why the term "faithless elector" has arisen to describe those who vote contrary to expectations. The term is not one of endearment, but rather one of derision. In spite of that, those who have voted faithlessly contend they are actually being *faithful* to the office of elector and thus the Constitution. The evolution of the position has changed considerably over time, and more is said of this in the following chapters. What is important here is that while most electors do see themselves as rubber stamps, some do not. Efforts have been undertaken to force electors to vote in accordance with the popular vote in their respective states, yet some electors continue to exert their independence. The "Hamilton elector" movement witnessed in the wake of the 2016 presidential election put the question of an elector's independence into the spotlight.

It would appear that it is not wholly clear what the representative function of presidential electors is. This ambiguity is complicated by the mandates issued (or not issued) to those who are selected as representatives (i.e., electors). As a consequence, there may be disagreement as to whom electors are supposed to represent structurally as well as individually. Even if we do have a guide as to what or whom representatives are supposed to serve, it is unclear how representatives see *their* role as representatives. Fairlie concludes that "representatives should be guided by their own immediate constituencies, by their party, or by their own views as to the best interests of the country as a whole" (1940, 466). He recognizes that each of these factors most likely affects how a decision maker acts. The certainty and intensity to which these issues are established will likely determine the extent to which one factor may be valued over another in the representative's actions.

Electoral Rules and Representation

Much can be learned about the values a society seeks to achieve regarding representation by examining the means by which it selects representatives. In their examination of alternative schemes to the Electoral College, Paul

Schumaker and Burdett Loomis adroitly state that "no method of aggregating votes satisfies all reasonable assumptions of a fair voting process" (2002a, 20). While it may be impossible to satisfy all Americans when it comes to creating a fair voting process, there may be ways to ensure that the goals of republicanism are satisfied as a means to represent people. The following section examines these issues in greater detail.

It is important that election rules produce outcomes the citizenry believes are consistent with the public's will. No system is perfect, but election rules that consistently yield outcomes the citizenry feels are out of touch with the public's wishes will likely contribute to tumult in the society. This may take the form of hyper-partisanship, policy gridlock, or citizen protests. It is important, then, that democratic systems devise rules that create a strong linkage between citizens and their elected representatives. A number of different structures have been created to ensure this takes place. Determining the *best* means to achieve this, however, is a complicated task.

Representative democracies come in many forms. Elections are carried out in myriad ways. This is true in the United States but also from a comparative perspective. The presidential system in the United States stands in contrast to the many parliamentary systems throughout Europe. The former focuses upon candidates, while the latter focus on political parties. Likewise, the wide use of single-member, winner-take-all districts is also very different from the pervasive use of proportional representation as a means to select representatives in many other countries. Regardless of these differences, it is the widespread acceptance that leaders have a right to their positions that marks the legitimacy of any democratic regime.

Among the choices a nation-state must make when determining how it devises its elections is the choice of what to emphasize in elections. One school of thought is to base representation on geographic districts. This is the norm in the United States. A primary argument for the Electoral College is based on the importance of geographic boundaries represented by statehood. This was a major concern at the country's founding and has continued to be so throughout American history.

Yet, many scholars and theorists argue that geographic representation, especially based on single-member districts, is a poor way to conceptualize representation. Eulau, Wahlke, Buchanan, and Ferguson note that geographic districts complicate the role of representation for legislators. While it is presumed they are to represent the interests that are distinct to their district, they are also charged with representing the interests of the nation as a whole. While these may be one and the same, they may also be at odds. They further question whether geographic units actually have interests that can be easily identifiable as distinct. They state (1959, 746):

> Implicit in this expectation is the assumption that a geographical unit has interests which are distinct from other units, and which should be represented in public decision-making. This assumption has been challenged on a variety of grounds; that the geographical area as such, as an electoral unit, is artificial; that it cannot and does not generate interests shared by its residents; that it has no unique interest; and so on.

Likewise, in *INS v. Chadha* (1983), Supreme Court Justice John Paul Stevens wrote that members of Congress are "servants of the people of the United States. They are not merely delegates appointed by separate states; they occupy offices that are integral and essential components of a single national Government." Hence, members of Congress are to represent both their district (and state) and the national interest. Representing the interests of the district (or state) may be in concert with what the legislator believes is in the best interest of the country, but that is not a certainty.

A second school of thought is to base representation on ideological alignment. Parliamentary systems emphasize the political party rather than candidate-centered campaigns. A fusion of power results due to the executive's emergence from the legislative body. Proportional representation is ubiquitous among parliamentary systems. Advocates of proportional representation over district representation suggest that more natural "interests" emerge from such schemes and ensure their representation in legislative bodies, where they may be neglected in winner-take-all, single-member districts. Citizens effectively vote for parties rather than candidates. Legislatures are then organized in proportion to the number of votes each party receives, provided they meet a minimum threshold. Governments using proportional representation typically result in multiparty systems as opposed to the American two-party system.

Traditionally, the United States has employed district representation through single-member, winner-take-all congressional districts. These electoral rules produce two-party systems. Many have lauded the stability of the two-party system in the United States. Proponents believe the two parties must offer generally moderate choices to attract large numbers of citizens to vote for them. However, the struggles accompanying efforts to redistrict every 10 years reveal decidedly partisan efforts to maintain power and weaken the power of the opposing party. As a result, congressional seats become less competitive. Less competition affects accountability, which may breed apathy, ideological extremism, and disaffection among the citizenry.

The Electoral College is grounded in district representation. It is a competition throughout 51 individual districts for votes in those "districts." Yet, how states award those votes is a decision they get to make. Almost all states have adopted the unit rule when it comes to their distribution of Electoral College votes. Maine and Nebraska stand alone in their use of the district plan. The campaigns of Obama (in 2008) and Trump (in 2016) spent time and resources in those states as part of their larger campaign strategies. Whether they would have done so absent the district plan is questionable. As we saw in Chapter 1, from time to time states consider making similar changes, but none of them have done so since Maine did in 1992. Discussion over the merits of the unit rule or some form of proportional representation in the Electoral College will likely persist. Understanding how other nation-states select their leaders is useful in order to evaluate the benefits and problems associated with the current Electoral College scheme in the United States.

In Chapter 1, we saw that the Electoral College has been among the most widely attacked institutions in all of American politics. In spite of these attacks, it has persevered. Electoral systems have traditionally been resistant to change. Writing two decades ago, Pippa Norris concludes that "until recently electoral systems in liberal democracies seemed set in concrete" (1997, 297) and that "electoral systems are inherently conservative" (1997, 298). Inertia regarding reform of the Electoral College likely reflects deference to the relatively long history of the body. Nonetheless, Norris finds that a great deal of experimentation with democratic systems emerged in the latter part of the 20th century. Much of that experimentation has occurred relative to the use of majority/plurality elections (as used in the United States) and proportional representation (PR) elections.

Some nation-states have implemented a mix of the two types of representation. In New Zealand, for instance, roughly half the seats in the national legislature are elected based on single-member districts, while the other half are selected on the basis of proportional representation. The rise of "cumulative voting" is another means of selection with which many governments have experimented. Under this model, votes are cast for individual candidates running in multimember districts. Voters may cast as many votes as there are seats to fill. However, they may cast all of their votes for a single candidate or disperse their votes across a variety of candidates if they so choose. A number of cities in the United States have adopted cumulative voting (Donovan and Bowler, 2004, 68).

Perhaps the most frequently employed form of proportional representation is the use of the single transferable vote (which is also referred to as ranked-choice voting or instant runoff voting) method to select legislators. This procedure has become an increasingly popular method of selection among many nation-states. Notably, citizens in Maine adopted this method of counting ballots through a state initiative in 2016. Typically, voters rank candidates based on their preferences, with one being their favorite candidate, two being their next favorite, and so on. If no candidate wins a majority after the first round of ballots, the candidates with the fewest votes are eliminated. If your preferred candidate is eliminated, your vote for your next preferred candidate who is still under consideration is then applied, until someone wins a majority.

In multimember districts, voters are able to vote for multiple candidates within a district. As long as a candidate receives a minimum number of votes, he or she is able to occupy a seat in the legislature. Although a voter's first preference may not receive the most votes, that candidate still can be selected provided he or she meets the minimum threshold in the district. This works to avoid the "wasted vote" concern associated with single-member, winner-take-all districts. The instant runoff variety provides a means to aggregate preferences so a single candidate is able to earn a majority of votes. The idea of an instant runoff in presidential elections has gained traction in recent years. Donovan and Bowler point out that "comparative studies of public opinion find greater satisfaction with democracy in PR nations and also find that voter turnout is higher in nations using PR election" (2004, 65).

While a robust body of research has been conducted on legislative electoral systems, few studies have assessed presidential electoral systems. Blais, Massicotte, and Dobrzynska's study of presidential elections across the globe serves as an important contribution to our understanding of how heads of state are selected. They find that a clear majority of republics have directly elected presidents. Of those, 89 percent employ either plurality rule or majority elections. Most (61 percent) utilize majority elections (1997, 446). The United States stands alone with its Electoral College process. They note that a handful of countries use a "more complex or mixed" procedure as evidenced through the Electoral College procedure (1997, 446). Writing about the American system, Fairlie states that "it has been urged that the President, elected indirectly by the whole nation, may be more representative of the entire country than the members of Congress elected by local constituencies" (1940, 238). However, agreement as to what constitutes the "whole country" has been a significant point of contention. While it is true that the presidency is the only nationally elected office in the United States, determining how we go about ensuring that all Americans are represented through that process is debatable.

Matt Golder's extensive review of electoral systems further supports the finding that majority rule has become more common in electoral systems. He states that "absolute majority rule has become the worldwide norm for electing presidents, and non-majoritarian systems have become more complex due to the increasing use of multiple tiers and mixed electoral formulas (Golder, 2005, 103). Golder finds that "the vast majority of presidential elections have used plurality (108) or absolute majority (108) rule" (2005, 116). He notes that "the key characteristic that defines a majoritarian system is that the electoral formula requires the winning candidate to obtain either a plurality or majority of the votes" (2005, 109). Of course, the Electoral College system requires a majority of electoral votes, not popular votes, which means candidates may win the presidency without a majority or even a plurality of the popular vote. Golder adds that "only a handful of countries have failed to use plurality, absolute majority, or qualified majority rule," and the United States is among that select group (2005, 117).

Robert Dahl points out that few other countries have adopted our constitutional system. He pointedly asks: "If our constitution is as good as most Americans seem to think it is, why haven't other democratic countries copied it?" (2003, 3). Looking at the Electoral College relative to other countries, Lineberry, Davis, Erikson, Herrera, and Southwell conclude that "American elections differ from those in other democratic countries by (1) the relative distance between popular participation and popular control of policy; (2) the indirect connection between the popular vote and the election of the chief executive; and (3) their stunningly low turnout rate" (2002, 163). Stein, Johnson, Shaw, and Weisberg conclude that the conventional wisdom regarding the Electoral College is that it "is inimical to wider citizen participation" (2002, 125). Moreover, they state that "for fans of expanded citizen participation . . . the Electoral College should join history's dustbin alongside the poll tax, literacy requirements, religious qualifications, male-only suffrage, and similar long-banished, undemocratic evils" (2002, 125).

The Give and Take of Political Representation

Bugh asserts that "representation is not a straightforward concept in the United States because it has different meanings" (2010b, 5). This is particularly true as the concept relates to the Electoral College. Political principles such as popular sovereignty, federalism, and legitimacy are intimately related to representation and are sometimes placed in conflict with one another through the Electoral College process.

Thorny issues can arise when the wants of those in particular states or regions of the country diverge from the wants of the masses across the country. This can be seen in issues relating to the give-and-take between the federal government and states' rights. Much of American history can be witnessed through these conflicts. The move from the Articles of Confederation to the Constitution was an early manifestation of this tension. The earliest political parties coalesced around what the proper balance was between national and state power. This can be seen in the Federalists and Jeffersonian Democrats. More recent examples can be seen in squabbles over the Affordable Care Act and issues relating to marriage equality. It is expected that differences will emerge between advocates of a stronger federal sovereign versus those who favor more localized self-government. Yet, it is imperative that all sides believe the government in power has legitimacy.

Legitimacy is a core principle relating to representation, which undergirds both popular sovereignty and federalism. Legitimacy requires that citizens widely accept that leaders have a right to their positions and have a right to rule. It is expected that electoral systems produce results that are considered legitimate. The unwillingness to accept the results of an election is a common indicator of corrupt regimes. Schumaker and Loomis argue that any alternative to the Electoral College must be justified not because it reflects the "true will of the people" but because it leads to "preferred outcomes about the broad function of the political system" (2002a, 21).

The issue of legitimacy was questioned during the 2016 presidential campaign. Donald Trump frequently brought up the legitimacy of American elections. In particular, he raised the issue of a rigged election by the Democrats. He warned his supporters that the Clinton campaign would try to steal the election and they had to be vigilant to make sure this would not happen. In a campaign stop, he stated: "Remember, we are competing in a rigged election . . . They even want to try and rig the election at the polling booths, where so many cities are corrupt and voter fraud is all too common" (Collinson, October 19, 2016). Four years earlier, Trump had criticized the Electoral College as being a "disaster" and a "total sham" (Abadi, November 9, 2016). In a deleted tweet, Trump claimed that Obama had "lost the popular vote by a lot and won the election. We should have a revolution in this country!" He concluded by tweeting that "More votes equals a loss . . . revolution!" (Abadi, November 9, 2016). That a future president would criticize the

Electoral College and use it as a means to call for revolution is noteworthy. Questioning the legitimacy of the process and the institution itself suggests some potentially serious flaws with the body.

The structure of the Electoral College seeks to balance many principles relating to representation. These attempts reflect the multiple perspectives of representation discussed by both Pitkin and Mainsbridge. For instance, the desire to represent geographic boundaries by providing that all states have two electoral votes based on their statehood violates the principle of one person, one vote as established in *Baker v. Carr*. Critics would charge that this malapportionment signifies a bias toward federalism over democracy. While true, it does not convey the whole picture, as the winner-take-all feature makes those states with large numbers of electoral votes attractive to campaigns. Rehfelt contends that any account of democracy must specify "how closely the laws of a nation should correspond to the preferences of the citizens governed by them" (2009, 214). He recognizes that deviations will often arise between the preferences of the citizenry and the laws of a nation, and those deviations may be justified because citizens may have no strongly formed opinion on an issue, their preferences may be incoherent, or their preferences may be out of alignment with "higher" principles relating to justice. While these deviations may occur, he argues that when they do occur, there must be a proper explanation and justification for them. That the popular vote winner does not win the Electoral College may frustrate many observers of American politics. Yet, the rules of the Electoral College are well established and known to all. Nonetheless, it may test the bounds of legitimacy for the winning campaign.

Of particular importance to understanding representation as it relates to the Electoral College is understanding who or what is being represented. Whether electoral systems are created to represent "the people," geographic districts, ideological groups, demographic groups, or political parties is not a wholly settled issue. Different components of the Electoral College process emphasize different forms of representation. The compromises throughout the Electoral College process complicate our understanding of which of these forms is most important at any given time. Compromises are often rife with conflict. Understanding the Electoral College as a formalistic means of representation allows us to embrace the fact that minimally, the rules of the game are known and it is up to campaigns to act accordingly. Campaigns emphasize different elements of representation as they see them as a means to win in the Electoral College.

In his discussion concerning the need to reevaluate democratic institutions, Douglas Chalmers provides relevant constructs to consider when examining the Electoral College. He contends that a "successful democratic system is one in which the output of laws and policies is favorable to the people" (2013, 14). He goes on to suggest that there needs to be a "high level of interaction with the people—including accountability to them" in order for this success to occur (2013, 14).

Central to his concern is that more participation does not necessarily lead to more favorable outcomes for the vast majority of the citizenry. He asks whether a democratic system "includes processes that compel the decision makers to frame policies and laws that benefit the people" (2013, 16). This is an argument that is made by both proponents and opponents of the Electoral College. Proponents note that without the institution, candidates would concentrate their resources in the most populated states, ignoring many others throughout the country. Conversely, opponents point out that the current system encourages candidates to concentrate their resources in a handful of competitive swing states, ignoring most other states throughout the country. The veracity of these claims is taken up in Chapter 5. The important point here is that institutions affect representation, and the Electoral College highlights this fact. Political scientist Harold Stoke sums these thoughts up nicely. He states:

> Originating as a device to discover the general interest, representative government functions ideally only when it completely reflects the great variety of interests and feeling within the state, when it represents most accurately every substantial element of the state which is politically significant. But where the state itself is a mosaic of the most diverse and antagonistic interests, the representative system, simply because its finest duty is to interpret faithfully this diversity, cannot itself be the means of compromising and composing the very differences it was designed to reflect. The more perfect the representative system, the more certain it is that opposing interests will face each other in the political arena. And the more numerous and divergent the interests, the less the likelihood that any kind of a program can emerge . . . [U]nless representative government uses . . . means of resolving its inherent contradictions, its decline would seem to be a consequence of its peculiar nature. (Quoted in Fairlie, 1940, 465)

The compromises implicit in the Electoral College were intended to provide a way to accurately reflect the will of the people from across the country. These compromises include attributing electoral votes on the basis of both statehood and population and permitting electors the discretion to choose candidates whom they believed were best suited for the office of president. These compromises were meant to guide outcomes based on the public's wishes. That criticisms abound whether this has been accomplished is not surprising. Rousseau's thoughts on the *general will* are instructive.

Speaking about legislative power, Rousseau argued that "sovereignty cannot be represented for the same reason that it cannot be alienated; it consists essentially in the general will, and the will cannot be represented" (quoted in Fairlie, 1940, 240). He goes on to say that "in their legislative power the people cannot be represented; but they can and should be represented in the executive power" (quoted in Fairlie, 1940, 240). The desire to have a sole figure who can speak on behalf of the country is a strong desire and one that has been articulated by scholars for generations. However, Schumaker and Loomis's observation that "there is no 'will of the people' independent of the methods used to represent it" (2002a, 21) is important to recognize and is especially relevant when considering any means to select a nation's chief executive.

Conclusion

Throughout this chapter, we have examined how representation has been conceptualized along a variety of fronts. These include Pitkin's observations regarding formalistic, descriptive, symbolic, and substantive representation. Mainsbridge expounds on these perspectives by identifying four related categories of representation: promissory, anticipatory, gyroscopic, and surrogate. Taken together, these perspectives illustrate the complex nature of representation. Different dimensions of representation are emphasized at different times and by different entities. How representatives view their own role further complicates how representation actually takes place in societies. Whether representatives see their role as delegate or trustee will determine how they will go about representing their district and their nation. Arguments relating to the merits or demerits of the Electoral College rarely identify these perspectives relating to representation in their arguments. Instead, issues relating to federalism and democracy often dominate debate over the institution.

This chapter reveals that confining the debate over representation in the Electoral College to one over the vices and virtues of federalism and democracy is incomplete. Both signify different elements of representation, but they do not embody all elements of representation. Consequently, we must consider multiple perspectives and how each relates to larger goals of the republic. Each will be relevant in our examination of how the Electoral College does or does not fulfill various norms of representation.

Donovan and Bowler note a persistent lack of trust in the American political system over the past 60 years (2004, 17). While nearly 75 percent of Americans stated they "trusted the federal government to do what is right" at least most of the time in 1958, just one in five respond the same way in recent years (Pew Research Center, November 23, 2015). Citizens' perceptions of government responsiveness have witnessed a similar decline over time. Donovan and Bowler argue that these trends "reflect, at least in part, that many Americans have lost faith in their electoral processes and, thus, do not feel that they are represented in the political system" (2004, 17). The 2016 presidential election was a tumultuous occurrence, and the Electoral College was at the center of the public's discord.

Although some attention has been devoted to the Framers' views of representation, the following chapter more specifically examines the creation and evolution of the Electoral College. Embedded in its creation is an investigation of the principles the Framers considered relative to representation. Understanding the intentions of the Framers regarding the Electoral College reveals a great deal about how we can evaluate its operation today.

3

The Founding and Evolution of the Electoral College

MOST ALL ARGUMENTS surrounding the Electoral College draw on the Framers' original intent regarding the body. Longley and Peirce rightly observe that it can be "illuminating to consider how this group of intelligent and well-meaning men sought to create a mechanism for selecting their nation's leader that would . . . stand the test of time" (1999, 16). At the same time, they urge caution in attaching too much weight to the wishes of the Framers in considering the actual practice of the Electoral College today. We have already seen that the Framers did not always speak with a consistent voice regarding their intentions. To this point, Michael Rogers concludes that "if one looks to the Framers' intentions for guidance on the Electoral College, one discovers their intentions were conflicting and diverse" (2010, 29). Similarly, David Siemers argues that the "founding was a political process, not a foreordained plan of demigods . . . that process was full of unexpected turns, reversals, and surprising results" (2002, xiii–xvii). Given the import of political goals over normative goals, Robert Dahl pointedly asks:

> Why should we feel bound today by a document produced more than
> two centuries ago by a group of fifty-five mortal men, actually signed
> by only thirty-nine, a fair number of whom were slaveholders, and
> adopted in only thirteen states by the votes of fewer than two thousand
> men, all of whom are long since dead and mainly forgotten? (2003, 2)

Indeed, the Electoral College represents one of the more divisive issues the Framers faced. The iterations of the process and the compromises involved represent many of the same arguments about the body today. Yet, significant arguments for the institution stem from the *politics* of that political era. An understanding of the initial vision for the selection of the chief executive and what ultimately resulted from the Constitutional Convention informs *and* complicates arguments regarding the Electoral College.

The Electoral College underwent drastic changes in relatively short order. In just over a decade, expectations of how the body would operate changed considerably. Longley and Peirce contend that "the founding fathers showed great wisdom in many of the features of the new Constitution they created in Philadelphia in 1787. In the case of the Electoral College system, however, it is difficult to attribute such virtue to them, for this institution never worked as intended by its creators" (1999, 26). The rise of political parties significantly changed the operation of the Electoral College, so much so that the original conception had to be altered through a constitutional amendment. These changes were sanctioned by the Framers and had significant consequences for the actual operation of the Electoral College. Therefore, they must be taken into consideration in any contemporary discussion of the benefits and problems associated with the institution.

This chapter examines the origins of the Electoral College and its subsequent evolution. I pay close attention to how the institution was supposed to function relative to the issues of representation we examined in Chapter 2. Understanding the tensions the Framers sought to resolve aids our evaluation of today's Electoral College. George Edwards identifies eight objectives of the Founders relating to their creation of the Electoral College; he contends they were concerned with issues relating to legislative intrigue, presidential independence, voter parochialism, population differences among the states, slavery, presidential power, the need to have independence in the selection of the president, and the desire to produce a system that was able to obtain a consensus at the Convention (2004, 80–89). While some of these issues speak to perpetual questions regarding government structure (e.g., separation of powers, political equality, federalism), others were relevant due to the circumstances of the moment in time in which the Framers were operating (e.g., slavery and the need to obtain consensus to ratify the new Constitution). These factors are important to keep in mind when assessing the intentions of the Framers.

The Principles at Stake

In 1781, the Articles of Confederation was ratified, becoming the first constitution of the United States of America. The document decidedly favored limited governmental power and emphasized the autonomy of the states. Under the Articles, each state maintained its sovereignty, and states were encouraged to act in concert with one another in mutual "friendship." The legislature was composed of a unicameral Congress where each state held one vote. The president of the Congress was the closest approximation to a chief executive. The president was to be appointed by the Congress and could serve no longer than a three-year term. The president generally was seen as the presiding officer of the Congress and held administrative functions relating to the business of Congress, particularly when the body was in recess. The position had little in common with what would become the American presidency.

The Articles of Confederation proved to be deficient in several important ways. State sovereignty came at a cost. Significant differences emerged between the states across many areas. Disunity in the areas of public finance, trade, and defense led many to suggest the need for greater federal power to ensure greater coordination among the states to promote the welfare of the country. Stabilizing the economy, providing a common currency, and producing a stronger military were important issues that needed to be addressed. Less than 10 years after the adoption of the Article of Confederation, the Framers convened in Philadelphia for the purpose of amending the document. It became apparent that rather than modifying the Articles, many of the Framers were intent on creating a new government with greater federal power. The push toward greater federal power was controversial and the subject of great debate.

The debates that unfolded throughout the Constitutional Convention continue to be relevant regarding Americans' views of government today. The Virginia Plan and the New Jersey Plan emerged as the "foundation documents" driving much of the discussion among the delegates (Slonim, 1986, 37). The former plan generally emphasized greater federal power, while the latter plan generally sought to maintain greater state sovereignty. Balancing representation among people and across states was a central concern throughout the Convention. As expected, the push toward a stronger federal government was met with great resistance by less populated states. Slave states, too, were concerned about potential federal encroachment on their sovereignty. These issues were particularly salient when it came to devising the legislative branch and the selection of the chief executive. In fact, the process of choosing the chief executive was one of the more difficult issues they faced. This can be seen in the debates among the Framers about the presidential selection process.

The *Federalist Papers*, written by John Jay, Alexander Hamilton, and James Madison, crystalized this view. The *Federalist Papers* were written both to inform Americans about the new constitution and to persuade them to adopt it. As such, they represent an important artifact detailing the Framers' thoughts about the document. Hamilton's discussion of the Electoral College in *Federalist 68* is commonly cited as a laudatory defense of the institution. Hamilton claimed that "the mode of appointment of the Chief Magistrate of the United States is almost the only part of the system, of any consequence, which has escaped without severe censure, or which has received the slightest mark of approbation from its opponents." Rogers argues that Hamilton's characterization of the Framers' views of the Electoral College represents a falsehood that cloaked the body in a "protective veil of tradition" that has served to maintain the institution because it aligns with the intentions of the Framers (2010, 40). Closer inspection reveals that the Electoral College was indeed, one of the most intractable issues the Framers confronted.

Slonim contends that "no other constitutional provision gave them so much difficulty in its formulation" (1986, 35). James Wilson, a delegate from Pennsylvania, stated that the presidential selection process had "greatly divided the House, and will also divide people out of doors. It is in truth the most difficult of all on which we have had to decide" (Kurland and Lerner, 1987, 545). Slonim concludes that "no other provision has drawn so much criticism or provoked so many constitutional amendments as has the Electoral College clause" (1986, 35). In spite of this, Farrand (1913) states that the Framers were perhaps more proud of their handiwork in creating the Electoral College than they were anything else they did in Philadelphia—going so far as to suggest that they believed they had devised the model for selecting a chief executive for all nations throughout the world. Yet, an examination of the debate over the Electoral College reveals that the Framers settled on the institution after much deliberation. Understanding their concerns is helpful in understanding their intent and how it relates to arguments over the Electoral College today.

The Debate in Philadelphia

Rogers contends that the Framers were seeking to balance a host of interests that were often in conflict with one another. These included "small states versus large states, northern free states versus southern slave-owning states, as well as those favoring more power nationally versus those desiring to keep power at the state level" (2010, 23). The balance of power between the federal government and state governments proved to be one of the most difficult issues to resolve. This balance reflects the multidimensionality of representation discussed in Chapter 2. The Framers were charged with creating a document that would satisfy multiple constituencies. Doing so meant they had to devise a government that was both national and federal in nature (Dahl, 2003, 12).

In regard to the Electoral College, the Framers aimed to maintain the separation of powers, attract quality candidates to the presidency, and limit chicanery in the electoral process. From this, three options dominated discussion in the debates over the Electoral College. These options were selecting the president by (1) a vote of Congress, (2) direct popular vote, or (3) a vote of state legislatures. At the outset, it is clear that what was to become the Electoral College was not on the minds of the Framers when they arrived in Philadelphia. However, elements of each of these options foreshadow what was to become the Electoral College. The amalgamation of these alternatives into the Electoral College led John Roche to famously conclude that it is nothing more than a "jerry-rigged improvisation which has subsequently been endowed with a high theoretical content" (1961, 811).

The selection of the chief executive vexed the Framers throughout the summer. After many iterations, they found common ground in the Electoral College. When considering the debate over the selection process, it is important to recognize the give-and-take of the Framers throughout the process. Edwards suggests that the delegates faced great pressure to avoid additional conflict, were fatigued and impatient due to their activity in Philadelphia, and were not immediately concerned about the actual operation of the institution as they were more concerned with concluding their business at the Convention (2004, 87). While they were often exasperated from the constant back-and-forth with one another, they were able to settle on a process that, while at times not preferable, was at least agreeable to all. This is an important point to consider.

Lutz, Abbott, Allen, and Hanson lament that too often those who debate the Electoral College do not take into account the distinction between "most preferred" versus "preferred by most" (2002, 48). Intense interests are able to shape what can be "preferred by most" given their strong advocacy on behalf of a certain policy or course of action. This is evident when examining the debate over the executive selection process. The coalition of less populated states and slave states held intense feelings about how representation in the legislature and executive ought to be conceptualized. They believed they had much to lose by acquiescing sovereignty to a national government, without adequate representation of their respective interests. This point becomes especially salient taking into account that they were moving from a confederal government to a federal government. State autonomy was the norm, and any deviation from that was considered a threat by many states. Dahl sagely notes that "the necessity for compromise and the opportunities this gave for coalitions and logrolling meant that the Constitution could not possibly reflect a coherent, unified theory of government" (2003, 12). The politics of ratification hung over most every decision the Framers had to make.

When the delegates gathered in Philadelphia, a deliberate attempt was made to model the new constitution after state constitutions. Doing so provided familiarity among those in attendance and provided reference points in their arguments over what had the potential to work best at the federal level. During this period, most state legislatures chose their state's chief executive. This was the case for Virginia, which also served as the model for the draft constitution. The received wisdom was that the same would be true for the federal chief executive (i.e., selection by the legislature). Rogers notes that "for much of the Convention the national legislature was the preferred mechanism for most participants" (2010, 26). Slonim points out that after much debate, midway through the Convention, it appeared that consensus was building for an executive who was "(1) to be elected by the legislature; (2) to serve for seven years; and (3) to be ineligible for a second term" (1986, 42). This arrangement is very different from what unfolded over the following month.

After some thought, the Framers became concerned that a chief executive chosen by the legislature would lack independence. Although it was expected that this would be the means of selecting the chief executive going into the Convention, arguments that legislative selection would weaken separation of powers and checks and balances began to hold greater sway. As the Framers began to question the legislature's involvement in selecting the chief executive, they turned to a discussion of popular selection.

At the time, governors were only popularly elected in Massachusetts, New Hampshire, and New York. James Wilson, a delegate from Pennsylvania, soon began to advocate for the direct popular election of the executive. Pointing to the examples of Massachusetts and New York, Wilson stated that direct election had proven to be a "convenient and successful mode" of executive selection (quoted in Slonim, 1986, 38). Gouverneur Morris argued that the executive should "be elected by the people at large . . . if the people should elect, they will never fail to prefer some man of distinguished character . . . if the legislature elect, it will be the work of intrigue, of cabal, and of faction" (Slonim, 1986, 40). Direct election, however, sparked a great deal of skepticism among many of the delegates. Some thought it was not practicable. Others thought it would supersede the sovereignty of the individual states. Both of these arguments persist to this day.

George Mason pointedly stated that "it would be unnatural to refer the choice of a proper character for a Chief Magistrate to the people, as it would, to refer a trial of colours to a blind man. The extent of the Country renders it impossible that the people can have the requisite capacity to judge of the respective pretentions of the Candidates" (Farrand, 1913, 31). Mason was not questioning whether citizens had the *right* to popularly elect the executive; instead, he questioned their *ability* to do so. The introduction of presidential electors, who would be chosen by the citizenry to cast their ballots for the executive, appeared to be a novel way to resolve the concerns over direct election. These electors were originally considered because citizens would not have enough information to make informed decisions about presidential candidates due to the lack of communication and information available at the time. It was thought that they would provide a means for direct popular control that was attached to the citizenry yet provided independence for the executive from the legislative branch. The creation of smaller electoral districts provided a mechanism to make a nationwide popular vote more practicable. Having citizens select electors who would in turn select the executive was viewed by many as the best way of achieving a democratic result without instituting a direct popular vote. Slonim states that "under the circumstances, popular election of the executive would have the trappings of representative democracy but not the essence" (1986, 41).

The concern that direct election would supersede the sovereignty of the states was tied both to the relative size of states and the knotty issue of slavery. Less populated states were concerned that more populated states would dominate the lawmaking process. The Connecticut Compromise ultimately resolved most of their fears by providing for a bicameral legislature where the lower house was apportioned on the basis of population and the upper house provided equality for each state. The Three-Fifths Compromise "solved" the issue as to how slaves would be counted in the census when it came to determining the number of seats each state would have in the House of Representatives. While this scheme proved workable among the delegates for the legislature, it proved to be difficult as they considered how the chief executive would be selected. Slonim (1986, 55) states that "the protracted discussion over the mode of electing an executive was but a continuation of the struggle that marked the debate on the composition of the legislature. The smaller states were no more prepared to concede to the large states domination of the process of selecting a chief executive than they were prepared to allow them to dominate the legislature."

Charles Pinckney, a delegate from South Carolina, made the now-familiar argument that "the most populous states by combining in favor of the same individual will be able to carry their points" (Slonim, 1986, 40). Just as defenders of the current Electoral College bristle at the notion of a direct popular election, Pinckney observes that the most populated states would have the greatest potential sway through a direct national election. This view favors a *federal* process of selecting the chief executive over a *national* view of selecting a chief executive. The concerns of larger states encroaching on the sovereignty of less populated states was unmistakable. Slave states, too, were highly cognizant that the selection of the executive was tied very closely with their political fortunes. For instance, Hugh Williamson, a delegate from North Carolina, made the dubious claim that direct election of the executive would disadvantage slave states as their "slaves will have no suffrage" (Farrand, 1913, 22). Consequently, both less populated states and slave states preferred legislative selection over direct election as each were able to benefit from compromises relating to representation in the legislative branch.

The resulting impasse forced the Framers to consider additional alternatives. Rogers concludes that "heading into the Convention the odds-on favorite was the national legislature, with direct popular election, at best, second. That neither materialized as the actual mechanism is a function of the deliberative political process and the Framers' tendency to seek compromise in the face of competing motives and goals" (2010, 27). Instead, the state-based approach become more workable in the context of the issues the Framers faced regarding other elements of the Constitution. While the Framers adopted many components of the Constitution from state constitutions, the Electoral College process was a process that was nonpareil. It is worth noting that no state since has adopted anything similar to the federal Electoral College process to select its chief executive. This is the case even though many of the same issues debated at the federal level have been present at the state level (e.g., how to represent citizens in states with large urban areas, along with rural voters). The argument that the politics of the time took precedence over timeless political principles is compelling when one takes into full account the debate over the institution during the Convention.

After consideration of both legislative selection and direct election, the Framers began to coalesce around the idea of a temporary body selected at the state level with the express purpose of choosing the chief executive. The chief architect of the Constitution, James Madison, seemed to prefer direct election. However, he also acknowledged deep concerns with such a process. He stated that "the people at large was in his opinion the fittest in itself" (Slonim,

1986, 43), but he was troubled by the variation in suffrage between Northern and Southern states. Specifically, he noted that due to slavery, Southern states would have little influence on the outcome of a national election if it were based on the popular vote. Building off this concern, on July 20, Oliver Ellsworth proposed that rather than a national legislature, state legislatures could appoint electors for the purpose of choosing the chief executive. This motion appeared to gain momentum but was abandoned just three days later in favor of selection by the national legislature.

Debate continued regarding the process of executive selection, but until August 31 it appeared the national legislature would ultimately choose the president. At that point, Morris moved to strike the provision that the national legislature would select the president from the draft constitution. His motion was approved almost unanimously (9–1–1). This was a surprising turn of events given the lack of debate over the issue in the preceding month. Although many motions had been made for alternatives, it had appeared that selection by the legislative branch was the expected means of selection. With little settled regarding presidential selection, the Committee on Unfinished Parts took up the matter for consideration. They emerged with what we now call the Electoral College.

It combined many of the ideas that had been under consideration as well as incorporating other features of the Constitution that seemed to make sense in light of the concerns of the Framers. The temporary body of electors was meant to ensure the independence of the executive. Yet, it was believed that few individuals other than George Washington would command a majority in the Electoral College, which would then put presidential selection into the hands of the legislature. Thus, the Electoral College was thought to be a nominating body of "the people" to provide viable candidates to the legislature for selection. Leaving the choice of how electors would be selected to the states helped maintain state sovereignty on the matter. Calculating representation based on the representation a state received in both houses of Congress appeased less populated states and slave states. This agreement was consistent with the already forged Connecticut Compromise and appeared to placate those concerned that parochialism would complicate the selection of the national chief executive.

Given the inability to find a workable solution to presidential selection and the fresh perspective offered by the Committee on Unfinished Parts, the newly devised Electoral College process was welcomed by the delegates. It is worth acknowledging that the solution was born more of compromise than through grand political theory. Gossett makes the point that "what really moved the delegates to accept the electoral system . . . were certain practical considerations, dictated not by political ideals but by the social realities of the time—realities that no longer exist" (1970, 1103). Jack Rakove less charitably makes a similar point: "The Electoral College was cobbled together nearly at the last minute and adopted not because the framers believed it would work, but because it was less objectionable than two more obvious alternatives: election of the president by the people or by Congress . . . It had no advantages of its own" (2000, A31). This point is underscored by the ratification debates that followed.

During those debates, at least 32 critics articulated 13 different criticisms of the institution in the wake of the Convention (Rogers, 2010, 30). Rogers argues that "many believed that, like the Constitution, the Electoral College was too complex and complicated" (2010, 30). The Electoral College faced its harshest critics in Virginia, Massachusetts, New York, and Pennsylvania. It is perhaps no accident that these were among the most populous states at the time and had the most to lose through the federal rather than national character of the institution. William Symmes Jr., a representative from Massachusetts, conveyed this point: "Whose voice are we supposed to hear in all public transactions? We Republicans say, the voice of ye. people. Who are ye. people? We answer, ye. majority. But a majority of States may chuse a President" (Kaminski and Saladino, 1988–2009a, 237). Likewise, DeWitt Clinton, a politician from New York, decried that the president and Senate would be "so far above the common people that they will care little about them" (Kaminski and Saladino, 1988–2009b, 407).

In spite of the intricate process they had crafted, many of the Framers believed the choice of the president would still be left to the legislature. They foresaw few candidates achieving a majority of the Electoral College vote, wherein the legislature would ultimately select the executive through the contingency process. George Mason was concerned that many outside of Independence Hall would object that "nineteen times in twenty the President would be chosen by the Senate, an improper body for the purpose" (Farrand, 1913, 500). Indeed, many scholars have concluded that "Congress was expected to select the president most or even all of the time" (Lutz, Abbott, Allen, and Hanson, 2002, 39).

Just as the Framers wrestled with the problem of presidential selection throughout the summer of 1787, many continued to wrestle with their solution throughout the ratification process. The Electoral College was not a universally acclaimed institution, nor was it the "most preferred" option among the Framers. Instead, "the historical record shows . . . that the Electoral

College emerged as a compromise solution for those favoring direct popular election and those seeking a state-based mechanism" (Rogers, 2010, 40).

To recap, the Electoral College was conceived out of much discussion and debate. To suggest that the body resulted from compromise is an understatement. The final version of the Electoral College looked nothing like what was proposed by the Framers throughout most of the Convention. In fact, no one had suggested an intermediary body would choose the chief executive when the Convention convened in May. It was not until late August that such an idea was offered. Moreover, the bargaining between the states to conceptualize representation among the states in the Electoral College went through many iterations. Ultimately, it would appear that momentum from the Connecticut Compromise largely influenced the final composition of the Electoral College. These decisions were not made by accident, but nor were they fully built on timeless principles relating to representation. The politics of ratifying a document all could live with (whether they preferred it or not) was an essential element in the creation of the Electoral College.

All of this goes to show that while the Framers were men of eminent talent and philosophical depth, they were also politicians. Although they relied heavily on principle, they were not beholden to absolutes. Instead, they sought common ground when possible. The debate over presidential selection reveals their willingness to compromise in order to find an agreeable solution to a rather difficult problem. Roche concludes that "the vital aspect of the Electoral College was that it got the Convention over the hurdle and protected everybody's interests. The future was left to cope with the problem of what to do with this Rube Goldberg mechanism" (1961, 811). Rather than standing on high ideals, the institution was the product of compromise. With any compromise, agents both "win" and "lose." While the Electoral College was not the first choice of those in Philadelphia, it became the most acceptable choice among those debating the issue. Consequently, future generations have continued to debate its merits and demerits. Perhaps more important is that the "mechanism" has undergone significant substantive changes from that which was devised at the Convention. It is to the evolution of the body to which I now turn.

The Evolution of the Electoral College

Michael Korzi provides a succinct way to think about debate concerning the Electoral College. He states that "there are really two Electoral Colleges: the one that the Framers envisioned and the one that evolved basically by the middle of the nineteenth century and which we still live with today" (2010, 47). He goes on to note that many treat the original body and the evolved body as the same thing. Yet, the Electoral College of today operates very differently from that which was originally conceived. Therefore, it is important to understand how changes to the institution have affected its operation as it relates to many of the issues brought up by the Framers. Even then, as we have just seen, relying too heavily on the Framers' intentions is likely inadequate due to the compromises and lack of unanimity among them regarding the Electoral College.

Several major changes have occurred that have significantly affected the operation of the Electoral College. In spite of the energy devoted to modify the Electoral College through constitutional means over the years, most of these changes have occurred at the state level and through political necessity (Longley and Peirce, 1999, 22). Longley and Peirce identify five major ways the Electoral College has evolved from its original conception: obedient electors, the move away from the Electoral College as a nominating body, the popular election of electors, the rise of the unit rule, and the 12th Amendment's prescriptions regarding the Electoral College process. Taken together, these changes democratized the presidential selection process and illustrated the ability of states and political parties to effect change regarding the Electoral College.

Recall that originally the top two candidates receiving votes in the Electoral College were elected as the president and vice president, respectively. Although this conception was to have the two most capable individuals occupy the presidency and vice presidency, it soon became apparent that these individuals would likely have different opinions on a number of issues. This became increasingly evident with the emergence of formal political parties. The appearance of party tickets further complicated matters as electors made no distinction in their ballots for president or vice president. Chapter 1 detailed the constitutional crisis this created with the tie between Thomas Jefferson and Aaron Burr in 1800.

As a result of that election, the practice and operation of the Electoral College changed dramatically. Preceding that election, electors were pledging themselves to vote for a particular ticket. This practice meant that electors were forgoing their independence and that citizens (or state legislatures) knew in advance of the meeting of the Electoral College how electors were expected to vote. This was a clear move away from a trustee style of representation among the electors toward a delegate style of representation. No constitutional amendment occurred to sanction this activity. No federal statutes have been enacted to enforce this practice either. Over time, political parties in a number of states have exacted pledges from their electors to ensure their loyalty when they meet as a college. These pledges have been ruled constitutional by the U.S. Supreme Court. Some states have gone farther by punishing electors who break their pledge. However, the Supreme Court has not ruled on the constitutionality of these "binding" laws. I revisit this issue in greater detail in Chapter 6.

The idea that the Electoral College would be a nominating body also went by the wayside with the establishment of party tickets. The development of political parties helped provide a means to achieve mass democracy in a way the Framers did not envision. Recall that selection by the legislature dominated much of the discussion about presidential selection in Philadelphia. While considerable debate was offered in favor of popular election, many of the Framers thought it was impracticable. The Electoral College was then offered as a compromise between the two. The rise of political parties provided an efficient means to democratize the presidential selection process. This is especially true given the advent of party tickets and electors who conveyed their loyalty to those tickets. In essence, then, "by identifying and campaigning for their strongest candidates, the parties became the nominators" (Lutz, Abbott, Allen, and Hanson, 2002, 39).

The 12th Amendment provided a formal push toward party governance and cleaned up the problems that surfaced in the election of 1800. Although hundreds of proposals have been offered to amend the Electoral College, this is one of only two that has been successful (the other being the 23rd Amendment). The amendment requires electors to cast two separate ballots, one for president and one for vice president; it also provides that if no candidate receives a majority of electoral votes, the House of Representatives would select from among the top three candidates receiving electoral votes rather than the top five. Scholars have pointed out that prior to its passage, political parties were faced with very strategic choices because the top two candidates receiving votes would earn the presidency and vice presidency respectively. A party with little chance of winning might consider (1) throwing its votes toward a preferred vice presidential candidate with the hope of quelling the power of the incoming president or (2) throwing its votes to the opposing party's weaker candidate in an effort to deny the presidency to its preferred candidate (Lutz, Abbott, Allen, and Hanson, 2002, 36). The passage of the 12th Amendment made these calculations obsolete. It also moved presidential selection "from one of largely elite competition toward mass participation" (Lutz, Abbott, Allen, and Hanson, 2002, 37).

The final two changes that have affected the Electoral College's operation occurred over time rather than all at once. They are also intimately tied to the party system encouraged by the 12th Amendment. The use of the unit rule further established the dominance of political parties (and the two-party system in particular) in American politics. States are free to choose how they apportion their Electoral College votes, and the advent of party tickets made adoption of the unit rule irresistible to party leaders. Almost all the states had adopted the unit rule to allocate their electoral votes by the 1830s. As we saw in Chapter 2, the use of the unit rule has important consequences for representation. It works to maintain the two-party system, thereby minimizing the influence of minor parties. Such systems may also lead to greater voter apathy. Proponents claim that two-party systems promote more centrist policy, simplify choices for voters, and encourage greater stability in government.

The Constitution leaves the manner of selecting electors up to the states. Originally, many state legislatures simply appointed electors. Only Delaware, Maryland, Pennsylvania, and Virginia allowed direct election by voters in the first presidential election in 1789. Connecticut, Georgia, New Jersey, and South Carolina had their state legislatures choose their electors. By 1800, it appeared that state legislative selection rather than a direct popular vote was going to be the norm. Ten of 16 states chose their electors through their state legislatures in that contest. However, with the addition of new states to the Union, the 1816 election saw an almost even split between state legislative selection and direct popular vote (9 to 10). By 1836, all states but South Carolina had chosen to select their electors through a popular vote. It was not until 1860 that the state finally moved to adopt the popular selection of its electors. The move toward direct election of electors signifies a clear move toward democracy.

The Electoral College has certainly undergone some significant change. Its operation is very different from what was originally conceived by the Framers. Apart from the 12th Amendment, its evolution was driven at the state level, by political parties, and often without much objection. Taken with the rise of party tickets and expected loyalty among electors, these changes suggest greater confidence in citizens' ability to choose their leaders and a move away from any notion that electors would serve as trustees of the citizenry. The thought that state legislatures rather than citizens would choose electors would be met with great resistance today.

Korzi's "evolved" body is very different from the "original" body. Today's Electoral College is far more democratic than the one conceived by the Framers. Historian H. W. Brands details the "appetite for democracy" that has grown throughout American history and in particular toward the Electoral College (March 31, 2016). He argues that over time, voters "demanded to choose presidential electors themselves . . . [They] made Andrew Jackson the first 'people's president,' to the dismay of the founding generation" (March 31, 2016). As we saw earlier, many of the Framers questioned not the right of the citizens to make choices but their ability to make choices. However, the rise of political parties and improvements in communication rendered obsolete many of the reasons why citizens would have difficulty making decisions. Moreover, an expectation that the citizenry would have a direct hand in selecting the president has been apparent for nearly 200 years. As a result, the body has changed a great deal. As Feerick states, "the system which emerged in practice is not the system contemplated by the founding fathers" (1968, 255).

Conclusion

Notwithstanding Hamilton's pronouncement that the Electoral College "was at least excellent," it is apparent the Framers considered a number of alternatives when devising the institution. These alternatives reflected various interests throughout the country. The resulting body took these interests into consideration, and the Electoral College was born. It was unlike anything that had been created to that point, and nothing like it was originally under consideration by the Framers. Instead, it was the result of a "complex compromise that reflected the interests of different states and the search for consensus" (Edwards, 2004, 90).

At the outset of this chapter, I noted that George Edwards identified issues the Framers struggled with regarding the presidential selection process, including the importance of presidential independence, concern over voter parochialism, concern over the population differences among the states, slavery, and the pressure to draft a system that would obtain a consensus at the Convention. In this context, the creation of the Electoral College makes great sense. Through the Electoral College process, the Framers were able to address all of these issues and ultimately produce consensus among the delegates. Edwards argues that the concerns of the Framers in crafting the original Electoral College are largely irrelevant given the changes that have taken place both in its evolution and in regard to today's American political landscape. He states:

> Legislative election is not an option, there is little danger that the president will be too powerful if directly elected, voters have extraordinary

access to information on the candidates, there is no justification at all for either electors or state legislatures to exercise discretion in selecting the president, defending the interests of slavery is unthinkable, and the short-term pressures have long dissipated. (2003, 89)

In short, Edwards concludes that almost all of the catalysts for the creation of the body no longer exist. Therefore, observers should evaluate the institution as it has evolved, not as it originated. The evolved body is quite different from the original body, and the rationale for the original Electoral College is largely no longer relevant.

In their examination of the Framers' intentions, Lutz, Abbott, Allen, and Hanson identify several "broad lessons" that can be gleaned from the history and evolution of the Electoral College. First, they contend that the institution was created as a "natural extension of the principles of federalism, separation of powers, and a deliberative process" that was consistent with other features of the Constitution (2002, 45). Second, they illustrate how incremental changes to electoral systems have had large effects on political institutions. The passage of the 12th Amendment and the adoption of the unit rule significantly altered the operation of the Electoral College. As we saw with the evolution of the body, the rise of political parties and the move to popularly select electors dramatically changed the Electoral College process as well. Third, they note the close tie between political parties and the Electoral College. The institution works to support the two-party system, and any change to it is often viewed through the lens of how that change would affect the strength of the two major parties. Finally, they point out how resistant the body is to change. This is especially the case when it comes to change at the federal level.

Korzi's observation of there being two Electoral Colleges—the one that was drafted and the one that has been in practice—is instructive. We have learned that the original vision of the Electoral College resulted from compromise and debate. It took many different ideas into account and was "approved by most" rather than being the "most preferred" option the Framers faced. The rise of political parties and the adoption of the 12th Amendment radically changed the practice of the Electoral College. It is a far more democratic institution than its original conception. The acknowledgment of these two Electoral Colleges (original versus evolved) explains much of the difficulty that is faced when evaluating the body. Individuals may be addressing one version of the Electoral College instead of another. Often, those arguing over the Electoral College are not arguing using the same facts. We must first agree on which body we are examining. This requires us to acknowledge the compromises of the Framers and the evolution of the body over time. Doing so allows us to appropriately evaluate the merits of the Electoral College. Any examination of the institution that fails to account for these matters is incomplete.

4

Federalism and the Electoral College

AT A PRESENTATION shortly after the 2016 election, I was greeted with a question I was not expecting. One of the audience members asked whether it was true that if you removed the results from Los Angeles County and the five boroughs of New York, Donald Trump would have won the popular vote. Stammering for an answer, I noted that because neither candidate campaigned in those areas, the answer to the question would be incomplete. Because Clinton was expected to win those areas in large numbers, it would be expected that Trump supporters would be less inclined to cast votes in those states. Moreover, the Senate race in California was a contest between two Democrats, with no viable Republican challenger. I then promised the audience I would get back to them with an answer.

It turns out it was true. Removing Los Angeles County and New York's five boroughs from the national vote would have given Trump over 300,000 more votes than Clinton nationwide. However, if one were to remove those same areas along with the entire state of Alabama from the national vote, Clinton would have defeated Trump by over 600,000 votes. Neither of the campaigns visited any of these states in 2016, and yet all were citizens of the United States. The very nature of the audience member's question reveals the emphasis on geographic boundaries when it comes to discussions of the Electoral College. This chapter takes this on by evaluating the Electoral College as it relates to federalism.

In Chapter 3 we examined debates over the Electoral College at the Constitutional Convention. The Framers ultimately favored a process emphasizing federal input over national input. This distinction, however, is not as clear as many proponents of the Electoral College purport it to be. Protecting state sovereignty was certainly at the front of many Framers' minds. After all, the first government of the United States was a confederacy, and the Convention was called to ameliorate issues resulting from the lack of coordination under the Articles. While greater efficiency and cooperation were at the heart of the Convention, striking a balance with states' autonomy made the move to a federal government tricky. This was especially the case due to the vast differences between the states relative to their demographics, their economies, and the cloud of slavery. The Electoral College provided a means to protect state interests while also seeking to reward candidates having national rather than regional appeal. Electors were expected to choose individuals who were not "favorite sons." Additionally, recall that many of the Framers considered an intermediary body of electors the next best thing to a popular election given the lack of communication and media at the time. While it emphasized the role of states, it also sought to create a system where electors were able to select a chief executive who would work to serve the best interests of the entire nation, rather than states writ large. Ultimately, the Framers wanted a chief executive with broad support throughout the fledgling nation.

The federal–national distinction brings several theories of representation to bear, most notably descriptive and substantive representation. This is especially the case when we consider the evolved Electoral College rather than the original body. Recall that within a generation, the institution changed considerably due to the rise and influence of political parties in the electoral system. Parties have become a major source for representation in American politics. As E. E. Schattschneider famously stated: "Modern democracy is unthinkable save in terms of parties" (1942, 1). After the presidency of George Washington, political parties have dominated electoral politics at the national level. The Electoral College is often cited as a reason for the existence and maintenance of the two-party system, given the widespread application of the unit rule throughout the states. While it is tempting to rely on the original intent of the Framers, doing so ignores the changes many of those same individuals participated in just a few years after the Electoral College's inception. It also disregards changes in our political culture that have direct bearing on arguments surrounding the Electoral College. Haider-Markel and his colleagues identified several of these changes. Most notably, they state that "the system has been transformed by the development of a competitive two-party system and by having electors pledged to party slates, by using state-wide popular elections (rather than state legislatures) to determine electors and by the winner-take-all feature most states use to award their Electoral College votes" (2002, 57). Likewise, they assert that "contemporary democratic theory and cultural norms emphasize that power and legitimacy are derived from popular 'majority rule' (as Andrew Jackson was to claim as the basis of his presidential power beginning in 1832)" (2002, 55–56). The principle of majority rule has become embedded in virtually every elective office throughout the country. Calls to have the president elected through a nationwide popular vote underscore this point.

George Edwards (2004) has made a strong case that the emphasis on the federal character of the body has been overstated and has had deleterious consequences for representation in the United States. His argument rests upon several points. First, he argues that federalism was more of a secondary rationale of the Framers. As discussed in Chapter 3, they were concerned with consensus building and believed that the Electoral College system would prevent regionalism and would likely yield presidents who campaigned with national interests in mind. Although the appearance is that protecting state sovereignty was paramount, the desire to produce a national figure who was able to command supermajorities is a more accurate explanation of the Framers' intentions for the body.

Second, he notes that the Electoral College represents the only national position in the United States and that the Electoral College system violates the bedrock principle that all votes should be treated equally. As we saw in Chapter 3, many of the Framers preferred direct election of the chief executive but were unable to convince enough of their colleagues that the citizens were well suited to do so. Few questioned the right of citizens to directly select their leaders; instead, they were concerned that poor communication significantly hindered mass participation. And while few states chose their electors by direct election in early races for the presidency, by 1836 virtually all states chose their electors by popular election. Combined with the direct election of US senators, the extension of suffrage to women and minorities, and the rise of direct democracy, it is expected that citizens should be responsible for choosing their leaders. Indeed, it would be unthinkable today if state legislatures decided to choose electors over the wishes of their state's citizenry.

Third, many have pointed out that arguments suggesting the Electoral College helps preserve federalism are overblown. To begin, differences among the states have become less marked over time. Communication, transportation, and the mass media have minimized differences throughout the United States. The absence of slavery and the greater enjoyment of civil rights across the country has also given pause to those emphasizing differences among the states. Second, and perhaps most important, the nationalization of conflict through the two-party system has stressed differences based on *ideology* rather than *location*. This relates to the evolved Electoral College and is often neglected in arguments examining federalism's relationship to the institution. However, the development of the two-party system has had enormous effects on political processes across the states.

Lastly, the diversity that exits between the states also occurs *within* the states. Few states are wholly agricultural or industrial, rural or urban, or Democrat or Republican. In short, differences that exist between states may also exist within states. This is a point that political scientist Daron Shaw, who was an advisor to George W. Bush's 2000 campaign, makes regarding the public's understanding of Electoral College campaign strategies. He states: "Categories of states are fine, but what happens, for example, when the campaign has to decide where to expend resources *within* the battleground states?" (2006, 52).

Because of the differences within states, the relationship between sparsely populated states and densely populated states is not a clear one. For instance, Jack Rakove asks: "What does Chicago share with Galena, except that they both are in Illinois; Palo Alto with Lodi in California; Northern Virginia with Madison's home in Orange County; or Hamilton, N.Y., with Alexander Hamilton's old haunts in lower Manhattan?" (December 19, 2000, A35). Edwards further points out that a great deal of diversity exists among the states with the fewest number of electoral votes (those with five or less). He states that:

> some of the states are quite liberal while others are very conservative, and their policies and levels of taxation reflect these differences . . . They represent a great diversity of core economic interests, including agriculture, mining, gambling, chemicals, tourism, and energy. Even the agricultural interests are quite diverse, ranging from grain and dairy products to hogs and sheep. In sum, small states do not share common interests. It is not surprising that their representatives do not vote as a bloc in Congress or and that their citizens do not vote as a bloc for president. (2004, 96)

Speaking to these points, there is little actual evidence that the Electoral College works to protect state interests, especially states with smaller populations. If anything, candidates spend their time in and speak to issues relevant to battleground states. As we will see, most battleground states have sizeable populations and possess relatively large blocs of electoral votes.

Lastly, Edwards contends that partisanship and ideology drive divisions in American politics far more so than one's state residency. Rather than focusing on the supposed interests that states have, those concerned over effective representation should be promoting elections that encourage competition among ideas. Even at the Founding, James Wilson asked: "Can we forget for whom we are forming a government? Is it for men, or for the imaginary beings called States" (quoted in Edwards, 2004, 95). Likewise, Madison stated that "the President is to act for the people not for States" (quoted in Edwards, 2004, 95). More recently, Haider-Markel and colleagues conclude that "the most desirable consensus in America today would focus less on agreement among state interests than agreement across the social cleavages that presently divide our country" (2002, 63). The current Electoral College does not fully enable voters with like minds to aggregate their votes across state lines to make a difference in a national election. The emergence of "vote swapping" in recent elections represents one attempt to solve this issue.

Although many advocates say that less populated states would be ignored without the Electoral College, an examination of where resources are deployed in presidential campaigns shows that these states are largely being ignored under the *current* Electoral College system. The same is true for many of the most populated states. Instead, it is competitive states that receive most of the candidates' attention. The concentration of campaign resources in these battleground states has consequences that directly relate to participation and representation in presidential campaigns.

Throughout the remainder of this chapter I revisit the rationale for the Electoral College as it pertains to federalism and how its evolution has affected its purpose. Further, I evaluate the effects of the Electoral College on how candidates campaign and what this has meant for citizen participation and representation. Lastly, I examine the merits of arguments that support the Electoral College as an important bulwark of federalism in the United States.

Background

The Electoral College was born out of compromise. What the Framers ultimately fabricated regarding presidential selection turned out to be much different than what many expected when they arrived in Philadelphia. Much of that was due to compromises that occurred relative to the legislative branch. This is particularly true as it relates to representation of states relative to the national government. Although the decision to have a body of electors vote for the president could be seen as a nod to state sovereignty, it also could be viewed as a nod toward popular selection. Recall that originally it was believed that the legislature would select the chief executive. This idea was abandoned due to concerns over separation of powers. The notion of having state legislatures choose the chief executive was discarded due to a concern over the possibility of "favorite sons" who could garner votes but would be incapable of securing widespread support across the country. The Electoral College then, would serve as a means to select (or at least nominate) candidates with broad-based appeal for the position of president. States would continue to be important players in the process, but they would not be the only players in the process. The desire to have presidents ascend to the office with widespread support was strong, and the Electoral College was thought to be an adequate means to produce such a result.

Still, there is little question that the Electoral College system emphasized the role of states in the process. It provided a means to enable all states to play a role in the presidential selection process. Although not all states would have an equal voice due to the distribution of Electoral College votes, less populated states would have a presumably greater voice than they would if presidential contests were left up to only the popular vote. Moreover, each state's having an equal vote in the House of Representatives in the occurrence of a contingent election indicated deference to statehood as an important principle of representation. The emphasis on statehood was particularly appealing to the natural coalition of less populated states and slave states. It provided these states with much greater weight in the electoral process than they otherwise would have had. The Electoral College was consistent with many other compromises the Framers made in an effort to secure the passage of the new constitution. Haider-Markel and colleagues state that the "Electoral College was developed as a method for selecting a president who would have a national perspective that was inclusive of state interests, by giving the states a significant but not overwhelming role in his selection" (2002, 55). Protecting the interests of states was a particularly sensitive issue as the Constitution was a grand movement toward greater federal power. In this context, the arrangement adopted by the Framers represents an attempt to satisfy concerns of national overreach rather than an endorsement of state power in national affairs.

The evolution of the institution and its subsequent operation have led some scholars to question whether federalism is actually supported by the body today. Others wonder whether the system makes any sense "in an era where every official besides the president is elected by the popular vote" (Haider-Markel et al., 2002, 53). Haider-Markel and colleagues suggest that the Framers were not as antidemocratic as they are often portrayed. They state that "a myth has developed that portrays the framers as 'antidemocratic,' fixated on minimizing the potential for liberty-threatening 'mobocracy.' In fact, the framers seemed more preoccupied with showing some deference to the states than with the evils of popular votes" (2002, 56). The Framers wanted a system that would "achieve fairly broad consensus or supramajorities, rather than bare-minimum majorities" (Haider-Markel et al., 2002, 56). Poor communication prevented many citizens from being well informed about candidates across the new nation. It would fall to electors to find candidates who would work toward national interests rather than parochial interests.

Judith Best (1975) has maintained that the Electoral College was designed to produce candidates who could obtain the most widespread support across all the states in the country rather than simply securing the most votes from across the country. The differences between the states (particularly those pertaining to slavery) were significant at the Founding. Attaching interests to statehood made a great deal of sense. At the same time, however, the Framers were not oblivious to the role of interests across the country. Although discussed, they jettisoned a proposal that gave all states an equal say in the Electoral College. While less populated states were disproportionally represented, larger states still had the greatest influence in the body due to their blocs of votes.

A number of scholars have made the case that geography was much more salient during the nation's formative years than it has been from the 20th century onward. From the outset, many Framers were skeptical of centralized power, and the adoption of the Articles of Confederation sought to disperse power among the states rather than grant it to a national government. The distinction between agrarian states and industrial states was relatively clear, as was the presence of those states practicing slavery and those that forbade it. The push toward a stronger national sovereign had to contend with these significant differences among the states. Although calls for state sovereignty persist today, it meant quite a bit more in the 18th and 19th centuries due to the presence of slavery. The balance of power between slave states and non-slave states was delicate and combustible. The move to the new constitution represented a significant step toward greater federal power. While state sovereignty was important to the Framers, the recognition that the national government was the "supreme law of the land" was an unequivocal statement regarding the relationship between the newly formed federal government and the states.

Debate over the importance of maintaining the federal principle as it relates to the Electoral College must take into account the evolved body, not just the original institution. Likewise, we should consider what we have learned about the nature of representation. As we saw in Chapter 2, representation takes many forms. Looking after the interests of one's own constituency is one of many considerations of a representative. This fact becomes even more critical when we consider how the Electoral College has changed, in addition to changes in American political culture.

Political equality has become an important principle in American politics. Evidence of this can be seen in the democratization of many institutions in American society. The landmark Supreme Court case *Reynolds v. Sims* (1964) ruled that political equality was required under the Constitution's Equal Protection Clause. Chief Justice Earl Warren stated that "Legislators represent people, not trees or acres. Legislators are elected by voters, not farms or cities or economic interests" (*Reynolds v. Sims*). Consequently, the Court concluded that congressional districts should have roughly equal populations relative to one another. Thus, the principle of "one person, one vote" was firmly established.

Nonetheless, the Electoral College process is a creature of the Constitution, and its scheme of awarding electoral votes on the basis of congressional and Senate representation is well established. Proponents of the body contend that it is an important institution to protect states' interests, particularly for less populated states. Despite these claims, its advocates may be disappointed with the scholarly record on the subject. Haider-Markel and colleagues conclude that "the current operation of the Electoral College may give states a smaller role in the selection of a president than originally envisioned" (2002, 61). Table 4.1 documents the relative voting power of the states in the 2016 election.

Several items stand out when examining Table 4.1. First, we can see the effects of the "bonus two Senate votes" for the least populated states relative to the most populated states. Less populated states maintain a disproportionate voting power relative to larger states. For instance, none of the states with three electoral votes make up any more than 0.32 percent of the national population, but all compose at least 0.56 percent of the Electoral College vote. The biggest differences occur with Wyoming (0.18 percent) and Vermont (0.19 percent). The bonus two votes provide these two states with nearly three times the voting power in the Electoral College than their populations would merit. Conversely, California makes up 12.15 percent of the US population but just over 10 percent of the votes in the Electoral College. Texas also suffers from malapportionment, as its citizens represent 8.62 percent of the population but just around 7 percent of the Electoral College vote. The discrepancies for many states are not as stark, but differences do occur in all

Table 4.1 Electoral Vote Allocation 2016

State	# of Electoral Votes	% of National Population	% of Electoral College Vote	Tipping Point Index*	Voter Power Index*
Wyoming	3	0.18	0.56	<0.1	<0.1
Vermont	3	0.19	0.56	<0.1	0.2
Washington, DC	3	0.21	0.56	<0.1	<0.1
Alaska	3	0.23	0.56	0.3	1.5
North Dakota	3	0.24	0.56	<0.1	0.1
South Dakota	3	0.27	0.56	<0.1	0.1
Delaware	3	0.30	0.56	0.3	1.1
Montana	3	0.32	0.56	<0.1	0.1
Rhode Island	4	0.33	0.74	0.4	1.1
Maine	4	0.41	0.74	0.5	1
New Hampshire	4	0.41	0.74	3	5.5
Hawaii	4	0.44	0.74	<0.1	0.2
Idaho	4	0.52	0.74	<0.1	<0.1
West Virginia	5	0.57	0.93	<0.1	<0.1
Nebraska	5	0.59	0.93	<0.1	<0.1
New Mexico	5	0.64	0.93	2.3	4
Kansas	6	0.90	1.12	<0.1	<0.1
Nevada	6	0.91	1.12	3.5	4.3
Arkansas	6	0.93	1.12	<0.1	<0.1
Missouri	10	0.93	1.86	<0.1	<0.1
Utah	6	0.94	1.12	<0.1	<0.1
Iowa	6	0.97	1.12	1.3	1.1
Connecticut	7	1.11	1.30	0.2	0.2
Oklahoma	7	1.21	1.30	<0.1	<0.1
Oregon	7	1.27	1.30	0.8	0.6
Kentucky	8	1.37	1.49	<0.1	<0.1
Louisiana	8	1.45	1.49	<0.1	<0.1
Alabama	9	1.51	1.67	<0.1	<0.1
South Carolina	9	1.54	1.67	0.4	0.2

Table 4.1 Continued

State	# of Electoral Votes	% of National Population	% of Electoral College Vote	Tipping Point Index*	Voter Power Index*
Minnesota	10	1.71	**1.86**	3.7	1.6
Colorado	9	1.72	1.67	6.7	3.2
Wisconsin	10	1.79	**1.86**	4.5	2
Maryland	10	1.86	1.86	<0.1	<0.1
Mississippi	6	1.89	1.12	<0.1	<0.1
Indiana	11	2.05	2.0	<0.1	<0.1
Tennessee	11	2.06	2.0	<0.1	<0.1
Massachusetts	11	2.11	2.0	<0.1	<0.1
Arizona	11	2.15	2.0	2.8	1.5
Washington	12	2.26	2.23	<0.1	<0.1
Virginia	13	2.60	2.42	6.4	2.2
New Jersey	14	2.77	2.60	0.6	0.2
Michigan	16	3.07	2.98	12.2	3.4
North Carolina	15	3.14	2.79	10.3	2.9
Georgia	16	3.19	2.97	1.7	0.5
Ohio	18	3.59	3.35	5.1	1.2
Illinois	20	3.96	3.7	0.3	<0.1
Pennsylvania	20	3.96	3.72	13.5	3.1
New York	29	6.11	5.40	<0.1	<0.1
Florida	29	6.38	5.40	17.10	2.5
Texas	38	8.62	7.06	0.3	<0.1
California	55	12.15	10.22	<0.1	<0.1

* The Tipping Point and Voter Power Indexes are derived from Nate Silver's final "Polls Plus" Forecast for the 2016 election. Tipping Point Index is "the probability that a state will provide the decisive vote in the Electoral College." Voter Power Index is the "relative likelihood that an individual voter in a state will determine the Electoral College winner."

Shaded cells indicate those states that were competitive as evidenced by their tipping point and/or voter power index.

Bold values indicate those states that had a higher percentage of the electoral vote relative to their percentage of the national population (i.e., they are disproportionately represented in the Electoral College).

but just one state. Maryland is the only state where the percentage of citizens in the state is equal to the percentage of the Electoral College vote of the state.

That differences occur for all but one state indicates the lack of political equality of citizens across the United States. Yet, proponents of the system point out that Americans live in a republic rather than a democracy. The Electoral College is not a national institution but a federal institution. However, as discussed earlier, the federal nature of the institution is not as clear as is often claimed. Taking into account the original debate over the body illustrates that protecting state sovereignty was one of many principles the Framers sought to address. The evolution of the Electoral College has democratized the process through direct election of electors, and the dominance of political parties has undoubtedly nationalized presidential campaigns.

Second, arguments examining the Electoral College's effects on political equality that are solely based on the relationship between a state's population and its share of the electoral vote are incomplete. While it is true that smaller states have a disproportionate share of the Electoral College vote, we must also take into account the relative importance of a state to political campaigns. John Banzhaf's (1968) pioneering study on *voter power* in the late 1960s produced a new research stream on the subject. Longley and Peirce (1999) further dedicated great energy to examining the Electoral College's effects on *state power* in presidential elections. Assumptions about both voter power and state power are now commonly integrated into most analyses used to predict presidential elections. The emphasis on the importance of specific states to the outcomes of elections is now commonplace.

In the days prior to the 2016 election, Nate Silver modeled what he referred to as "tipping point" states ("the probability that a state will provide the decisive vote in the Electoral College") as well as a "voter power index" ("the relative likelihood that an individual voter in a state will determine the Electoral College winner") (November 8, 2016). These variables build off the work started by Longley and Peirce decades ago. The last two columns of Table 4.1 document Silver's final "polls plus" forecast on the day of the 2016 election. Several findings stand out when looking at these columns. First, we see that most of the states with the highest probability of being a "tipping point" state have populations that are *underrepresented* in the Electoral College. For example, Florida was viewed as the most likely state to determine the outcome of the election, yet its percentage of electoral votes is a full percent lower than its percentage of the national population. In fact, all four of the highest-rated "tipping point" states have populations that would warrant more Electoral College votes based on a purely proportional scheme.

The importance of the unit rule cannot be understated. The large numbers of electoral votes at stake in these states make them very appealing (and necessary) for campaigns to pursue.

We see that none of the least populated states show up as significant "tipping point" states, nor do voters in those states appear to have great voting power, according to Silver. Although voters theoretically have greater voting power in less populated states relative to more populated states due to malapportionment, scholars have found that battleground status is most important to one's likelihood of affecting the outcome of a presidential election. This can be seen in Silver's model. He surmised that voters in Michigan, Wisconsin, Florida, North Carolina, and Pennsylvania were among the most likely to cast decisive votes in the election. In the days following the election, it became clear that these states were indeed critical to Trump's victory. The margins in these states were very close (3.66 percent in North Carolina, 1.1 percent in Florida, 0.77 percent in Wisconsin, 0.72 percent in Pennsylvania, and 0.23 percent in Michigan), and without victories in at least three of these states, Trump would have lost the Electoral College vote. Alaska was the only state with three electoral votes to make Silver's list of the top 15 states with the most voting power. Similarly, none of the smaller states were viewed as being important players in deciding the outcome of the election. Alaska was viewed as the 20th most likely state to affect the outcome of the election—the highest among all the states with three electoral votes.

Although attention is often focused on the disproportionate influence small states have on the Electoral College process, we can see that there is a great deal of incentive to appeal to voters in those states with large numbers of electoral votes. In 2016, the ten most populated states composed 54 percent of the national population but just 48 percent of the total number of votes in the Electoral College. Still, these 10 states represented 256 of the 270 electoral votes necessary to win the presidency. By contrast, the 10 least populated states composed less than 3 percent of the population but 6 percent of the Electoral College vote (just 32 electoral votes). In sum, while malapportionment exists in the Electoral College, the large numbers of votes available from the most populated states largely drowns out the voices of citizens in less populated states.

Third, Table 4.1 provides us with an opportunity to examine Edwards's claims that the Electoral College provides protection for smaller states. When looking at many of the least populated states, it is difficult to see unanimity in their demographics, economies, ideologies, or partisanship. Put another way, there is a good deal of diversity among the least populated states. New

Hampshire, Maine, Delaware, Vermont, and the District of Columbia have been far more likely to vote for Democrats at the national level than have Wyoming, Montana, Alaska, North Dakota, and South Dakota. Yet, we have seen robust party competition at the subnational level in these states. Democrats and Republicans have been represented in statewide offices in virtually all of these states over the past few decades. It would be difficult to argue that these states are monolithic in their values, economies, and ideologies. These points echo Edwards's cynicism that the Electoral College works to protect the interests of smaller states. If the interests of smaller states are disparate and not clearly articulated, it makes little sense that a mechanism for protection in a presidential election should exist.

Among the arguments most often made in support of the Electoral College is that without it, campaigns would flock to the coasts and neglect the heartland. Many states would all but be ignored without the Electoral College. It is argued that the institution, then, is an important safeguard of federalism and minority interests. In this case, minority interests are thought to include rural states. Lutz, Abbott, Allen, and Hansen contend that "the notion of minority rights assumes that the important interests of an intense minority are seriously threatened and need protecting" (2002, 49). Applying this view to states has been met with skepticism. Lutz, Abbott, Allen, and Hansen question whether "states with small populations scattered across a continent are likely to have similar interests" (2002, 48). Edwards similarly questions how North Dakota has much in common with Rhode Island or how Wyoming and Delaware are similar (2004, 95–97). He goes further by noting the diversity within these states—often sending senators of different parties to Washington, or selecting legislatures and governors of opposing parties.

As argued previously, it would appear that a system based on protecting interests (that can be aggregated with similar interests) would make more sense if we are to consider how individuals in the least populated states are to gain a significant voice in national elections. The current "benefit" these states receive from malapportionment does little in the face of the widespread use of the unit rule. This is evidenced by the lack of attention given to these states in presidential campaigns. They are not visited, no money is spent in them, and they are essentially taken for granted by the two major parties. Again, the 10 smallest states only hold 32 electoral votes. Florida currently has 29 electoral votes alone and has been very competitive in presidential elections, making it an integral state in campaigns for the presidency. And this becomes one of the most revealing issues we can see when it comes to the "protection" of states and the Electoral College. If any states are advantaged by the current system, it is those states considered as swing states. This illustrates that not only are all citizens unequal when it comes to the Electoral College, all states are unequal as well.

These points speak to a broader argument that national forces rather than state forces are paramount to presidential campaigns. Haider-Markel and colleagues conclude that while "the Electoral College originally had features that valued the 'states qua states,' but these features have become less relevant as the system has evolved" (2002, 63). Instead, they contend that "powerful economic, demographic, and technological forces" have created a "national consciousness" that has permeated American politics (2002, 63–64). National security, economic prosperity, health care, and education are but a few issues that transcend state boundaries and are at the center of many political campaigns. Even concern over immigration, which was a contentious topic in the 2016 election, was not confined to states on the southern border. Many voters throughout the Midwest expressed great interest in the topic throughout the campaign.

The Electoral College process precludes those with different interests within a state from aggregating their votes with others with similar interests from across the nation. It is issues, rather than one's statehood, that often divide people. This is another consequence of the party system, which is intimately tied to the evolved Electoral College rather than the original Electoral College. The political parties run on platforms that are national in scope. Moreover, the adoption of the unit rule (at the insistence of the parties) minimizes the voices of those who fail to gather a plurality of the vote in a state. Conversely, district representation, proportional representation, or the single-member, transferrable vote procedure would yield very different outcomes that would likely more accurately reflect public opinion found throughout the states.

Many proponents of the Electoral College contend that it forces candidates to run broad campaigns and gives a voice to less populated states, and without it campaigns would only focus on the coasts. Yet, it is widely recognized that presidential campaigns mainly take place in a handful of swing states, largely ignoring the vast majority of states. During his victory tour in the wake of the 2016 election, Trump proudly proclaimed that he visited 17 states in the general election, and that was due to the Electoral College! That two-thirds of the states received no visits hardly amounts to a widespread campaign across the country, which is among the chief arguments in support of the body. It is no secret that candidates focus their campaigns in a few states. The following section examines the effects of this practice and evaluates its significance relating to arguments over representation and the Electoral College.

Battleground States and the Electoral College

Before going further, it is appropriate to provide a brief summary on political participation in the United States. Socioeconomic factors have been shown to be intimately related to political participation. Generally, political scientists have found that "American voters comprise an unrepresentative sample of the nation; they are older, more affluent, better educated, and more likely to be white than they would be if everyone were to participate at equal rates" (Gimple, Kauffman, and Pearson-Merkowitz, 2007, 787). Verba, Scholzman, and Brady (1995) point to a deficit in civic resources between voters and nonvoters as an important set of variables scholars must consider when examining political participation. They conclude that nonvoters either (1) lack necessary civic resources, (2) do not have adequate knowledge or interest in politics, or (3) are not mobilized to participate. The last two categories are especially relevant to the potential effects of the Electoral College on campaign strategies. This is the case due to the campaign strategies deployed in presidential campaigns. Citizens in battleground states are exposed to a barrage of political stimuli, while citizens in safe states rarely see political advertisements or host candidate visits. Likewise, political campaigns expend great energy mobilizing voters in swing states and largely neglect voters in safe states. Scholars have examined whether these practices have had an effect on political participation among citizens in battleground and non-battleground states. These studies have a direct bearing on any evaluation of how the Electoral College is related to representation in the United States.

Critics of the Electoral College claim that it encourages campaigns to narrow their focus to only those states that are competitive and thereby neglect the remainder of the states. In essence, presidential campaigns take place in a handful of battleground states. Candidates spend most of their time and resources in these states, giving little attention to those states not "in play." Reflecting on his role as an advisor to George W. Bush's presidential campaign, political scientist Daron Shaw remarked that it was indeed "true that campaigns do not consider all states equally important" as battleground states get most all the attention in presidential contests (2006, 51). Consequently, we could expect this practice to have an effect on voter information, voter turnout, candidate promises, and policy agendas. This is significant as "campaigns are usually conceived of as *essential* contact points between voters and public officials in the United States" (Shaw, 1999, 893, emphasis added). A number of studies have looked at how the Electoral College affects presidential campaigns and what this means for political participation.

Studies Examining Battleground States

Shaw has contributed a great deal to our understanding of how the Electoral College determines the choices campaigns make during the election cycle. Not surprisingly, he has found that resources are concentrated in battleground states. The more competitive and the closer the contest, the more visits will be made to the state, the more television buys will be made, and the more money will be spent. In his examination of presidential campaigns over the past 30 years, Shaw develops five distinctions campaigns make among the states: states that are base Republican, marginal Republican, battleground, marginal Democratic, and base Democratic. He observes that while different states move from one category to another in any given election, most do not. Rarely does a state move more than one category at a time. That is, it is unlikely a state will move from being a "base state" to a "battleground state" in a single election cycle. Thus, presidential campaigns typically start from very similar places from one election to another. Shaw suggests that changes in how candidates choose to target different states generally occur due to the number of electoral votes at stake in a state, the television advertising costs in a state, the competitiveness of a state, the interaction between competitiveness and electoral votes, and the interaction between competitiveness and the cost of television advertising (1999, 904).

Table 4.2 documents the campaign visits of the Bush–Cheney and Gore–Lieberman campaigns from the 2000 presidential election. That contest resulted in a razor-thin Electoral College majority for Bush (271 electoral votes), while Gore narrowly captured the popular vote (48.4 percent to 47.9 percent). A slim 537-vote margin in Florida secured the win for Bush. As Table 4.2 shows, the campaigns rightly spent more time in Florida than any other state (47 visits). The campaigns also targeted Michigan (39 visits), Pennsylvania (36 visits), California (34 visits), Wisconsin (31 visits), Missouri (30 visits), Illinois (29 visits), Ohio (27 visits), and Iowa (27 visits). Together, these nine states accounted for over a third of all electoral votes at stake. Iowa held the least number of electoral votes with seven. Most of these states were competitive. By contrast, 36 states received less than 10 visits and 24 states received no visits at all! The latter group of states accounted for 37 percent of the Electoral College votes. Of the least populated states (those with three

Table 4.2 Candidates' Visits to States in 2000

	Electoral Votes	Visits by Bush or Cheney	Visits by Gore or Lieberman	Total Visits
Florida	25	21	26	47
Michigan	18	27	12	39
Pennsylvania	23	24	12	36
California	54	24	10	34
Wisconsin	11	13	18	31
Missouri	11	15	15	30
Illinois	22	17	12	29
Ohio	21	17	10	27
Iowa	7	10	14	24
Tennessee	11	9	9	18
Washington	11	10	8	18
Oregon	7	10	6	16
New Mexico	5	7	5	12
Arkansas	6	6	5	11
Kentucky	8	5	5	10
Maine	4	4	5	9
Louisiana	9	5	3	8
New Hampshire	4	4	3	7
Nevada	4	4	2	6
New Jersey	15	0	6	6
Minnesota	10	2	3	5
West Virginia	5	4	1	5
North Carolina	14	3	1	4
Georgia	13	1	2	3
Delaware	3	1	1	2
Arizona	8	1	0	1
Colorado	8	1	0	1
Alabama	9	0	0	0
Alaska	3	0	0	0
Connecticut	8	0	0	0
Washington, DC	3	0	0	0
Hawaii	4	0	0	0
Idaho	4	0	0	0
Indiana	12	0	0	0
Kansas	6	0	0	0

Table 4.2 Continued

	Electoral Votes	Visits by Bush or Cheney	Visits by Gore or Lieberman	Total Visits
Maryland	10	0	0	0
Massachusetts	12	0	0	0
Mississippi	7	0	0	0
Montana	3	0	0	0
Nebraska	5	0	0	0
New York	33	0	0	0
North Dakota	3	0	0	0
Oklahoma	8	0	0	0
Rhode Island	4	0	0	0
South Carolina	8	0	0	0
South Dakota	3	0	0	0
Texas	32	0	0	0
Utah	5	0	0	0
Vermont	3	0	0	0
Virginia	13	0	0	0
Wyoming	3	0	0	0

Source: Shaw 2006, 86–87.

electoral votes), only Delaware received any visits from any of the candidates. None of the candidates set foot in the remaining seven least populated states.

Shaw finds that a similar pattern holds for media buys in the 2000 election. Most of the same states that received face time with the candidates were also the main targets for television advertising for the campaigns. Not surprisingly, Shaw observes (2006, 79–80) that the campaigns spent the most money in Florida (over $27 million), Pennsylvania (over $24 million), and Michigan (over $22 million). Not one dollar was spent toward advertising in 25 states (2006, 79–80). Put plainly, in one of the closest presidential contests in history, the candidates did not spend any advertising dollars in half of the states, nor did they even set foot in nearly half of the states. Rather, a state where the margin of victory was less than 0.01 percent was the main target of the campaigns, both in candidate visits and in media buys.

Table 4.3 provides similar information for the 2016 presidential campaign. Like the 2000 campaign, the candidates spent most of their time in a select group of states. Nearly 70 percent of all campaign events were held

Table 4.3 Candidates' Visits to States 2016

State	Electoral votes	Clinton–Kaine Events	Trump–Pence Events	Total Events
Florida	29	36	35	71
North Carolina	15	24	31	55
Pennsylvania	20	26	28	54
Ohio	18	18	30	48
Virginia	13	5	18	23
Michigan	16	8	14	22
Iowa	6	7	14	21
New Hampshire	4	6	15	21
Colorado	9	3	16	19
Nevada	6	8	9	17
Wisconsin	10	5	9	14
Arizona	11	3	7	10
Georgia	16	0	3	3
Maine	4	0	3	3
New Mexico	5	0	3	3
Indiana	11	0	2	2
Minnesota	10	0	2	2
Missouri	10	0	2	2
Nebraska	5	1	1	2
California	55	0	1	1
Connecticut	7	0	1	1
Illinois	20	1	0	1
Mississippi	6	0	1	1
Texas	38	0	1	1
Utah	6	0	1	1
Washington	12	0	1	1
Alabama	9	0	0	0
Alaska	3	0	0	0
Arkansas	6	0	0	0
Delaware	3	0	0	0
District of Columbia	3	0	0	0
Hawaii	4	0	0	0
Idaho	4	0	0	0
Kansas	6	0	0	0

Table 4.3 Continued

State	Electoral votes	Clinton–Kaine Events	Trump–Pence Events	Total Events
Kentucky	8	0	0	0
Louisiana	8	0	0	0
Maryland	10	0	0	0
Massachusetts	11	0	0	0
Montana	3	0	0	0
New Jersey	14	0	0	0
New York	29	0	0	0
North Dakota	3	0	0	0
Oklahoma	7	0	0	0
Oregon	7	0	0	0
Rhode Island	4	0	0	0
South Carolina	9	0	0	0
South Dakota	3	0	0	0
Tennessee	11	0	0	0
Vermont	3	0	0	0
West Virginia	5	0	0	0
Wyoming	3	0	0	0
Total	538	151	248	399

Twenty-five states representing 176 electoral votes received no visits (including all states with three electoral votes).

From Fairvote.com (http://www.fairvote.org/fairvote_s_2016_presidential_tracker).

in just six states (Florida, North Carolina, Pennsylvania, Ohio, Virginia, and Michigan). If we expand our analysis to six more states, we find that 94 percent of all campaign speeches, rallies, or town hall meetings took place in just 12 states. Put another way, 94 percent of all campaigning occurred in less than a quarter of the country! Figure 4.1 graphically depicts where the candidates spent their time. As in 2000, half of the states failed to see a single visit from the two major parties. Trump and Pence failed to set foot in 26 states, while the Clinton–Kaine ticket neglected nearly three-fourths of the country, holding events in only 14 states. Together, the campaigns neglected 25 states, representing 176 electoral votes. Although many proponents contend that small states would be neglected without the Electoral College, none of the states holding three electoral votes received a visit from the presidential or vice presidential candidates from both major parties.

FIGURE 4.1 Candidate visits during the 2016 presidential campaign
From National Popular Vote (https://www.nationalpopularvote.com/campaign-events-2016).

Florida once again was the main target of the two campaigns. Pennsylvania, Michigan, Ohio, and Iowa were also heavily courted in the 2016 election. In the 16 years since the 2000 election, North Carolina and Colorado have emerged as much more competitive states, and this can be seen in the number of visits to them by the candidates. The Trump campaign held nearly twice as many events than the Clinton campaign did in the very closely contested states of Michigan and Wisconsin. As in 2000, *not one* of the states with the fewest electoral votes received a single visit from the candidates during the home stretch of the campaign.

These findings offer little evidence that smaller states would be ignored without the Electoral College. This is because they are already being ignored under the Electoral College. The current system does not encourage candidates to campaign in those states, and many larger states are also ignored due to the Electoral College. Edwards nicely sums up the current state of research on Electoral College strategies. He states that the "Electoral College actually distorts the campaign so that candidates ignore many large and most small states and devote most of their attention to competitive states" (2004, 121). The fact that campaigns spend most of their resources in a handful of states is expected to have consequences on political participation.

A burgeoning research program has examined the effects of the Electoral College on political participation. Verba, Scholzman, and Brady's (1995) resource model of political participation suggests that citizens in battleground states would be better informed and more likely to participate than those voters in safe states. Hill and McKee assert that "because campaign resources are finite, campaigns must allocate them in a way that will maximize their effectiveness in reaching the goal of 270 [Electoral College] votes" (2005, 702). They contend that "competitive states are privileged because the objective is to win states, not the most votes" (2005, 702). Wolak theorizes that "because battleground environments are saturated with political information, even infrequent news consumers are exposed to campaign details" (2006, 354). In essence, campaign costs are lowered for voters in swing states relative to those who are not in swing states. Information is abundant and voters rarely have to search for it. Because of this, a different challenge may exist for voters in battleground states—the cost of evaluating the abundance of information. And yet, the pressure to participate is extremely high in these states.

Voters are told that they matter and that their vote may hold the key for the outcome of the election. This is a heavy burden and one that inflates voters' perception that their vote counts. This message is not one that is conveyed in base states. This is because no message is conveyed at all. Scholars have largely determined that the desire to satisfy one's "civic duty" is one of the chief reasons many Americans ultimately choose to vote. This is a point that is driven home among voters in swing states. They hear about it through a media barrage, candidate visits, and party mobilization strategies. Citizens in battleground states are saturated with information and have ample opportunities to hear from the campaigns, whether through campaign surrogates or the candidates themselves. Given the ubiquity of political activity, it would be expected that in battleground states, "the motivation to follow politics may reflect the social elements of the campaign or aspects of civic duty" (Wolak, 2006, 354).

Studies have shown that citizens in battleground states do participate at higher levels than their safe state counterparts. Building on the work of Shaw, Hill and McKee find that "media spending and candidate visits have a positive impact on turnout" (2005, 715). In their examination of the 2000 election, they found that citizens in battleground states were 1 to 2 percent more likely to vote than citizens in non-battleground states, once they controlled for state-level contextual and political factors (2005, 715–716). Similarly, Lipsitz examines the Electoral College's effects on participation by examining presidential elections from 1988 to 2004. She finds that citizens in battleground states were 3 percent more likely to vote in 1988 and 2000 (2009, 202). She found the largest difference occurred in the 2004 election, where there was a

6 percent expected difference between citizens in battleground states and safe states (2009, 202). However, she found virtually no difference in the expected turnout rates among voters in the 1992 and 1996 elections, which were viewed as much less competitive contests. She finds similar patterns for political participation in terms of one's likelihood of attending a meeting and one's likelihood to discuss politics with others. In both cases, citizens in battleground states were more likely to engage in these activities in those elections that were more competitive (1988, 2000, and 2004).

Gimple, Kauffmann, and Pearson-Merkowitz (2007) voice concern that the participation gap emerging from Electoral College strategies is most profoundly felt among low-income voters. They contend that voters who are least likely to be engaged become so only when extraordinary effort is taken to engage them. This mainly occurs in battleground states. They find that "poor voters who live in battleground states report significantly higher political interest levels than their low-income brethren in safe states" (2007, 791). Moreover, they observe that low-income voters are far more likely to be contacted in battleground states than they are in safe states. Rosenstone and Hansen (1993) have detailed the important role of mobilization to increase voter turnout. Because the Electoral College confines campaigns to a relatively small number of states, those citizens least likely to participate will continue to stand on the sidelines as they are not being mobilized to vote in states that are not up for grabs. While battleground states provide significant opportunity for citizens to become engaged in the political process, the fact remains that only a handful of states achieve this status.

Lipsitz provides a different perspective to examine the participation effects flowing from Electoral College strategies. She argues that concerns over the Electoral College's impact on participation may be overstated. She emphasizes that differences in participation largely evaporate in less competitive races, and those that do occur happen because of pronounced turnout in battleground states rather than a lack of participation in base states. This is a rather sanguine interpretation of the participation effects of the Electoral College. That turnout differences spike in competitive elections should be troubling. This suggests that when participation is especially critical, the increased effort that is made to court voters in swing states has a disproportionate effect on participation across the states. Rather than allaying concerns, Lipsitz's findings further reveal the Electoral College's differential impact on participation among the states.

In sum, studies of participation relative to the Electoral College suggest that where people live affects their likelihood of political participation. This is attributed to the exposure citizens receive to the candidates through campaign visits and media advertising. Voter mobilization strategies are also more likely to occur in battleground states than safe states. Taken together, these factors work to lower costs for voters and increase the perception that their vote will matter in the election. Interestingly, some voters in safe states have sought creative ways to help influence the outcome of presidential contests. More conventional activities include canvassing in nearby states, making phone calls to voters in swing states, and making campaign contributions. A more unconventional approach has occurred with the practice of vote swapping.

Vote swapping (also known as vote pairing) made its debut in the turbulent 2000 presidential election. It occurs when individuals from different states agree to vote for specific candidates who have little chance of winning in their own state but may be competitive in another state. Advances in communication (chiefly the Internet and mobile applications) have made vote swapping much easier to achieve. Kerbel, Cornfield, Randon Hershey, and Merelman provide a nice summary of the goings-on in 2000:

> In 2000, a number of people who wanted to support Ralph Nader but feared that their vote would benefit George W. Bush—their third choice after Nader and Al Gore—took to the Internet to participate in an ingenious vote-swap arrangement. Nader voters in competitive states pledged to cast their vote for Gore having found, on the Web, a Gore voter in a noncompetitive state who would in turn vote for Nader. This arrangement used media technology to circumvent one of the dilemmas posed by the Electoral College—that popular voters are not created equal. (2002, 122)

Nader supporters were dubbed "Nader's Traders" and represented another interesting episode in the closely contested 2000 race.

A similar effort was undertaken in 2016. Several websites and mobile applications popped up that sought to pair Hillary Clinton voters with supporters of Jill Stein or Gary Johnson. In the days preceding the election, as many as 55,000 people had visited vote-swapping sites to make a swap or look for a swap (BBC News, November 7, 2016). While representing only a fraction of the national vote, the location of those votes could have proven consequential to Trump's victory given the close margins in several of the key states. The federal courts have ruled that vote swapping is constitutionally protected as a form of free speech. Theoretically, the practice has the potential to overcome the geographic barriers created by winner-take-all systems in safe states for those citizens of the minority party. This point is intimately tied to theories of representation—particularly those emphasizing trustee governance and those emphasizing surrogate representation. Each of these theories stress that representatives often must consider how policies affect those who reside beyond their geographic districts. Mainsbridge notes that surrogate representation is especially relevant for single-member, winner-take-all districts—which is applicable with the Electoral College.

A final consideration regarding the importance of battleground states revolves around the characteristics of these states. Wolak suggests that "battleground states are characterized by partisan diversity—a close division between Democrats and Republicans, as well as a base of voters interested but uncommitted to a particular candidate" (2006, 354). Table 4.3 details how the six most targeted swing states in the 2016 election relate to the nation as a whole. One argument that is rarely made in defense of the Electoral College is that it provides an efficient means to campaign in a vast country. If battleground states exhibit similar characteristics to states across the nation, then arguments that the Electoral College is unfair to larger states or to smaller states may be overblown.

As we have seen, one reason a state becomes a battleground state is due to robust party competition within the state. Many battleground states often have a senator from both parties and divided governments at the state level. Competition between the parties in these states is often fierce and expensive. When looking at swing states such as Ohio, Florida, and Michigan, we observe great diversity not only among their political interests but also in their demographic and economic structures. These states generally have diverse economies that rely on a mix of agricultural, manufacturing, technological, and service industries. Likewise, as Table 4.4 illustrates, their populations closely mirror the demographics of the entire nation along a number of dimensions. Notable exceptions include the percentage of Hispanics or Latinos, foreign-born persons, and households that speak multiple languages. As these demographics continue to rise relative to the White population, these battleground states will be less representative of the nation as a whole from a purely descriptive perspective. Florida stands alone among these states as having significant populations representing these demographics. Apart from these differences, these battleground states are generally reflective of the nation as a whole. This does not suggest that the Electoral College, then, represents the interests of the entire country, nor does it offer support that the body represents the interests of states across the country. At best, it indicates that attention to battleground states may represent a microcosm of what we

Table 4.4 Characteristics of Battleground States in the 2016 Election

	Michigan	Pennsylvania	North Carolina	Florida	Ohio	United States
Population estimates	9,928,300	12,784,227	10,146,788	20,612,439	11,614,373	323,127,513
Persons under 5 years	5.80%	5.60%	6.00%	5.50%	6.00%	6.20%
Persons under 18 years	22.10%	20.90%	22.70%	20.10%	22.50%	22.80%
Persons 65 years and over	16.20%	17.40%	15.50%	19.90%	16.20%	15.20%
Females	50.80%	51.00%	51.40%	51.10%	51.00%	50.80%
White alone (a)	79.60%	82.40%	71.00%	77.60%	82.50%	76.90%
Black or African American (a)	14.20%	11.80%	22.20%	16.80%	12.80%	13.30%
Hispanic or Latino (b)	5.00%	7.00%	9.20%	24.90%	3.70%	17.80%
Foreign-born persons, 2011–2015	6.30%	6.30%	7.70%	19.70%	4.10%	13.20%
Persons per household, 2011–2015	2.52	2.49	2.54	2.63	2.46	2.64
Language other than English spoken at home, percent of persons age 5 years and up, 2011–2015	9.20%	10.60%	11.20%	28.10%	6.70%	21.00%
High school graduate or higher, persons age 25 years and up, 2011–2015	89.60%	89.20%	85.80%	86.90%	89.10%	86.70%

(continued)

Table 4.4 Continued

	Michigan	Pennsylvania	North Carolina	Florida	Ohio	United States
Bachelor's degree or higher, persons age 25 years and up, 2011–2015	26.90%	28.60%	28.40%	27.30%	26.10%	29.80%
In civilian labor force, total, population age 16 years and up, 2011–2015	61.20%	62.80%	61.80%	58.80%	63.30%	63.30%
Total retail sales per capita, 2012 (c)	$12,071	$14,008	$12,376	$14,177	$13,301	$13,443
Median household income (in 2015 dollars), 2011–2015	$49,576	$53,599	$46,868	$47,507	$49,429	$53,889
Persons in poverty	15.80%	13.20%	16.40%	15.70%	14.80%	13.50%
Population per square mile, 2010	174.8	283.9	196.1	350.6	282.3	87.4

(a) Includes persons reporting only one race.

(b) Hispanics may be of any race, so also are included in applicable race categories.

(c) Economic Census—Puerto Rico data are not comparable to U.S. Economic Census data

Data from https://www.census.gov/quickfacts/fact/table/MI,PA,NC,FL,OH,US/PST040216

Shaded cells indicate those areas of divergence between the battleground states and the US population.

would see if campaigns were indeed national contests for votes. This suggests we should consider the claim that social cleavages, rather than one's residency, are at the heart of most political conflict in the United States.

Haider-Markel and colleagues claim that "most citizens now have an identity that is grounded in being an 'American' as opposed to being an Alabaman, a Texan, or a Floridian" (2002, 63). To be sure, calls for smaller government are often code for protecting state sovereignty. Nonetheless, state consciousness has largely been replaced with a "national consciousness" imbued with partisanship and ideology (Haider-Markel et al., 2002, 62–63). This change speaks to larger issues of representation. The ubiquity of political parties in the American system combined with the use of the unit rule has made surrogate representation a chief lens many representatives employ when making decisions. Recall that surrogate representation occurs when legislators cross constituent lines to advocate on behalf of principles. Most often, these principles are intimately tied to one's party identification. Given the national focus and discipline within the two major parties, there has been little room for legislators to negotiate on behalf of their states over that of their parties in recent years. As we saw in Chapter 3, the Electoral College has evolved from one that was grounded in protecting the interests of states to one that has moved to protecting the interests of parties. Representation through the two-party system has become the *sine qua non* for governance in the United States. Recognizing this requires observers of the institution to consider whether the body continues to support state sovereignty or whether it is more a means to preserve the two-party system. Haider-Markel and colleagues question the rationale that the institution is a bulwark for states' rights: "Although the Electoral College surely prompts candidates to be attentive to state electorates in their campaigns, it is difficult to see how the current operation of the Electoral College helps produce presidents who are sensitive to preserving state power and curtailing national power" (2002, 62).

Conclusion

This chapter set out to discuss how the Electoral College was designed to preserve federalism and how its evolution has affected its purpose. In addition, this chapter looked at the effects of the Electoral College on presidential campaigns. Determining whether or not the Electoral College works to protect state interests (particularly those of smaller states) is a central argument made in favor of the body.

While the institution was created in part to protect the interests of states, changes to the Electoral College process have largely redefined this relationship. Parties rather than statehood have come to dominate voters' relationship to the federal government in the United States. As Clinton Rossiter famously proclaimed:

> The most momentous fact about the pattern of American politics is that we live under a persistent, obdurate, one might almost say tyrannical, two-party system. We have the Republicans and we have the Democrats, and we have almost no one else, no other strictly political aggregate that amounts to a corporal's guard in the struggle for power. (1960, 3)

Any analysis of the Electoral College that does not take into account the role of the two-party system is incomplete at best and disingenuous at worst. Further, there is little evidence that the Electoral College protects the interests of any states other than those that are considered to be swing states. These states tend to have relatively large populations and are generally representative of the nation at large. Notable exceptions include demographics relating to race. These battleground states receive a disproportionate amount of attention compared with most other states. Nearly half of all states routinely receive no campaign visits, television advertising, or voter outreach from the presidential campaigns. This is particularly the case for the least populated states across the country.

Shortly after Trump was inaugurated, discussion concerning the Electoral College continued. In a meeting with congressional leadership, it was reported that Trump was interested in using the national popular vote rather than the electoral vote to determine the presidency (Seipel, January 27, 2017). When confronted about losing the popular vote, Trump rightly countered that absent the Electoral College, he would have campaigned much differently. How and where he would have campaigned becomes an integral question to anyone considering change to the Electoral College. Although the expectation is that campaigns would flock to the coasts, the reality is that campaigns would deploy their resources wherever they felt they could maximize votes. Campaigns would undoubtedly take into account where large blocs of voters reside, but they would also have to take into account media buys, ideological alignment, and the likelihood they could get citizens to turn out to vote for them. New York, California, Georgia, and Texas would likely see far more campaigning occur in their states, but it is also likely that

Montana, Wyoming, Delaware, and Vermont would also witness a surge in campaign activity compared to the status quo.

This point underscores the significance of the Electoral College to campaign strategies in presidential elections. The institution affects where and how candidates campaign. Wolak indicates that these strategies create very different learning environments for citizens living in battleground states compared to those living in safe states. She contends:

> For residents of battleground states, the drive to work reveals campaign yard signs, billboards, and bumper stickers. Around the water cooler at work, conversation is likely to turn to campaign news. Dinner that night is likely to be interrupted by calls from parties seeking volunteers or donations, campaign messages from interest groups, and queries from campaign pollsters. Evening television watching is interspersed with campaign spots. On the local news, headlines feature the latest visit to the area from the presidential candidates. The sum of these presents a force more potent than simply exposure to ads or campaign events—it marks an appreciable change in the information environment. (2006, 353)

The Electoral College has ensured that citizens across the United States have very different experiences in presidential elections. Citizens in battleground states cannot avoid campaign commercials, Internet advertisements, or visits from the candidates or their surrogates. Conversely, citizens in safe states must rely on national broadcasts or seek information on their own if they wish to be active participants in presidential contests.

The recognition that votes in states rather than votes aggregated across the country determine the Electoral College outcome has led many to examine presidential politics at the state level. States find themselves being colored "red" or "blue" on election night as they are called for Republicans or Democrats respectively. Some have argued that the very regionalism the Electoral College was intended to avoid has appeared with greater frequency in recent elections: a solid Republican South and Plains, coupled with solid Democrat states on the coasts, with a few battleground states up for grabs. Figure 5.1 illustrates this point. This phenomenon is made possible by the Electoral College and has become a major talking point among many pundits examining American politics.

The emphasis on winning the popular vote in states rather than the nation is among the most contentious issues relating to the Electoral College.

The selective application of when the popular vote should be followed is worth noting. On the one hand, it is believed that the popular vote should be followed on a state-by-state basis. On the other hand, a national popular vote is seen as a threat to various interests within states. The same types of concerns that are present in national elections are present in statewide elections. The possibility that urban areas may dominate rural areas, problems associated with intrastate regionalism, and the potential for voter suppression or fraud within a state exist at the state level. Yet, no state uses an electoral process modeled after the Electoral College in its gubernatorial elections. Likewise, Republicans have been able to win statewide offices in deep blue states such as New Jersey, California, and New York. Democrats have been able to win in deep red states such as Mississippi, West Virginia, and Kentucky. The Electoral College discourages campaigns to reach out to voters in states that are uncompetitive. Apart from the novel use of vote swapping, citizens in safe states are not able to join with likeminded voters across the country. It is hard to argue to voters in these states that their vote actually does make a difference in a presidential campaign. This is true for Democrats, Republicans, and individuals of all stripes.

As we witnessed in the 2016 election, the winner-take-all practice most states employ, coupled with the apportionment of electoral votes based on House and Senate representation, does not ensure the nation's popular vote winner will ascend to the presidency. The presidency is the only office in the United States where the individual receiving more votes from the citizenry than his or her opponent is not proclaimed the winner. Although consistent with the Constitution, such an outcome necessarily brings up questions of legitimacy. We turn to a discussion of the popular vote and misfire elections in the following chapter and examine how they relate to concerns over legitimacy for incoming administrations.

5

The Popular Vote and Misfires in the Electoral College

THE 2016 ELECTION marked the second time in five elections that the popular vote diverged from the electoral vote. Over the course of American history, six presidential elections have shared this outcome. Peirce and Longley label these as misfire elections—hardly a term of endearment (1981, 116–119). Table 5.1 documents these contests. In each instance, the Electoral College came under great scrutiny. The idea that the person receiving the most votes from across the country does not win the election is baffling to many. Defenders of the institution quickly point out that the United States is a republic rather than a democracy, and the Electoral College is one means to support this notion.

Relying on formalistic representation, proponents can argue that the Electoral College has well-established rules, and candidates campaign according to these rules. If Americans wish to have a popularly elected leader, then they should rely on another formalistic procedure to do so—the amendment process. Given the difficulties inherent with the amendment process, the argument to move to a direct election of the president and vice president would need to be quite compelling across the states. As we saw in the previous chapter, the Electoral College does not motivate candidates to campaign throughout the country. Instead, they focus their resources in a handful of battleground states that are not necessarily representative of the country. Large populations across the country, including rural and urban areas, get little face time with candidates. This lack of engagement runs counter to claims made by proponents of the Electoral College. In a more practical sense, it may yield chief executives who are less responsive to those populations (i.e., substantive representation) or the perception that a president is less responsive to those

Table 5.1 Misfire Elections

Year	Candidate	Popular Vote	Electoral College Vote
1824	John Q. Adams*	113,122	84
	Andrew Jackson	151,271	99
	William Crawford	40,856	41
	Henry Clay	47,531	37
1876	Rutherford Hayes*	4,034,311	185
	Samuel Tilden	4,288,546	184
1888	Benjamin Harrison*	5,443,892	233
	Grover Cleveland	5,534,488	168
1960	John F. Kennedy*	34,049,976**	303
	Richard Nixon	34,108,157	219
2000	George W. Bush*	50,456,169	271
	Al Gore	50,996,062	266
2016	Donald Trump*	62,984,825	304
	Hillary Clinton	65,853,516	227

* Winning candidate.

** *Congressional Quarterly* tabulation based on proportional allocation of Alabama Democratic electors' votes.

populations (i.e., symbolic representation). Nevertheless, while attempts to move to a popular vote have been frequently undertaken, none of them have gained enough momentum to be referred to the states.

Misfire elections test the value citizens attach to varying perspectives of representation. No doubt Hannah Pitkin's observation that representation is a highly complex phenomenon is especially relevant when it comes to the Electoral College. Formalistic representation relies on authority, accountability, and ultimately legitimacy. These values are intimately tied to symbolic and descriptive representation. Voters should reasonably assume strong linkages between votes and outcomes. This chapter examines how the Electoral College process relates to claims of legitimacy. Misfire elections may not affect one's authority, but they can affect one's legitimacy and potentially one's accountability. Because of issues relating to malapportionment, the Electoral College process may insulate presidents from sanctions for their actions by a plurality of the citizenry. Thus, presidents need only be responsive to citizens in their electoral coalitions based on geography, which may ignore large populations of citizens throughout the country. This has a direct bearing on the accountability of office seekers.

Recall the Framers' intent to create a system that worked against regionalism. Madison argued that "local considerations must give way to the general interest" and that even he, as a Southerner, "was willing to make the sacrifice" (Slonim, 1986, 46). Yet, it is worth noting that the Electoral College process is not alone in this criticism. A direct popular vote could also lead to large numbers of Americans who may not feel represented by a presidential victor. This could particularly be the case in a multi-candidate election. Assessing the balance between republicanism and democracy in the American electoral system directly relates to questions of legitimacy.

The remainder of this chapter examines the role of the Electoral College in yielding broad electoral support and legitimacy for presidents. We saw in Chapter 3 that the Framers were concerned with the issue of legitimacy regarding the selection of the chief executive. They sought a system that ensured a nationally selected figure who held broad support from across the country. They wished to avoid scenarios where candidates with regional appeal were able to ascend to the presidency. Many of the compromises relating to the Electoral College reveal the Framers' fears regarding regionalism and the role of factions in selecting the chief executive. Yet, regionalism has consistently been part of the presidential selection process throughout American history. The basis of support for each of the parties has varied over the years but often revolves around different geographic locations. We saw in the previous chapter that the institution does not produce national campaigns and instead provides incentives for candidates to campaign in a relatively limited number of states. The likelihood of producing victors with widespread legitimacy may be hampered in close electoral contests, especially those that result in misfire elections (which has happened in more than 1 in 10 presidential contests).

Legitimacy and the Electoral College Process

Free and fair elections are expected to produce leaders who may claim legitimacy. All voting systems have limitations and biases. As we saw in Chapter 2, representation is a complicated concept and no one voting system is able to capture all of the dimensions associated with it. Indeed, in his assessment of the Electoral College and alternatives to it, political scientist Paul Schumaker concludes that "no electoral method is perfect" (2002a, 6). Still, elections function, in part, to provide legitimacy to those who represent others. The Framers were concerned with this and sought to create a process that took into account the popular will, or at least an informed popular will. Whittington argues that rather than serving as another check against the excesses of democracy, the Electoral College was created as a means to institutionalize democratic control, given the circumstances of the time (2017, 2). He argues that short of a national popular vote, it was the best they had. It is important to note the intended connection to the will of the people as it speaks to the Framers' recognition that the consent of the governed mattered.

Legitimacy is an important attribute in all democratic republics. Leaders who have legitimacy are able to claim electoral mandates in order to carry out campaign promises and put pressure on lawmakers to address their policy proposals. Leaders who lack legitimacy have a much more difficult time persuading both the public and lawmakers to work toward implementing their wishes. It is not a far stretch to suggest that a candidate who wins the electoral vote but loses the popular vote will have a harder time ensuring legitimacy among the electorate than a leader who is able to claim both the popular vote and the electoral vote.

Writing after the 2000 election, Loomis, Cohen, Oppenheimer, and Pfiffner indicated that "no system is immune from challenges to legitimacy, especially when elections are close" (2002, 76). They note that such challenges can be especially significant "when elites question election results within an institutional context" (2002, 76), which is exactly what occurred after the 2016 election. After the election, claims of widespread voter fraud circulated and were supported by Donald Trump. These claims suggested that as many as 5 million people voted illegally. Interestingly, one poll found that a majority of Trump's voters believed he won the popular vote (Shepard, July 26, 2017). Whether this illustrates the strength of the allegations of voter fraud, a misunderstanding of the presidential election process, or ignorance is an open question. Loomis and colleagues conclude that "the most important goal of the electoral system is to produce a clear and legitimate winner" (2002, 74). It would appear that the Electoral College process complicates this end.

Trump's criticisms of the Electoral College process are well noted: he called it a "travesty" and "disaster" after the 2012 election. While he later praised the institution, he also suggested he was open to shifting presidential elections to a national popular vote. Immediately after the 2016 election, in an interview with "60 Minutes," Trump affirmed his support that the president should be selected through a national popular vote (Blake, November 14, 2016). This underscores the importance of the national popular vote to the legitimacy of the victor. Indeed, it came as a great surprise to many that Trump continued to discuss the institution after he assumed office. Within his first few days, Trump indicated that he would have won the popular vote by wide margins had 3 to 5 million illegal votes not been counted (Abby and DeBonis, January 23, 2017). It was also reported that he broached the topic of getting rid of the Electoral College in favor of a popular vote to Senate Majority leader Mitch McConnell (Seipel, January 27, 2017). However, McConnell urged Trump not to pursue that course of action, suggesting that a national popular vote could lead to lengthy recounts like the one that occurred in Florida after the 2000 election (Seipel, January 27, 2017).

Herron, Francisco, and Yap contend that "election rules that contribute to the perception that the public will has been subverted may undermine social stability. Rules that lead to the exclusion of minority opinions, particularly in societies divided along cultural, religious, racial, regional or other lines, can lead to instability" (2010, 144). Such claims were made in the wake of the 2016 election. Just over 77,000 votes in the states of Michigan, Pennsylvania, and Wisconsin provided the 46 electoral votes that secured the presidency for Trump. This represents just 0.06 percent of all votes cast across the nation.

Green Party candidate Jill Stein requested recounts in both Michigan and Wisconsin in the days following the election. Concerns over voter suppression, faulty voting machines, and Russian interference were made in the wake of the election. Journalist Ari Berman vociferously argued that the strict enforcement of voter identification laws may have depressed turnout for Clinton, particularly in Wisconsin (May 9, 2017). Whether these laws contributed to Trump's victory is debatable. While scholars have found conflicting evidence regarding the effects of voter identification laws on the relative turnout among partisans (see, for example, Citrin, Green, and Levy, 2014, and Hajnal, Lajevardi, and Nielson, 2017), a number of studies conclude that photo identification laws do have a negative effect on turnout in general. Similarly, a number of studies have linked the quality of voting machines with voter turnout. These studies indicate that poorer-quality voting machines are often used in low-income, high-minority, and poorer voting precincts (see, for example, Barreto, Cohen-Marks, and Woods, 2009). Nearly a year after the election, it was revealed that voters in Wisconsin and Michigan were the targets of Facebook advertisements linked to the Russian government (Raju, Byers, and Bash, October 4, 2017). Many of the advertisements were designed to foment anti-Muslim animus. The effects of this campaign are unclear but worth noting given the close electoral margins in these states (a difference of less than 11,000 votes in Michigan and less than 23,000 votes in Wisconsin). Whether these issues altered the outcome of the election, they likely had an effect on Trump's claim to legitimacy. Writing about the Electoral College nearly 20 years ago, Loomis and colleagues concluded that "any ambiguity or perceived unfairness will diminish both the office and its incumbent" (2002, 77).

These concerns can be magnified given the state-by-state process of the Electoral College. Because each state can have different requirements regarding electoral processes, significant differences can emerge among the states relative to these processes. Election laws (and rules) may increase or suppress voter turnout from state to state. Whether these benefit or harm political parties equally matters a great deal, particularly in close electoral contests. Just as redistricting is politicized, efforts to increase or decrease the franchise in a state are also politicized, with the respective political parties seeking to gain an advantage relative to one another. Depending on partisan advantages in a particular state, the Electoral College may maximize rather than minimize social cleavages, as the rules of the game can be very different from one state to another.

Campaign efforts made to cobble together states with enough electoral votes to win may lead candidates to offer pledges to satisfy specific constituencies to the detriment of a more nationally oriented set of policies. Some scholars lament that the Electoral College process has already created an "interest-group presidency . . . working against policy making that addresses some overall sense of national well-being" (Loomis et al., 2002, 82). During the Convention, Madison had presaged such concerns, arguing that the "President is to act for the people not for the States" (Slonim, 1986, 50). Shankman (2017) points out a type of "schizophrenia" in how the Electoral College is currently perceived from various populations. Writing after the 2016 election, he argued that Trump supporters demanded "that electors obey the popular vote within their states," which then ignored the popular vote of the nation (2017, 20). Concerns over legitimacy are an important consideration regardless of the electoral practice under examination.

The Electoral College and the Popular Vote

Arguments for a popular rather than electoral vote to determine the election are not new. As we have seen, many of the Framers advocated for a popular vote. Slonim notes that "the Convention's records indicate that many delegates favored direct popular election of the executive, but for the reasons noted, were unable to institute such a system" (1986, 56). James Wilson was among the most vociferous advocates for the direct election of the president. Wilson argued that while direct election might seem "chimerical," it was actually a "convenient and successful mode" in the states that practiced it (i.e., Massachusetts and New York). George Mason apparently liked the idea but thought it was too unworkable in the fledgling country.

Recall that at the outset, the selection of the chief executive was to rest in the hands of the legislature. Over the course of the Convention, however, several delegates sought to lodge the power to select the president in the hands of the citizenry. For instance, on July 17 Gouverneur Morris moved to replace "National Legislature" with "citizens of the U.S." He argued that the people would likely select a highly qualified leader with high character, while the legislature would select a leader who would be answerable to the body and lack the necessary independence of the office (Slonim, 1986, 40). Morris declared that "if he is to be the Guardian of the people let him be appointed by the people (Slonim, 1986, 42). Not surprisingly, delegates from less populated states voiced familiar concerns that their votes would be drowned out by those of more populated states. Others were concerned not with the *right* of people to choose but their *ability* to choose, arguing that citizens would not have the necessary information available to them throughout the states to cast their ballots for someone other than their favorite sons. While the Electoral College process ultimately prevailed, it is important to acknowledge the politics involved in the determination of that process.

In short, the same types of arguments relating to representation due to geographic boundaries were present at the Founding. The belief that direct election would advantage more populated states over less populated states was among the chief reasons why direct election was not adopted. Explaining the events of the Convention to the Maryland legislature, one delegate noted that "those who wished as far as possible to establish a national instead of a federal government, made repeated attempts to have the President chosen by the people at large" (Slonim, 1986, 56). Similar arguments relating to federal or national representation continue today.

In his evaluation of alternative methods of selecting the president, Schumaker concludes that "no method of aggregating votes satisfies all reasonable assumptions of a fair voting process" (2002b, 20). William Riker posited that populist voting methods (e.g., a national popular vote) may reinforce "the normal arrogance of rulers with a built-in justification for tyranny, the contemporary version of the divine right of rulers" (1982, 65). For

Riker, no one system can adequately convey the preferences of voters without some form of manipulation. Voters are largely constrained by those who are on the ballot, although the candidates may not fully represent the voters' true preferences. Therefore, the belief that the elected truly represent those who voted for them will always be somewhat incomplete. Schumaker sums this up thusly: "There is no one best, most fair method of adding up citizens' votes to determine what the 'will of the people' is—*there is no 'will of the people' independent of the methods used to represent it*" (2002b, 21, emphasis in original).

Nevertheless, some scholars have denounced the Electoral College as being undemocratic. Robert Dahl criticizes the institution on several fronts (1990, 79–82). First, he voices concern about the possibility of the popular vote winner losing the Electoral College vote. Second, he points out that the current system is apt to produce winners who fail to obtain a majority of the popular vote. Third, he contends that if a runoff system were implemented, many outcomes would likely have changed in favor of a "most preferred" candidate, due to multi-candidate fields. Lastly, he notes that the Electoral College system violates the principle of "one person, one vote," providing unequal electoral weight to less populated states. Although the United States is widely acknowledged as a republic and not a democracy, the impulse of citizen rule is strong and has grown over the course of American history.

Perhaps the most unsettling of Dahl's concerns is the occurrence of misfire elections. The existence of and continued prospects for misfires are of great concern and deserve greater consideration. The ability to justifiably claim victory is an important aim for many leaders, and a divergence between the electoral and popular vote totals complicates one's ability to claim victory. Almost all presidents come to the office hoping to achieve a mandate to act. Patricia Heidotting Conley notes that "mandates imply that politicians receive direction from the voters who elected them" (2001, xiv). The notion of a mandate is central to democratic theory and one that newly elected presidents seek to assert. Large electoral wins confer legitimacy and an ability to act on those who can rightfully claim victory. However, because choices are seen as binary, many voters are ill informed, and cynicism about politics is pervasive, the notion that mandates exist is often contested. Dahl takes issue with the concept of mandates, referring to them as "myths" (1990). He argues that those subscribing to mandate theory believe that presidential elections (1) provide constitutional and legal authority; (2) convey the preferences of a plurality of voters for the president; (3) reveal that a majority of voters prefer the president's agenda and want the victor to pursue it; and (4) suggest that the president's agenda should prevail over the wishes of the legislature since the office reflects the collective wishes of the American people (1990, 361–362). Relying on theories of representation relating to both Burke and Pitkin, Dahl contends that points three and four are problematic. Recall that these theorists indicate that leaders should not be fully bound to public opinion given the need for compromise or judgment in order to govern effectively. It is also questionable whether voters know the positions of candidates or whether the positions of the candidates are truly the preferred policy positions of voters. For these reasons, Dahl warns that claims of electoral mandates are harmful because they are "almost always employed to support deceptive, misleading, and manipulative interpretations" (1990, 365). Mandates are often a result of how successful a president is at convincing others that he or she has a mandate. While a large electoral victory may make this easier, it by no means makes it certain in the minds of others. Ultimately, a mandate may be in the eyes of the beholder.

While presidents seek to have some guidance for their actions, they also seek to use their victories as leverage to accomplish their policy agendas. It would seem that misfire elections undoubtedly make the claim of a mandate very difficult to achieve. Heidotting Conley asserts that "presidents who believe that they represent the voice of the people will claim a mandate and work to change the national policy agenda" (2001, xi). As Dahl notes, winning in the Electoral College enables victors to justifiably state they are representing "the people." Loomis and colleagues argue that legitimacy provides presidents with "political capital in order to govern as effectively as possible" (2002, 80). The idea of an electoral mandate is often cited by those claiming the voters have spoken and have empowered newly elected leaders to govern as they wish. Immediately following his victory in 2004, George W. Bush declared: "The people made it clear what they wanted . . . I earned capital in the campaign, political capital, and now I intend to spend it" (Stevenson, November 5, 2004).

Elections that result in misfires can complicate matters for incumbent presidents. They can rightfully claim victory through the established procedures of the Electoral College, but they cannot escape the fact that their opponent received more votes from citizens across the country than they did. Although 12 percent of all presidential elections have resulted in misfires, peaceful transitions of power accompanied each of those contests. Nonetheless, the question of how these awkward outcomes may affect the success of the winning ticket is worth considering. It can reasonably be expected that candidates losing the popular vote but winning the electoral vote may have a more difficult time persuading policymakers and the general public to pursue their agenda. Indeed, Herron, Francisco, and Yap contend that the public's will can be "subverted if the winner claims a mandate that does not conform with election results" (2010, 146). This is a concern that directly confronts one's ability to be held accountable.

Short of misfire elections, presidential election results illustrate that winning a simple *majority* of the popular vote has been an elusive quest in many contests. Candidates have won the office with a *minority* of the popular vote in nearly 40 percent of all presidential elections since the 1824 election.[1] The frequency of minority-elected presidents has led many to call for instant runoff elections to ensure a majority winner. This possibility is explored in greater detail in the concluding chapter. Coming to office with a minority of the popular vote would seem to dampen the agenda of the incoming president relative to those who are able to muster a majority of votes from across the country. Those winning the office with the lowest percentages of the popular vote include John Quincy Adams (31.9 percent), Lincoln (39.8 percent), Wilson (41.9 percent), Nixon (43.4 percent), and Clinton (43.0 percent). Table 5.2 documents those contests where presidents were elected with a minority of the popular vote.

Yet, some proponents of the Electoral College argue that the process helps to ensure greater legitimacy for victors, especially in closely contested races. Most often, the Electoral College outcome magnifies the winning ticket's margin of victory relative to the popular vote total. It is rare that popular and electoral vote totals coincide. Table 5.3 reveals many examples where the popular vote and the electoral vote are not in concert with one another. The lack of alignment between the two is mostly due to the adoption of the winner-take-all method of counting votes by most states. For instance, in 1980, Ronald Reagan won just over 50 percent of the popular vote but nearly 91 percent of the Electoral College vote. In 1912, Woodrow Wilson captured 42 percent of the popular vote but 82 percent of the Electoral College vote. As Table 5.3 illustrates, Electoral College vote totals are not typically an accurate reflection of how citizens voted across the states. A close alignment between the popular and electoral vote totals has happened in just a handful of elections. Interestingly, George W. Bush's victories represent two of the most closely aligned popular–electoral vote totals in history. Altogether, only 13 of 49 presidential elections have had less than a 10 percent margin between

---

1. Popular vote totals are unavailable for presidential elections prior to 1824.

Table 5.2 Elections Where the Winner Was Selected by a Minority of the Population

Year	Winner	Electoral College Vote %	Popular Vote %	Votes	Margin	Runner-up
1824	John Quincy Adams	32.18%	30.92%	113,142	−38,221	Andrew Jackson
1844	James Polk	61.82%	49.54%	1,339,570	39,413	Henry Clay
1848	Zachary Taylor	56.21%	47.28%	1,360,235	137,882	Lewis Cass
1856	James Buchanan	58.78%	45.29%	1,835,140	494,472	John Frémont
1860	Abraham Lincoln	59.41%	39.65%	1,855,993	474,049	John Breckinridge
1876	Rutherford Hayes	50.14%	47.92%	4,034,142	−252,666	Samuel Tilden
1880	James Garfield	57.99%	48.31%	4,453,337	1,898	Winfield Scott Hancock
1884	Grover Cleveland	54.61%	48.85%	4,914,482	57,579	James Blaine
1888	Benjamin Harrison	58.10%	47.80%	5,443,633	−94,530	Grover Cleveland
1892	Grover Cleveland	62.39%	46.02%	5,553,898	363,099	Benjamin Harrison
1912	Woodrow Wilson	81.92%	41.84%	6,296,284	2,173,563	Theodore Roosevelt
1916	Woodrow Wilson	52.17%	49.24%	9,126,868	578,140	Charles Evans Hughes
1948	Harry Truman	57.06%	49.55%	24,179,347	2,188,055	Thomas Dewey
1960	John Kennedy	56.42%	49.72%	34,220,984	−112,827	Richard Nixon
1968	Richard Nixon	55.95%	43.42%	31,783,783	511,944	Hubert Humphrey
1992	Bill Clinton	68.77%	43.01%	44,909,806	5,805,256	George H. W. Bush
1996	Bill Clinton	70.45%	49.23%	47,400,125	8,201,370	Bob Dole
2000	George W. Bush	50.37%	47.87%	50,460,110	−543,816	Al Gore
2016	Donald Trump	56.50%	45.98%	62,979,636	−2,864,974	Hillary Rodham Clinton

Created by author.

Table 5.3 Popular–Electoral Vote Alignment

Year	Winner	Electoral College Vote %	Popular Vote %	Difference	Runner-up
1980	Ronald Reagan	90.89%	50.75%	40.10%	Jimmy Carter
1912	Woodrow Wilson	81.92%	41.84%	40.10%	Theodore Roosevelt
1984	Ronald Reagan	97.58%	58.77%	38.80%	Walter Mondale
1936	Franklin Roosevelt	98.49%	60.80%	37.70%	Alf Landon
1972	Richard Nixon	96.65%	60.67%	36.00%	George McGovern
1864	Abraham Lincoln	90.99%	55.03%	36.00%	George McClellan
1852	Franklin Pierce	85.81%	50.83%	35.00%	Winfield Scott
1932	Franklin Roosevelt	88.89%	57.41%	31.50%	Herbert Hoover
1940	Franklin Roosevelt	84.56%	54.74%	29.80%	Wendell Willkie
1964	Lyndon Johnson	90.33%	61.05%	29.30%	Barry Goldwater
1956	Dwight Eisenhower	86.06%	57.37%	28.70%	Adlai Stevenson
1952	Dwight Eisenhower	83.24%	55.18%	28.10%	Adlai Stevenson
1944	Franklin Roosevelt	81.36%	53.39%	28.00%	Thomas Dewey
1840	William Henry Harrison	79.59%	52.87%	26.70%	Martin Van Buren
1988	George H. W. Bush	79.18%	53.37%	25.80%	Michael Dukakis
1992	Bill Clinton	68.77%	43.01%	25.80%	George H. W. Bush
1872	Ulysses Grant	81.25%	55.58%	25.70%	Horace Greeley
1928	Herbert Hoover	83.62%	58.21%	25.40%	Al Smith
1832	Andrew Jackson	76.57%	54.74%	21.80%	Henry Clay
1996	Bill Clinton	70.45%	49.23%	21.22%	Bob Dole
1868	Ulysses Grant	72.79%	52.66%	20.10%	Horatio Seymour
1860	Abraham Lincoln	59.41%	39.65%	19.80%	John Breckinridge
1924	Calvin Coolidge	71.94%	54.04%	17.50%	John Davis
1892	Grover Cleveland	62.39%	46.02%	16.37%	Benjamin Harrison
1920	Warren Harding	76.08%	60.32%	15.80%	James Cox
2008	Barack Obama	67.84%	52.93%	14.90%	John McCain
1908	William Taft	66.46%	51.57%	14.90%	William Jennings Bryan
1904	Theodore Roosevelt	70.59%	56.42%	14.20%	Alton Brooks Parker

Table 5.3 Continued

Year	Winner	Electoral College Vote %	Popular Vote %	Difference	Runner-up
1900	William McKinley	65.23%	51.64%	13.60%	William Jennings Bryan
1856	James Buchanan	58.78%	45.29%	13.50%	John Frémont
1968	Richard Nixon	55.95%	43.42%	12.50%	Hubert Humphrey
1828	Andrew Jackson	68.20%	55.93%	12.30%	John Quincy Adams
1844	James Polk	61.82%	49.54%	12.30%	Henry Clay
2012	Barack Obama	61.71%	51.06%	10.70%	Mitt Romney
2016	Donald Trump	56.50%	45.98%	10.50%	Hillary Rodham Clinton
1888	Benjamin Harrison	58.10%	47.80%	10.30%	Grover Cleveland
1880	James Garfield	57.99%	48.31%	9.70%	Winfield Scott Hancock
1896	William McKinley	60.63%	51.02%	9.60%	William Jennings Bryan
1848	Zachary Taylor	56.21%	47.28%	8.90%	Lewis Cass
1948	Harry Truman	57.06%	49.55%	7.50%	Thomas Dewey
1836	Martin Van Buren	57.82%	50.79%	7.00%	William Henry Harrison
1960	John Kennedy	56.42%	49.72%	6.70%	Richard Nixon
1884	Grover Cleveland	54.61%	48.85%	5.80%	James Blaine
1976	Jimmy Carter	55.20%	50.08%	5.10%	Gerald Ford
1916	Woodrow Wilson	52.17%	49.24%	2.90%	Charles Evans Hughes
2000	George W. Bush	50.37%	47.87%	2.50%	Al Gore
2004	George W. Bush	53.16%	50.73%	2.40%	John Kerry
1876	Rutherford Hayes	50.14%	47.92%	2.20%	Samuel Tilden
1824	John Quincy Adams	32.18%	30.92%	1.30%	Andrew Jackson

Created by author.

popular and electoral vote totals, and nearly 40 percent of all elections have diverged by more than 20 percentage points.

Some argue that the magnification effect helps confer greater legitimacy on the winning candidate. Ross argues that:

> The Electoral College system, when combined with the winner-take-all rule, tends to magnify the margin of victory, giving the victor a certain and demonstrable election outcome. The magnification of the electoral vote can work to solidify the country behind the new President by bestowing an aura of legitimacy. (November 1, 2004)

Yet, the magnification effect has been criticized on several fronts. Edwards contends that such logic (1) relies on a counting system that works to "fool people as to the actual outcome"; (2) fails to recognize that "there is no evidence that anyone ignores the popular vote in favor of the electoral vote"; and (3) rests on a faulty assumption that "the electoral college vote increases the probability that a president will successfully claim a mandate" (2004, 44).

Likewise, Herron, Francisco, and Yap note that the mathematical legerdemain of the amplification effect can have negative consequences:

> The Electoral College may also inflate the victory margin, conferring upon the victor the perception of a more substantial victory than he enjoyed in the popular vote and thus a "contrived majority." The Electoral College "mandate" can convey greater legitimacy to the winner by implying that his victory was supported by a majority of the population. If the assumption of a clear electoral mandate extends to policies, the chief executive could assert that his policy preferences enjoy majority support and should be enacted regardless of legislative preferences. By asserting a mandate that does not reflect popular vote outcomes, a president could incite opposition that would lead to conflict. (2010, 146)

The claim of a mandate from minority-elected presidents has happened many times in recent memory. In 1992 Bill Clinton won just 43 percent of the popular vote but nearly 70 percent of the Electoral College vote. In his first few months in office, he tackled controversial issues including health care reform and the "don't ask, don't tell" policy regarding homosexuality in the military. Although his own party controlled both houses of Congress, he failed to generate broad-based support and those initiatives did not translate into public policy. Just two years later, the so-called Republican Revolution occurred, with a major transfer of power in the legislature: Republicans gained 54 seats in the House and 8 seats in the Senate, which resulted in Republican control of both Houses.

More recently, Trump came to office with 46 percent of the popular vote and 56 percent of the Electoral College vote. In his first year, he too sought to govern as though he had an electoral mandate. Like Clinton, Trump's party held both the House and the Senate. In spite of this, he was unable to fulfill his signature promise to repeal and replace the Affordable Care Act (otherwise known as Obamacare) in his first year. Although he was able to claim a legislative victory with a tax reform bill at the end of his first year, again, like Clinton, none of Trump's major initiatives were able to generate bipartisan support. Similar to Clinton, Trump's party lost control of the House of Representatives, losing 40 seats, likely stalling his agenda over the remainder of his first term.

The claim that a large Electoral College victory is able to erase the fact that a president was elected by a minority of the electorate is dubious. Examples from 1992 and 2016 suggest this is true even when the president's party controls the legislature. Whether the Electoral College enables one to claim broad electoral support is similarly questionable. As we saw in the previous chapter, candidates typically begin the race for the presidency chasing after a relatively small percentage of the national vote in a handful of states. It would be difficult to argue that such a system works to yield a broad-based coalition. Instead, the structure of the institution is decidedly tipped toward the federal representative impulse over the national representative impulse. This is an issue of concern to those who point out that the presidency represents the only nationally elected office. Political parties can play a mediating role, provided they are competitive across the country. Absent this competition, party regionalism can be an obstacle to national policymaking.

The United States has witnessed the peaceful transition of power on a regular basis throughout most of its history. It is uncertain whether this is due to the existence of the Electoral College or in spite of it. These considerations reveal that presidential contests are often much closer than their outcomes suggest. While some have argued that the Electoral College is an effective process to grant legitimacy to victorious candidates, others contend that the process often works to the detriment of winning candidates. Both of these arguments come into sharp focus in close presidential contests. The following section more fully examines the relationship between popular and electoral vote totals and what it means to an incoming president's legitimacy.

Hairbreadth Elections in the Electoral College

In one of the most influential books on the Electoral College, Longley and Peirce spend an entire chapter on what they term "crisis elections." In addition to misfire elections, they also identify what they call "hairbreadth elections." Table 5.4 identifies those contests that are considered to be hairbreadth elections. These are elections "where a minor vote shift could have changed the outcome" (1999, 34). These changes could occur in a single state or in a group of states. For instance, a change in just 116 votes in South Carolina would have given Samuel Tilden the Electoral College vote in 1876. Similarly, a change in less than 3,300 votes scattered across Georgia, Maryland, and Delaware in 1848 would have thrown the election to Democrat Lewis Cass of Michigan over Zachary Taylor. Longley and Peirce note that the vote shifts required to change the outcomes of specific elections should be approached with caution as they do not fully take into account the distribution of votes within each state. Many factors are at play in any given election and in any given state. It is unlikely that uniform shifts of votes occur absent these factors. Still, scholars have found that many citizens are relatively ambivalent about whom they will cast their ballot for in the days leading up to the election. For example, Blais (2004, 802) finds that as many as 4 percent of Americans change their minds the day of the election! Such indecision makes hairbreadth elections especially important to evaluate. This capriciousness is particularly relevant in close elections, and Longley and Peirce's analysis points out that close elections are the norm rather than the exception.

Table 5.4 reveals that hairbreadth elections are commonplace. Indeed, half of all elections can be identified as hairbreadth elections (where a change in 75,000 or fewer votes would have changed the outcome of the election). Nearly 40 percent of all elections would have resulted in either a different winner or an Electoral College deadlock with a change in less than just 30,000 votes. And 20 percent of all presidential elections have come down to less than just 10,000 votes between the winning ticket and the losing ticket.

Table 5.4 illustrates that misfire elections have been far more likely than we typically recognize. Among the arguments for the Electoral College is that it has misfired on just a few occasions, working relatively well throughout most of American history. However, the success of a system that has created six so-called wrong winners is debatable (Abbot and Levine, 1991). Moreover, the fact that a shift of a few thousand votes strategically scattered throughout the states could tip half of all elections is of note to those examining the integrity of the process. In their evaluation of the merits of the Electoral College,

Table 5.4 Hairbreadth Elections

Year	Shift Needed	States	Outcome
1828	11,517	OH, KY, NY, LA, IN	Other candidate wins
1836	14,061	NY	Deadlock
1840	8,386	NY, PA, ME, NJ	Other candidate wins
1844	2,555	NY	Other candidate wins
1848	3,227	GA, MD, DE	Other candidate wins
1856	17,427	IN, IL, DE	Deadlock
1860	18,050	CA, OR, IL, IN	Deadlock
	25,069	NY	Deadlock
1864	38,111	NY, PA, IN, WI, MD, CT, OR	Other candidate wins
1868	29,862	PA, IN, NC, AL, CT, CA, NV	Other candidate wins
1876	116	SC	Other candidate wins
1880	10,517	NY	Other candidate wins
1884	575	NY	Other candidate wins
1888	7,189	NY	Other candidate wins
1892	37,364	NY, IN, WI, NJ, CA	Other candidate wins
1896	20,296	IN, KY, CA, WV, OR, DE	Other candidate wins
1900	74,755	OH, IN, KS, NE, MD, UT, WY	Other candidate wins
1908	75,041	OH, MO, IN, KS, WV, DE, MT, MD	Other candidate wins
1916	1,983	CA	Other candidate wins
1948	12,487	CA, OH	Deadlock
	29,294	CA, OH, IL	Other candidate wins
1960	8,971	IL, MO	Deadlock
	11,424	IL, MO, NM, HI, NV	Other candidate wins
1968	53,034	NJ, MO, NH	Deadlock
1976	11,950	DE, OH	Deadlock
	9,246	HI, OH	Other candidate wins
2000	269	FL	Other candidate wins
	3,606	NH	Other candidate wins
	10,799	NV	Other candidate wins
	20,489	WV	Other candidate wins
	25,086	AR	Other candidate wins
	39,393	MO	Other candidate wins
	40,115	TN	Other candidate wins
2004	59,388	OH	Other candidate wins
2016	61,804	FL, MI	Other candidate wins
	67,830	FL, WI	Other candidate wins
	34,906	MI, PA, ME (District 2)	Deadlock
	38,872	PA, MI, WI	Other candidate wins

Created by author.

Herron, Francisco, and Yap voice concern over those electoral systems that may be prone to claims they subvert the public will. They state:

> The 2000 U.S. presidential elections yielded a victor who could not claim majority or plurality support in the popular vote. While the election of minority presidents in the past did not directly lead to social instability in the United States, the failure to gain a popular victory along with an electoral victory may undermine a president's ability to govern and indirectly contribute to instability. (2010, 146)

Recall that a shift in less than 39,000 (0.006 percent of all votes cast) votes in Pennsylvania, Michigan, and Wisconsin would have given Hillary Clinton 278 electoral votes and the presidency. Coupled with her nearly 3-million-vote margin in the popular vote, such an outcome would have been closer than expected, but expected nonetheless. Although it would not have ended in a misfire, it instead would have joined the ranks of other hairbreadth elections.

In the wake of the 2000 election, calls were renewed to abolish the Electoral College. The 2004 election almost provided an additional push to do so. In the months and days preceding the election, many once again expected a close Electoral College race. George W. Bush bested his opponent John Kerry by just over 3 million votes in the popular vote and by a 286–251 margin in the Electoral College. Yet, a shift in less than 60,000 votes out of more than 5.6 million total votes cast in Ohio would have earned Kerry the presidency with 271 electoral votes in spite of trailing Bush by 3 million votes cast from across the country. Had this happened, calls to abolish the Electoral College likely would have emerged from the "unusual suspects"—many less populated states that Bush had won. Bush performed far better in many of those states than he had four years earlier, and the national vote totals reflected that fact. It is also likely that many of those who were criticizing the system a few years earlier would likely have found new value in it since their party seemingly benefited from it.

Hairbreadth elections underscore the importance of the consistency of electoral rules, whether votes are summed on a state-by-state basis or from across the nation. Recall from Table 5.2 how frequently the popular and electoral vote diverge from one another. The most extreme case of this divergence occurs with misfire elections. After a long absence these results have occurred in two of the past five elections. Changing demographics suggest misfire elections will likely occur with greater frequency in the future.

Not surprisingly, arguments about the Electoral College and the nature of representation come squarely into focus in the aftermath of these contests. Questions relating to legitimacy are often at the heart of the unease. The following section examines elections that have resulted in Electoral College misfires with an eye toward evaluating how those outcomes affected the incoming president's legitimacy to act on his policy agendas.

Electoral College Misfires

As we have seen throughout this chapter, there is good reason to think that the factors surrounding one's election affect one's ability to govern once in office. Winning the electoral vote but losing the popular vote would seem to muddle matters for the victor. The following section examines how misfire elections may have affected the newly elected president's ability to govern.

We have witnessed misfire elections in 1824, 1876, 1888, 1960, 2000, and 2016 (see Table 5.1). The 1824 and 1960 elections deserve special consideration as misfire elections. In 1824, no candidate received a majority of Electoral College votes, so the House contingency procedure was put to use for the first time after the passage of the 12th Amendment. Although Andrew Jackson secured 42 percent of the popular vote to John Quincy Adams's 31 percent and led Adams in electoral votes 99–84, the House selected Adams as the president. Thus, while the House ultimately chose Adams, it is a clear example where the Electoral College process subverted the popular vote across the country. I set aside whether doing so was appropriate or not. Instead, I am devoting attention to those races where the popular vote winner did not win the presidency. Consequently, I treat it as a misfire election.

The election of 1960 is another contest that is often overlooked as a misfire election. In that election, the state of Alabama had six unpledged electors and five loyalist electors composing the Democrats' full slate in the general election. At the time, electors' names appeared on the ballot and voters were able to cast ballots for electors from different parties or within a party, as was the case in this election. An unpledged Democratic elector received the highest number of votes (324,050), while the highest total among the loyalist electors was 318,303. It is suspected that most often the same people voted for both the unpledged and loyalist electors. However, the unpledged electors were not supportive of Kennedy, and counting their votes among Kennedy's popular vote total would be in error. In fact, all six of those electors cast their Electoral College ballots not for Kennedy but for Harry Byrd. To determine the popular vote in Alabama, scholars have adopted a formula crediting Kennedy with 5/11 of the party's total in the state, leaving the remaining 6/11 of the popular vote to the unpledged electors in the state. This results in Kennedy earning just over 147,000 votes compared to Nixon's nearly 238,000. This is seen as a more accurate accounting of how citizens in Alabama cast their votes in the election (see, for example, Edwards [2004], Gaines [2001], and Longley and Peirce [1999]). Doing so also tips the popular vote across the nation from Kennedy to Nixon by about 58,000 votes, resulting in a misfire election. Elections in 1876, 1888, 2000, and 2016 are more commonly recognized as misfire elections. Altogether, 12 percent of all presidential elections have resulted in the popular vote winner losing in the Electoral College.

Just as the Electoral College counting process could have a magnification effect by amplifying a candidate's margin of victory, that same process could also dampen one's victory due to the disconnect between popular and electoral votes. While the lack of alignment between popular and electoral votes likely has little effect in most elections, misfire elections attract a great deal of attention to this phenomenon. Given their frequency, they are worth exploring in greater detail. Electoral College victors receiving fewer popular votes than their opponents would seem to face much greater scrutiny than those where the popular and electoral votes are in alignment. This scrutiny may translate into a harder time earning legitimacy from the public. Even though the rules are set in advance and misfire winners play by those rules, the expectation that the individual receiving the most popular votes should prevail is a strong impulse and one that has grown with the expansion of democratic practices over time.

It is worthwhile examining how those ascending to the presidency through a misfire election fare relative to their peers. Historians and political scientists have developed numerical rankings of presidents to determine the best and worst among our nation's leaders. Attempts to rank presidents are replete with all types of pitfalls. Cronin and Genovese caution that presidential ratings are "fraught with potential biases" and that "the actions of presidents may look different from different historical vantage points (2010, 48). They question whether it is even possible to compare leaders from different historical eras. Nonetheless, many rankings exist, and great stability has emerged in presidential ratings across various lists. One's success is undoubtedly linked to one's ability to claim legitimacy.

Figure 5.1 depicts presidential rankings by electoral and popular vote shares. The data reflect the first time the president won office and do not include any presidents elected before 1824 as popular vote totals are not available for those contests. The latter excludes some of the highest-ranked presidents by historians, including George Washington (ranked 2nd), Thomas Jefferson (ranked 7th), and James Monroe (ranked 13th). On inspection, several items are worth noting in Figure 5.1. First, as previously discussed, the misalignment between the electoral and popular votes is observed in almost all presidential elections. This is true among some of the highest-rated presidents as well as some of the most maligned presidents.

Second, Figure 5.1 would seem to suggest that one's margin of victory (whether in the Electoral College or by the popular vote) does not have much bearing on how a president is ultimately evaluated. For instance, three of the four highest-rated presidents all enjoyed at least 71 percent of the electoral vote and 55 percent of the popular vote in their contests. Similarly, four of the five *worst-rated* presidents all obtained over 76 percent of the electoral vote and at least 51 percent of the popular vote in their victories. Those presidents rated as average are more likely to have both lower margins of victory and more closely aligned margins between the Electoral College and the popular vote.

Third, presidents who were elected in misfire elections congregate in the bottom quartile of all presidents. Given the nascency of Trump's presidency, he is excluded from these rankings. Trump's public approval ratings are worth noting as they were among the lowest of any newly elected president (Jones, January 22, 2018). Of the five remaining presidents who won the presidency in a misfire election, John F. Kennedy is the only president who ranks among the top 10 (8th). John Quincy Adams ranks among the middle (21st out of 43) of

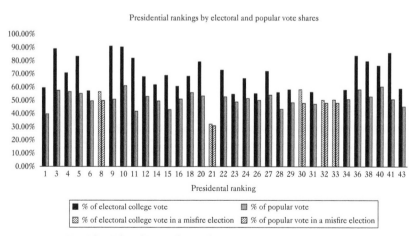

FIGURE 5.1 Presidential ranking and vote share

Created by author. Rankings from Christiano Lima (https://www.politico.com/story/2017/02/all-time-best-president-united-states-rankings-235149).

all presidents, while the remaining three presidents are rated 30th (Harrison), 32nd (Hayes), and 33rd (George W. Bush). For some perspective, this means that Harrison, Hayes, and George W. Bush are rated worse than 70 percent, 74 percent, and 77 percent of all presidents who have served. However, this does not mean that misfire elections necessarily result in inept presidencies. To this point, Loomis and colleagues suggest that the composition of the incoming Congress is more likely to account for a president's success or failure than the circumstances of victory (2002, 81).

As might be expected, the margin between electoral and popular vote shares in misfire elections tends to be smaller than most. These races highlight the importance of the magnification effect in close electoral contests. Recall that this effect occurs due to the winner-take-all process and malapportionment created by the addition of two electoral votes for Senate representation. It is in misfire elections that we can see the most salient impact of the magnification effect. It is difficult to determine from Figure 5.1 how much this phenomenon affects one's potential for greatness. As might be expected, a close examination of misfire elections reveals that they represent some of the most contentious contests in American history. In most instances, voters faced choices offering very different prescriptions for the future. Examining misfire elections may shed light on how they contributed to the president's ability to enact his legislative agenda.

The 1824 Election

The 1824 election represents the second time the House contingency procedure had to be used to determine the president of the United States. The collapse of the Federalist Party and the inability of the Democratic-Republican Party to agree on a candidate led to a crowded field. John Quincy Adams, John Calhoun, William Crawford, Henry Clay, and Andrew Jackson all vied for the presidency. Adams, Calhoun, and Crawford were all members of sitting president James Monroe's cabinet. Clay was the Speaker of the House of Representatives and Jackson had distinguished himself as a military hero in the War of 1812. Calhoun dropped out of the race prior to the general election but aligned himself with Jackson.

The 1824 election also represents the first time a majority of states chose to use a popular vote scheme to select their electors. Combined with the lack of clear party choices and a broad field, this led to a vote distribution that broke down largely along geographic lines. The Framers' concerns about "favorite sons" dominating the popular vote was well rooted. Jackson won

Pennsylvania, the Carolinas, and most of the West. Adams won the New England states, New York, and a few additional districts. Crawford and Clay won in their home states as well as a few others but finished well behind both Jackson and Adams. This resulted in four candidates receiving electoral votes but no candidate receiving a majority of electoral votes (131). Jackson ended up with the most electoral votes (99), followed by Adams (84), Crawford (41), and Clay (37). This left the outcome to the House of Representatives, which was empowered to choose among the top three candidates receiving electoral votes as established under the two-decade-old addition to the Constitution—the 12th Amendment. The 1824 election is the first and only time the House contingency procedure as ordained by the 12th Amendment has been used.

Two months after the general election, the lame duck House met to select the next president from among Jackson, Adams, and Crawford. Supporters of Jackson pointed out that he had won a plurality of both the electoral vote and the popular vote. However, this rationale did not carry the day. Instead, Adams won a slim majority of the state delegations (13 out of 24), while Jackson received the vote of seven delegations and Crawford received support from the remaining four. Many have attributed Clay's influence to Adams's victory, noting that he threw his support behind him during the interregnum period. As the Speaker of the House, he wielded great influence. Edwards notes that Clay's support was not without controversy. Before the House vote, some claimed that Clay had brokered a deal with Adams to support his candidacy in exchange for being named his Secretary of State. Clay denied the charges and even requested to duel those who made the claim. Adams did tap Clay to be his Secretary of State, and the entire affair came to be known as the "corrupt bargain." The outcome of the election gives Jackson the distinction of being the only president to not ascend to the presidency after winning both the most electoral votes and the most popular votes.

Edwards argues that "the charges and controversies resulting from Adams's victory in the House haunted him throughout his term and were a decisive issue against him" (2004, 60). Throughout his tenure, Adams faced opposition from loyal Jacksonians in Congress. While he proposed an ambitious federal program to fund infrastructure across the country, he was unable to muster the necessary support to enact the legislation. His proposal to provide land to Native Americans in the West also failed to gain traction in Congress.

In 1828, Adams found himself again facing Jackson for the presidency. The electorate had expanded considerably in a short time. However, Jackson soundly beat Adams, capturing 56 percent of the popular vote and 68 percent of the Electoral College vote. This marked only the second occasion that a president had failed to win a second term (Adams's father, John, had been the first). After a short respite, John Quincy Adams returned to politics, serving in the House of Representatives until his death in 1848.

The 1876 Election

The nation continued to heal in the decades following the Civil War. In the decade prior to the 1876 election, the country had witnessed the assassination of Abraham Lincoln, the impeachment of Andrew Johnson, and the election of former Union General Ulysses S. Grant. Reconstruction and a recession took a toll on the recovering nation during Grant's terms in office. His administration further dealt with charges of corruption and graft. With no heir apparent, a spirited campaign was undertaken for the Republican nomination in 1876. Rutherford B. Hayes, governor of Ohio, and James Blaine, Speaker of the House, vied for the nomination. After seven ballots, Hayes defeated Blaine and moved to the general election.

Hayes faced Democrat Samuel Tilden, governor of New York. The election was bitterly contested, with some warning of "dire consequences" if voters were not wise in their choice (Edwards, 2004). When the election concluded, Tilden held a 250,000-vote margin in the popular vote over Hayes. However, the results in Florida, Louisiana, and South Carolina were very close. The parties in these states both claimed victory, sending conflicting returns to Washington. All three states would need to fall to Hayes in order for him to claim victory in the Electoral College—by one vote. In the meantime, it was discovered that a Hayes elector in Oregon was ineligible to serve as he was also a federal officeholder, which is one of the few stipulations the Constitution has when it comes to the eligibility of presidential electors. Oregon's governor, a Democrat, promptly filled the position with a Democrat elector, thus adding another level of intrigue to the race. The ballots from these states were turned over to a 15-member commission appointed by Congress to judge all disputed returns. After much wrangling, the bipartisan commission was ostensibly composed of eight Republicans and seven Democrats. Five members came from the House, five from the Senate, and five from the Supreme Court. Once the composition of the commission became clear, it also became clear that Hayes was likely to become the next president. The slight Republican majority resulted in party-line votes where all of the disputed returns were counted in favor of Hayes. During this time, however, Democrats sought to extract concessions from Republicans to withdraw federal troops from the

South and hasten the end of the Reconstruction period. Hayes agreed, and when the commission completed its work, he bested Tilden in the Electoral College by a 185–184 vote.

Writing about this episode, historian Edward Stanwood laments: "It is to be hoped that the patriotism of the American people and their love of peace may never again be put to so severe a test as to that which they were subjected in 1876 and 1877" (1898, 393). Nearly 10 years later, the Electoral Count of 1887 was passed in an effort to avoid controversies like those experienced in the 1876 election.

As president, Hayes made good on his promise to withdraw federal troops from the South. While he sought to protect the rights of African Americans in the South, the lack of federal oversight and rising power of Democrats foiled many of his initiatives. Congress was controlled by Democrats, and they were often at odds with Hayes. Throughout his term, Democrats referred to Hayes as "Rutherfraud" and "His Fraudulency." The opposition he faced was very similar to the acrimony the Jacksonian loyalists had toward Adams. The importance of congressional control to a president cannot be overstated. This may be especially true in the wake of a controversial election. Loomis and colleagues' insights regarding institutional context are noteworthy for both Adams and Hayes. Moreover, any attempts he made to placate Southern Democrats worked to antagonize his fellow Republicans. Given his tough battle for the nomination, this further eroded his support. Hayes chose not to run for a second term and was succeeded by fellow Republican (and Ohioan) James Garfield.

The 1888 Election

In 1884, Democrat Grover Cleveland edged Republican James Blaine in one of the closest presidential elections in history. Cleveland won 48.85 percent of the popular vote to 48.28 percent for Blaine. Cleveland carried 20 states, Blaine 19. Cleveland bested Blaine in the Electoral College by a 219–182 vote. However, if 575 voters in Cleveland's home state of New York had voted for Blaine instead, the latter would have won the Electoral College and this section would be discussing the election of 1884 as a misfire election. Nevertheless, the closeness of this election reveals an electorate that was evenly divided and foreshadowed the misfire occurring in the very next contest.

In 1888, Cleveland faced Benjamin Harrison, a Republican from Indiana. Like the previous election, the popular and electoral vote totals were once again very close. As in 1884, Cleveland narrowly won a plurality of the popular vote, 48.6 percent to 47.8 percent. And like four years before, the race was decided by the state of New York. This time, however, Cleveland lost his home state by less than 15,000 votes out of nearly 1.2 million votes cast. As in each of these races coming down to one or a few states, the winner-take-all format handed all 36 electoral votes to Harrison, leaving Cleveland well short of an Electoral College majority. None of the tumult that accompanied the elections of 1824 or 1876 surfaced in the aftermath of the 1888 contest.

In office, Harrison sought to expand American influence abroad, pushing for the annexation of Hawaii and the protectorate status of the Samoan islands. His presidency witnessed extraordinary efforts to establish and protect public lands. His support for the McKinley Tariff and Sherman Silver Purchase Act likely contributed to the economic collapse of 1893, which was the greatest depression in American history at that time. The economic angst of the time weighed heavy on the minds of voters in 1892. That election witnessed a rematch between Cleveland and Harrison. This time, Cleveland beat Harrison, becoming the first president to return to office after being defeated.

The 1960 Election

For reasons already discussed, the 1960 election is often overlooked as a misfire election. Yet, close inspection reveals that Nixon likely won a razor-thin plurality of the popular vote. Because Kennedy won a relatively convincing victory in the Electoral College, Nixon did not contest the outcome. It is worth noting that Nixon carried 26 states to Kennedy's 22 and that Southern Democrat Harry Byrd received 15 votes in the Electoral College. In fact, a stealth campaign among presidential electors emerged with the idea to throw their votes to Byrd in an effort to select someone other than Kennedy or Nixon. In the end, an elector from Oklahoma followed through on the plan, casting his vote for Byrd. The following chapter examines this and other Electoral College lobbying campaigns in greater detail.

Kennedy's brief tenure is marked by several significant events. Under his leadership, events in the Cold War intensified as evidenced by the Bay of Pigs invasion, the Cuban missile crisis, Kennedy's historic speech at the Berlin Wall, and increased involvement in Vietnam. Kennedy's establishment of the Peace Corps is often cited as one of his signature achievements as president. Although he lobbied for a tax cut and a civil rights bill, he was not able to see either come to fruition. At number eight, Kennedy is rated the highest among all of the misfire presidents, but this may have more to do with his promise than his actual performance. His assassination in 1963 cut his presidency short and is often associated with a loss of political innocence in the United States. Distrust and cynicism toward government have increased to considerable levels in the years since Kennedy's assassination.

The 2000 Election

In 2000, Democrat Al Gore, the sitting vice president, ran against Republican George W. Bush, governor of Texas. Gore was the son of a US Senator and Bush's father was the 41st president of the United States. The night of November 7, 2000, was a wild one. As results were tabulated it became clear the race was going to be close and would likely be decided by Florida. By 8 p.m. the networks called Florida for Gore, but by 10 p.m. they retracted their predictions and placed Florida as "undecided." Several hours later, they declared Bush had won Florida and the presidency. Gore reportedly called Bush and conceded the election. However, by 4:30 a.m., Gore retracted his concession as votes were still being tabulated and it appeared that the margin was infinitesimal. The final tally had Bush ahead of Gore in the state by just 537 votes out of nearly 6 million cast.

The 2000 election shares characteristics with several of the misfires that have already been discussed. As in 1824, we saw the son of a president seeking the same seat as his father. Like 1876, great controversy enveloped how electoral votes would be counted due to contested ballots. Rather than duplicate tallies submitted by both parties, questions of voter intent ran rampant in the state of Florida during its infamous recount. The political and legal wrangling made its way to the Supreme Court, which in a controversial 5–4 decision ruled that all recounts would cease, thereby ending any chance Gore had to overtake Bush in the Electoral College. Both the 1888 and 2000 elections came down to several hundred votes in one state and witnessed a very close alignment between the popular vote and the electoral vote. Lastly, as was the case in 1960, the 2000 election witnessed a surreptitious movement to change the outcome by appealing directly to members in the Electoral College.

In the wake of a closely contested presidential contest, President Bush was greeted by a legislature that was equally divided. Republicans controlled the House of Representatives by a handful of seats and the Senate was split evenly. Much of Bush's presidency is defined by the September 11, 2001, attacks and the US response to them. His leadership was lauded in the hours and days after those attacks, but over the course of his presidency public support for military actions in Afghanistan and Iraq waned. A sluggish economy further contributed to low public approval for the president's policies. In spite of this, Bush won reelection in a closely contested race against Democrat John Kerry. This is the only time a president selected through a misfire election has been able to win a second term. Bush also currently holds the distinction as the lowest-rated president among those who won office in a misfire election.

Virtually all presidents face crises during their tenure. In the case of presidents who lose the popular vote but earn an Electoral College victory, it is fair to say that they face their first crisis before they even take the oath of office. While this alone does not determine a president's level of success, it can serve as an early drag on the president's ability to generate legislative momentum. This can be seen in each of the misfire elections examined above. In addition to the electoral dynamics, institutional dynamics are also important to acknowledge. Members of Congress who find their party on the wrong end of a misfire election will be unlikely allies for the incoming president at best and thorns in his or her side at worst. If the president's party controls the legislature, these dynamics become less important. However, if the legislature is split or the opposing party has control, misfire presidents face a doubly difficult task relative to those who win the presidency with both the popular and electoral vote. Even though the notion of electoral mandates is questionable, a president who fails to win the popular vote has even less leverage with Congress. Indeed, it would seem that presidents who lose the popular vote need to work to earn legitimacy from the public in a way that a popularly elected leader would not.

Conclusion

This chapter set out to examine the relationship among the electoral vote, the popular vote, and legitimacy in presidential elections. As noted throughout this examination, the concept of representation is difficult to ascertain. It is multidimensional and may consist of conflicting goals. The Electoral College process is the result of much haggling between the Framers about how representation should be realized. These same issues have since been taken up by lawmakers across the states. We have learned that no electoral system is capable of fully incorporating the many aims of effective representation.

These issues are more than academic. For republics to properly function, it is expected that leaders can obtain guidance for their actions or support for their policies. Moreover, it is essential for citizens to *feel* like they are represented. Few presidential elections have resulted in constitutional crises, yet many have prompted great controversy and many more have managed to narrowly avoid such outcomes. Four in 10 presidents have been elected without a majority of the popular vote. Similarly, nearly 40 percent of all presidential elections have been decided by less than 75,000 votes out of millions cast. One in five presidential elections have come down to a difference of just 10,000 votes! As we have seen, the "wrong winner" has been chosen six times in American history. Deep divisions accompanied most of these elections, and historians have been unkind in their rankings of these presidents. Indeed, few achieved great success during their terms. The Electoral College process alone is not responsible for their ineffectualness, but it likely did not help.

Students often ask whether their vote matters. Absent a national popular vote, *where* one casts one's ballot largely determines how impactful the vote can be. The previous chapter illustrates this point. Votes of the minority party are drowned out in states with little party competition. The inability to sanction presidential candidates in these states undercuts the norm of accountability that is expected in democratic regimes. The addition of the two Senate votes for each state provides far greater voting power for citizens in less populated states relative to their population. In the case of misfire elections, these features come sharply into focus. Indeed, Longley and Peirce referred to these contests as crisis elections. Yet, while some took to the streets in the wake of the 2016 misfire election, another peaceful transition of power occurred. Hillary Clinton even attended Trump's inauguration a month after the Electoral College met.

The following chapter turns to an important but overlooked feature of the Electoral College that serves as a direct form of representation—presidential electors. Created by the Constitution and legislated by the states, electors compose the Electoral College. They alone are empowered to ultimately select the president and vice president of the United States. While many believe they have become party automatons simply following their party's wishes, a closer investigation of these mysterious figures reveals that much more is happening beneath the surface.

6

Presidential Electors as Agents of Representation

ONE OFTEN OVERLOOKED feature of the Electoral College is one of the most obvious features relating to representation. Not one citizen who votes actually votes for the president and vice president of the United States. Instead, they vote for electors, who in turn cast one vote for president and one vote for vice president. Most Americans do not realize they are voting for these virtually anonymous individuals, and many overlook the day the actual Electoral College meets weeks after the general election. Thanks to the tumult associated with the 2016 election, Americans were reminded that electors were given the task of ultimately choosing the president rather than the citizenry.

As we saw in Chapters 2 and 3, the system of electors was born out of the disagreements about how the president was to be selected. Ultimately, the Framers settled on a transitory body composed of "esteemed men" whose sole purpose was to select the president of the United States. Once their duty was performed, their service would be complete. It was understood that they would serve as trustees rather than delegates. In *Federalist 68*, Hamilton states that electors would consist of "a small number of persons selected by their fellow citizens from the general mass" who would "be most likely to possess the information and discernment requisite to such complicated investigations" (Rossiter, 1961, 412). It would fall on these "men of discernment" to select the chief executive. Although they were to take the popular will into account, it was up to them to use their own judgment to determine whom they felt would best be able to serve as the leader of the fledgling country. The rise of political parties, the advent of party tickets, and the decision to award electors using the winner-take-all system in most states rendered this original conception of electors obsolete very quickly.

Today, however, few recognize this as the role of presidential electors. Indeed, one treatment of electors suggests that "the legitimacy of the popular election of the president is buttressed by the probability that many, if not most, citizens who now go to the polls, think that they are voting for president, not a slate of electors." (Loomis, Cohen, Oppenheimer, and Pfiffner, 2002, 77). In spite of this, some electors have refused to follow their party's will and have cast ballots contrary to expectations. While a very small percentage have gone this route, research suggests that many more have considered doing so (Alexander, 2012). In 2016, 10 electors sought to cast faithless ballots, representing the largest number of potential faithless votes in American history.[1] It would seem, then, that there is a disconnect between what the citizenry thinks the role of an elector is (i.e., a delegate) and what many electors think it should be (i.e., a trustee). Because electors ultimately select the president and vice president, it is essential that we fully understand exactly how citizens view the role, how electors view their role, and whether these are in alignment. If they are not, then an important component of representation in presidential elections is left wanting.

This chapter examines the position of elector and how the office has evolved over time. Surprisingly little is known about those who serve as electors and how they conceive of their duties. In order to understand these important issues, I draw from surveys of electors from each of the last five meetings of the Electoral College. This unique dataset yields surprising information about who these figures are, what they think about the institution, and how they see their role in translating the popular vote into the electoral vote. It turns out that many electors believe they should have the right to act as trustees, many are lobbied to change their votes, and a substantial number considered doing so in each of the elections under examination.

Presidential Electors, Then and Now

The Constitution dictates that electors cannot be members of Congress or "persons holding an office of trust or profit under the United States." This prohibition was meant to support the notion of separation of powers and mitigate against cabal and intrigue in the presidential selection process. This independence would further enable electors to act freely and vote for candidates without regard for the preferences of the three federal branches.

---

1. This excludes faithless votes cast as a result of the death of a nominee.

While some debate has occurred on the issue, it is largely accepted that the Framers originally believed that electors were to be chosen from among society's most distinguished citizens. Robert Bennett provides a succinct statement of their intentions:

> The electors were to be independent decision makers, "men," in Alexander Hamilton's words, "most capable of analyzing the qualities adapted to the station and acting under circumstances favorable to deliberation, and to a judicious combination of all the reasons and inducements which were proper to govern their choice." They were to deliberate and then exercise choice to come up with the best person(s) for the job of president. With only the one job assigned to them as electors, it appears to have been assumed that they would operate with a large measure of independence from their respective state legislatures, even if they had been chosen directly by those legislatures . . . If it all worked, highly distinguished electors would be able to operate largely free not only of legislative interference or fealty on both the state and the federal level, but of interest group pressure. The electors would exorcize political haggling from a task that should have none of it. (2010, 14)

Echoing this sentiment, George Edwards states that "the framers intended that electors would be distinguished citizens, and such they were in some early elections" (2004, 3–4). The procedures used in devising the system would appear to support the notion of independent-minded statesmen coming together to select the president and vice president. There would be no need to hold separate meetings throughout the states, nor would there be a need to secure pledges from electors if they were not originally intended to have an independent voice. These early conceptions of the office of elector lead Bennett to note the inconsistency of what we term "faithless electors" today: "The irony is that it is only they [faithless electors] who are faithful to at least a part of the original conception of how the electors were to decide on the presidency of the United States" (2010, 45). This irony represents the divergence between the original and evolved conceptions of the role of electors.

Presidential electors were to be drawn from the highest quarters of society and were supposed to be independent of the federal government. Although some argued that governors or state legislatures should choose the president, the Convention ultimately determined that the method of elector selection should be left to the states. Indeed, many prominent statesmen have served as electors over time. In recent elections, a number of governors or former governors (William Janklow, Ted Strickland, Mike Rounds, Winfield Dunn, and David Paterson) and statewide officeholders (Mary Landrieu, Eliot Spitzer, Dennis Daugaard, and Lee Fisher) have served in the position. It is of interest that two years after his service, Janklow was elected to Congress but resigned before his term expired due to his conviction on second-degree man-slaughter charges from a traffic incident. Spitzer went on to become governor of New York shortly after his service but also resigned from office early, in response to a sex scandal. Just as not all electors are scoundrels, they are not all statesmen either. Few citizens knew they were voting for Hall of Fame foot-ball star Franco Harris or winner of "The Amazing Race 4," Chip Arndt, to cast their ballots for president and vice president of the United States in 2008. Even fewer knew they were voting for the likes of Ned Helms, A. G. "Bobby" Fouche, Patricia Marcus, or Lesley Ahmed (all were electors in 2008).

Conventional wisdom indicates that most electors are chosen as a re-ward for their party activities. These activities can take the form of financial contributions or work at the grassroots level. Although scant research exists on the topic, most assume that presidential electors are both loyal and ac-tive partisans. Much of the research presented here investigates the extent to which these assumptions are accurate. While little is known about electors themselves, scholars have learned a great deal about active partisans. Chief among these findings are that active partisans are highly educated, have greater wealth, and are far more ideological than are the vast majority of American citizens (Green, Jackson, and Clayton, 1999). These factors are considered in this investigation of presidential electors.

The office of presidential elector has changed significantly over time. Following the presidency of George Washington, the Federalists and the Democratic-Republicans each offered candidates for president. John Adams narrowly won in 1796, while his political nemesis Thomas Jefferson was elected vice president, illustrating an unforeseen problem with the selection process. It quickly became apparent that the president and vice president would likely be rivals, thereby impeding the president's ability to act. Despite the Framers' stated distaste for political parties, they quickly became enmeshed in the pres-idential selection process.

During the 1796 election, one newspaper stated: "The President must not be merely the creature of a spirit of accommodation or intrigue among electors. The electors should be faithful agents of the people in this very im-portant business" (Longley and Peirce, 1999, 109). Accordingly, in the first campaign where pledges were secured, it was expected those pledges would be honored. In effect, the rise of party prominence in the selection process rendered obsolete the original intent of elector independence. Since that time, electors have come to be defined by faithfully carrying out their party's will by casting ballots for their party's ticket.

Examples abound detailing the seemingly ritualistic nature of the position. For instance, James Bryce notes in his classic treatise, *The American Commonwealth*, that "presidential electors have become a mere cog-wheel in the machine; a mere contrivance for giving effect to the decision of the people" (1995, 38). A more sardonic portrayal is offered by Justice Robert Jackson, who wrote in 1952 that electors, although often personally eminent, independent, and respectable, officially become voluntary party lackeys and intellectual nonentities to whose memory we might justly paraphrase a tuneful satire: "They always voted at their party's call / And never thought of thinking for themselves at all" (quoted in Longley and Peirce, 1999, 110). This sentiment reflects the notion that electors are to be mere tabulators of the popular vote in their state. This conception of the office has dominated opinion relating to the position for over 200 years, which is why faithless electors are strongly discouraged in contemporary elections. Even one of the institution's most ardent proponents, Tara Ross, has argued against elector independence. She states that "if any change is to be made to the presidential election system, it should be to eliminate the role of elector and automate the process of casting the states' electoral votes" (2004, 114).

Originally, the names of electors were typically printed on ballots and citizens cast their votes specifically for electors. This left open the possibility that citizens could even select electors from different political parties. Today, however, just a handful of states list the names of electors on their ballots. Instead, most indicate that one's vote is for a slate of electors in support of candidate A, B, or C. Richard Briffault notes that even among states that do list the names of electors, most "list them in brackets in small print below the large print candidate names" (November 16, 2016).

When electors meet, they are often provided with preprinted ballots that leave them virtually no choice in how they cast their vote. This actually came into play in 2016, when a Colorado elector had just one box to check (that for Hillary Clinton). Instead, he handwrote the name of John Kasich on the ballot. He was promptly removed and replaced by the Colorado Secretary of State.

Today, most observers of American politics believe that presidential electors are partisan faithful who are rewarded for long service to the political party. Longley and Peirce assert that electors are likely nothing more than "political hacks and fat cats" (1999, 105). Research has found that most are indeed party professionals who are far more educated, politically active, and likely to contribute money than are the rest of the citizenry (Alexander, Brown, and Kaseman, 2004, 837).

This brief précis indicates several things. First, citizens likely have little idea that they are voting for electors rather than a presidential ticket. Second, even if they did know they were voting for electors, they would have little way of knowing who those electors are. Third, voting for a slate of electors pledged to support a particular ticket implies that those electors will be faithful to those pledges. This has been the practice of presidential electors for over two centuries. It would be a stretch to think that citizens expect electors to exercise their own judgment after the voters have spoken in the general election.

The original operation of the Electoral College has undergone significant changes. This is especially apparent with the office of presidential elector. The position has evolved into a ceremonial one where electors are to carry out the will of their political party. To avoid any deviation in this practice, it is the received wisdom that faithful party members are rewarded with the position of elector. One respondent from my surveys supports this sentiment with her claim that "in a lifetime of rewards, this was the greatest" (#314, 2008 Survey).

Selecting Electors

The Constitution dictates that state legislatures are empowered to select electors, but how states choose to do so is left up to them. Within a short while, states chose to select electors by popular vote. This has been the case for over 150 years. State parties offer slates of electors who are chosen by citizens in the states to vote for the winning party's ticket. If a plurality of voters in a state choose a party's slate, those electors are then selected to become members of the Electoral College, provided the vote is certified by the chief election official in each state.

States currently use a variety of methods to nominate slates of electors. Selecting electors who will not stray is of paramount importance to both the party and the party's ticket. Three main procedures dominate the method of choosing electors at the state level (Table 6.1). Selection at the state convention is the most popular form of elector selection, and approximately half of the states use this method. In these states, potential electors run for the office of presidential elector at their state's respective party convention. In 14 states, parties have greater latitude as to how they select electors (what I refer to as the "party option"). This may mean they use an ad hoc party committee to

Table 6.1 Nomination Procedures for Presidential Electors

Party Convention (25)	Party Option (14)	Party Committee (10)	Personal (2)
Colorado	Arizona	District of Columbia	California
Connecticut	Alaska	Florida	Pennsylvania
Delaware	Alabama	Iowa	
Hawaii	Georgia	Kansas	
Idaho	Louisiana	Massachusetts	
Illinois	Maryland	Missouri	
Indiana	Mississippi	New York	
Kentucky	Montana	South Carolina	
Maine	New Jersey	Wisconsin	
Michigan	Oregon		
Minnesota	Tennessee		
North Carolina	Texas		
North Dakota	Utah		
Nebraska	Washington		
New Hampshire			
New Mexico			
Nevada			
Ohio			
Oklahoma			
Rhode Island			
South Dakota			
Virginia			
Vermont			
West Virginia			
Wyoming			

Compiled by author.

nominate electors. It may also be that party figures in the state (i.e., the state chair) are empowered to nominate electors. Selection by party committee is the next most frequent method of elector selection; 10 states use this method. Most variations on this theme charge the party's central committee, along with the assistance of statewide officeholders, to serve as a nominating body for the party's slate of electors. Longley and Peirce suggest that this method of selection often seeks to produce balanced elector slates. For instance, the party committee actively seeks to reward specific party constituencies (e.g., labor, agriculture, minority) and produce an elector slate mirroring the party demographically.

Two states stand out when it comes to elector selection—California and Pennsylvania. These states have distinctive features linking them to candidates rather than parties. As such, I classify their processes as personal methods of selection. In California, the parties nominate their electors by having each of their candidates for the U.S. House of Representatives and U.S. Senate select an individual. In at least one instance, this resulted in an elector being chosen by having his name pulled out of a hat at an event for the candidate for the House of Representatives. Of all the states, Pennsylvania provides the closest connection between a presidential elector and a presidential ticket. Pennsylvania's electors are chosen directly by their party's candidate. One would expect this method of selection would be most satisfying for presidential candidates and those concerned about potential renegade electors.

These various patterns of nomination provide a window to examine whether and to what extent different modes of selection affect the level of commitment electors have to their party's presidential ticket. It can be gathered that most methods ensure loyalty to the party rather than loyalty to a party ticket. Future aspirations within the party would seem to incentivize loyalty to the party's ticket. Still, a significant number of electors struggle over these loyalties.

Faithless Electors in the Electoral College

Faithless electors are understood to be electors who vote against the party's (and voters') wishes, casting a ballot for another candidate. Thus, they are not being faithful to their party or the voters in their state. As noted by Bennett, the term "faithless elector" is an oxymoron, given the Framers' original conception that electors would use their independent judgment. An elector who votes accordingly is actually being faithful to the original intent rather than what the office has come to be. This view distinguishes electors as trustees rather than delegates. Yet, today, most Americans expect electors to follow the will of the citizenry in their state and see the meeting of the Electoral College as nothing more than a formality. An elector who strays from the party's ticket is consequently viewed as being faithless to the citizenry's wishes. In sum, today, most Americans expect electors to serve as delegates rather than trustees.

Shortly after seven electors cast faithless ballots in 2016, I argued against elector independence, suggesting that the "Constitution provides for many other more suitable checks than elector discretion to prevent the concentration of power in the hands of a despot" (January 3, 2017). I maintained that one individual should not be able to change the wishes of hundreds of thousands of voters, which "produces unnecessary uncertainty in an already maligned process and runs counter to the expectations of the office of presidential elector" (January 3, 2017). In my mind, the office has evolved from one viewed as a trustee to one viewed as a delegate. Whether one is considered to be faithful or faithless highlights the distinction between the original and the evolved body. In response to this argument, William Greene, an elector (and fellow political scientist), wrote that electors who exercise their own judgment are not faithless but are instead faithful to the Constitution and the Founders' intentions. As it turns out, Greene was a Republican elector in the 2016 Electoral College and cast his ballot not for Donald Trump but for Ron Paul. He wrote:

> When American voters go to the polls on the first Tuesday in November, they don't vote for president and vice president; they vote for electors, who get to cast the actual votes for president and vice president a month later. Those electors are, indeed, "expected" to take into account the results of that November "popular" vote when they make their decisions in December, as most of them have done since states began allowing voters to choose the electors in the 1800s. However, nowhere in the Constitution does it say that electors are required to abide by those "straw poll" results. The intent of the founders was that each elector should vote for whomever he believed would be the best person, in the entire United States, to be president. (January 9, 2017)

Recall that the names of electors no longer appear on most state ballots. To suggest that the general election is a straw poll for electors to consider ignores the electoral practices of the past 200 years. It also requires one to take extraordinary leaps regarding the expectations and execution of the office in the eyes of loyal partisans as well as lay citizens. As indicated previously, the expectation of electors has changed considerably from its original conception. Electors are chosen by political parties for their obedience, not for their independence. This is why a majority of states extract pledges and even go so far as to criminalize the abrogation of those pledges. Ross contends that "it is hard to see how independent deliberation by electors in this day and age will do anything to advance the goals of the Electoral College . . . to the contrary, the public is more informed about the character and policies of presidential candidates than they are about those of the electors. In many cases, they may not even know the names of electors" (2004, 119).

Acknowledging the distinction between the original and evolved Electoral College is essential in any discussion of the role of presidential electors. Doing so informs whether electors are being faithful or faithless.

The number of faithless votes cast over time is a matter of debate. Estimates range from as high as 167 to as low as 16. Confusion results in the classification of what constitutes a faithless vote. For instance, in 1872, 63 electors failed to cast ballots for Horace Greeley, as he died during the interregnum period between the general election and the casting of electoral votes. The same thing happened in 1912, when eight Republican electors did not cast ballots for their recently deceased vice presidential candidate, James Sherman. Because their candidates had died after the election and prior to the electors' votes, many do not consider that these electors acted faithlessly. For this reason, a common classification of a faithless vote occurs when an elector votes for a different candidate than *expected* by his or her party. Using this standard, there have been approximately 96 faithless electors in American history (FairVote, 2018). It is instructive to look at several of these individuals.

Little systematic research has been conducted on faithless electors. Elsewhere, I have noted that "faithless electors are not unicorn-like creatures of fantasy," as they have occurred in 3 of the last 5 elections (Alexander, 2012, 29). The Federalist Samuel Miles has the distinction of being the first faithless elector in American history. During the 1796 campaign, state parties began securing pledges from their electors. In that election, Miles broke ranks with his Federalist brethren and voted for Thomas Jefferson. His actions evoked the following rebuke from a fellow Federalist: "What, do I chuse Samuel Miles to determine for me whether John Adams or Thomas Jefferson shall be President? No! I chuse him to act, not to think" (Peirce and Longley, 1980, 36). And thus the contempt for faithless electors was born.

In addition to Miles, another early faithless elector was William Plumer of New Hampshire. In the 1820 election, Plumer cast a vote for John Quincy Adams (who was not running) rather than for James Monroe (to whom he was pledged). One report claims that Plumer cast this vote because he believed that only George Washington should be unanimously elected by the Electoral College. Others suggest that he cast the vote to draw attention to Adams as a potential candidate for president and to protest what he viewed as wasteful extravagance in the Monroe administration (Wilmerding, 1958, 176).

In recent years, the appearance of faithless electors has increased. After a 30-year absence, faithless electors have appeared in 10 of the last 18 presidential elections. Several of these individuals deserve particular attention. The motivations for these individuals are varied yet give some clues regarding the types of people who might cast faithless ballots.

In 1956, W. F. Turner, a Democrat from Alabama, voted for a local circuit judge instead of his party's nominee, Adlai Stevenson. Turner claimed he was not being faithless but instead was fulfilling his duties to "the white people" of Alabama (Longley and Peirce, 1999, 112). The Electoral College lobbying campaign of 1960 did yield one faithless elector—Henry Irwin, a Republican from Oklahoma. Irwin broke his pledge to Richard Nixon and instead voted for Senator Harry Byrd of Virginia. He explained his actions by arguing that he was standing up against socialism. In 1976, Mike Padden, a Republican elector from Washington, failed to vote for Gerald Ford and instead voted for Ronald Reagan. Padden questioned Ford's commitment to the pro-life movement. In 1988, Margaret Leach (a Democrat from West Virginia), on hearing that she was not required to vote for the candidates to whom she was pledged, decided to cast her votes in protest of the practice. Consequently, she cast her presidential ballot for the vice presidential nominee (Lloyd Bentsen) and her vice presidential ballot for the presidential nominee (Michael Dukakis). She reportedly tried to convince other electors to do the same thing, but none followed her lead. Thus, she cast a faithless vote to protest her ability to cast a faithless vote! These stories suggest that Alexander Hamilton's claim that the Electoral College would be beyond the reach of "cabal, intrigue, and corruption" is highly questionable. The Hamilton elector movement of 2016 illustrates the potential for chicanery by members in the institution.

Although no faithless elector has ever changed the outcome of who would become president, faithless electors did have an effect upon a vice president's selection. In 1836, 23 Virginia electors withheld their votes from vice presidential nominee Richard Mentor Johnson because of his relationship with an African American woman. Johnson was a paradoxical figure: he owned slaves yet married a mixed-race slave and by many accounts treated her lovingly. Johnson "defended his domestic arrangements saying that 'Unlike' Thomas Jefferson, Henry Clay, and 'others,' whose relationships with black women were hidden and abusive, 'I married my wife under the eyes of God, and apparently He has found no objections'" (Troy, November 20, 2016). Troy contends that the members of the Virginia delegation punished Johnson by refusing to cast their ballots for him. Their rebuke left him one vote shy of a majority in the Electoral College. For the first time, then, the 12th Amendment's contingency procedure was used to select the vice president. On their first ballot, the members of the Senate selected Johnson to serve as Martin Van Buren's vice president by a 33–16 vote.

Longley and Peirce surmise that "incentives for elector defections occurring on a multiple basis would be much greater in the case of a very close election. Should an electoral college majority rest on a margin of only one or two votes, then we might well witness faithless electors appearing in order to gain personal fame or draw attention to some favorite cause or issue" (1999, 113–114). This is exactly what happened in 2000 when Barbara Lett-Simmons failed to vote for Al Gore in an attempt to protest the lack of full voting participation in the Congress for the District of Columbia.

Keeping Electors Faithful

As noted above, the election of 1796 brought the first faithless elector when Samuel Miles voted for Thomas Jefferson instead of John Adams. This was the first campaign where state parties secured pledges from their respective electors affirming that they would vote in accordance with the party that nominated them. In effect, these pledges severely constrained the idea that electors would be independent, free-thinking individuals. Although these pledges have been subsequently challenged, the Supreme Court affirmed their constitutionality in *Ray v. Blair* (1952). The presence of a pledge directs an elector to act as a delegate rather than a trustee. In most cases, the failure to follow the party's pledge results in the removal of the elector and empowers the party to replace him or her with a member who will abide by the party's wishes.

While much has been done to guard against faithless electors at the state level, no federal statute prohibits their actions. When it is brought to their attention, most Americans are at best annoyed and at worst incensed to find that they vote for electors rather than for candidates. The latter sentiment takes over once citizens realize that constitutionally, electors retain the independence to vote for any candidate they so choose.

To guard against faithless electors, a number of states have passed legislation binding presidential electors to their pledged tickets. Table 6.2 shows that 30 states and the District of Columbia have laws requiring electors to cast their votes for their party's ticket, although most of these states specify no punishment if electors fail to honor their pledges. Interestingly, it appears that the occurrence of a faithless elector likely stimulates the passage of legislation punishing such behavior. Four of the seven states that sanction faithless electors have witnessed unexpected electoral votes cast in their past.

On occasion, state parties recognize that pledges are not enough and exercise their power to remove electors about whom they have doubts. This

Table 6.2 State Control over Presidential Electors

Legal Requirements or Pledges	No Legal Requirements
31 states and the District of Columbia (310 electoral votes)	20 states (228 electoral votes)
Alabama, 9 electoral votes	Arizona, 10 electoral votes
Alaska, 3 electoral votes	Arkansas, 6 electoral votes
California, 55 electoral votes	Georgia, 15 electoral votes
Colorado, 9 electoral votes	Idaho, 4 electoral votes
Connecticut, 7 electoral votes	Illinois, 21 electoral votes
Delaware, 3 electoral votes	Indiana, 11 electoral votes
District of Columbia, 3 electoral votes	Iowa, 7 electoral votes
Florida, 27 electoral votes	Kansas, 6 electoral votes
Hawaii, 4 electoral votes	Kentucky, 8 electoral votes
Maine, 4 electoral votes	Louisiana, 9 electoral votes
Maryland, 10 electoral votes	Missouri, 11 electoral votes
Massachusetts, 12 electoral votes	New Hampshire, 4 electoral votes
Michigan, 17 electoral votes	New Jersey, 15 electoral votes
(Violation cancels vote and elector is replaced.)	New York, 31 electoral votes
Minnesota, 10 electoral votes	North Dakota, 3 electoral votes
(Violation cancels vote and elector is replaced.)	Pennsylvania, 21 electoral votes
Mississippi, 6 electoral votes	Rhode Island, 4 electoral votes
Montana, 3 electoral votes	South Dakota, 3 electoral votes
Nebraska, 5 electoral votes	Texas, 34 electoral votes
Nevada, 5 electoral votes	West Virginia, 5 electoral votes
New Mexico, 5 electoral votes	
(Violation is a fourth-degree felony.)	
North Carolina, 15 electoral votes	
(Violation cancels vote; elector is replaced and is subject to $500 fine.)	
Ohio, 20 electoral votes	
Oklahoma, 7 electoral votes	
(Violation of oath is a misdemeanor, carrying a fine of up to $1,000.)	
Oregon, 7 electoral votes	

Table 6.2 Continued

Legal Requirements or Pledges	No Legal Requirements
South Carolina, 8 electoral votes **(Replacement and criminal sanctions for violation)**	
Tennessee, 11 electoral votes	
Utah, 5 electoral votes **(Violation cancels vote and elector is replaced.)**	
Vermont, 3 electoral votes	
Virginia, 13 Electoral Votes **(Virginia statute may be advisory; "shall be expected" to vote for nominees.)**	
Washington - 11 Electoral Votes **($1000 fine.)**	
Wisconsin, 10 electoral votes	
Wyoming, 3 electoral votes	

Source: National Archives and Records Administration.

is exactly what happened in 1972 when Democrats removed a Minnesota elector after they became convinced that he would not vote for Democratic candidate George McGovern (Longley and Peirce, 1999). Election law in Michigan, Minnesota, North Carolina, Utah, and South Carolina specifies that electors who violate their pledge are to have their votes canceled and are to be replaced with another elector. Robert Hardaway points out that these laws may have little effect in prohibiting faithless votes:

> . . . even if such laws were enforceable, they could not change a faith-less elector's vote. The only recourse would be to punish the elector after the fact. The electors meet at a specific time and place to cast their ballots for president. The whole ceremony is over in a matter of minutes. There is simply no time to rush to court and obtain a court order to vote for a particular candidate. Once the vote is cast, it is not retractable. (1994, 50)

Several states go farther by criminalizing the behavior. Oklahoma and Washington provide for $1,000 fines for electors who fail to honor their pledges. In North Carolina, not only are faithless electors to vacate their office, they are also levied a $500 fine. Finally, New Mexico's law makes a violation of the party oath a fourth-degree felony. Despite these efforts, Edwards concludes that "the preponderance of legal opinion is that statutes binding electors, or pledges that they may give, are unenforceable" (2004, 26).

The Electoral College revolt of 2016 presented a major test of these binding laws. As of this writing, courts have upheld the $1,000 fine for each of the faithless electors from the state of Washington. It may be that the Supreme Court will ultimately hear their case and settle the constitutionality of binding laws once and for all. Similarly, the Court has yet to rule on the constitutionality of the laws that replaced the electors who cast faithless ballots in Minnesota and Colorado. If these laws are viewed as constitutional, it is likely that many more states will adopt them, thereby removing the possibility of elector independence in future elections. This would undoubtedly settle the question of elector representation by dictating that electors act as delegates rather than trustees.

The mere presence of these laws suggests the very real concern citizens and political parties have regarding the possibility of the faithless elector. While the constitutionality of these laws may be dubious, political parties have developed extensive control over who becomes a presidential elector. My interviews with electors revealed great anxiety over the potential for faithless electors. Many were troubled by the notion and made it clear to me that parties must choose their electors very carefully to avoid such problems.

Despite elector pledges and laws prohibiting faithless electors, myriad instances exist illustrating the problems political parties have with elector fidelity. Over the years, political parties have coordinated campaigns to both ensure elector discipline and induce elector faithfulness. A Senate select committee observed in 1826 that electors were "usually selected for their devotion to party, their popular manners, and a supposed talent for electioneering" (Longley and Peirce, 1999, 104). In 1876, Republican elector James Russell Lowell was coerced to change his vote from Hayes to Tilden but responded, "[The Republican Party] did not choose me because they have confidence in my judgment but because they thought they knew what my judgment would be. If I had told them I should vote for Tilden, they would have never nominated me. It is a plain question of trust" (Longley and Peirce, 1999, 114).

In 1980, president-elect Ronald Reagan reportedly sent letters to each of his electors reminding them of their duty to vote as anticipated (Longley and Peirce, 1999, 80). More recently, as a result of the miscast electoral vote in

Minnesota during the 2004 election, the state promulgated a statute guarding against faithless votes by (1) making all electoral votes public and (2) removing those electors from their office if they cast faithless votes. Several electors noted on their surveys that their state gave them no choice other than that of their own party's ticket at their Electoral College meeting. Some added that they were insulted by the procedure.

Ordinary citizens are not alone in their concern over faithless electors. Political parties and state legislatures have introduced many safeguards to eliminate the possibility of faithless votes. However, attempts to curtail the faithless elector rest on questionable constitutional grounds. Because no constitutional provision prevents rogue electors, the potential for faithless electors remains. This fact also provides an additional venue to campaign for the presidency. The following section examines lobbying campaigns aimed at presidential electors.

Lobbying the Electoral College

In *Federalist 68*, Alexander Hamilton (Rossiter, 1961, 412) argued that the Electoral College was "peculiarly desirable to afford as little opportunity as possible to tumult and disorder." Many of the Framers argued that allowing for both popular and geographic representation would engender an environment of consensus and produce a president who would be appealing to voters throughout the country. Rather than having the legislature involved in selecting the president, Hamilton argued that having a transient body selected by the people would guard against those who would bring mischief to the electoral process:

> The business of corruption, when it is to embrace so considerable a number of men, requires time as well as means. Nor would it be found easy suddenly to embark them, dispersed as they would be over thirteen States, in any combinations founded upon motives which, though they could not properly be denominated corrupt, might yet be of a nature to mislead them from their duty. (Rossiter, 1961, 413)

Hamilton then suggested that lobbying the Electoral College would be fruitless because electors would be both beyond reproach and physically difficult to contact.

However, because the Electoral College is a transient (and virtually anonymous) body, members are not obliged to act according to the "shadow of the future" and may therefore be receptive to those seeking to lobby them on behalf of a candidate or a cause (e.g., that the popular vote winner should be the electoral winner). The Electoral College we have now is far different from the one Hamilton envisioned. Changes in communication have brought citizens from across the United States together in ways Hamilton could not have imagined. These changes have increased opportunities to lobby electors.

Schumaker and Loomis contend that "after a close election, a candidate who is within an electoral vote or two of victory might approach some of his opponent's electors with inducements to switch" (2002b, 200). This was the case in the 2000 election, when the race was decided by just two electoral votes. Surveys of electors from that election reveal they were flooded by Electoral College lobbyists. Subsequent surveys find that electors are routinely targeted during the time between the citizenry votes and when they cast their ballots in the Electoral College. History has shown that such lobbying campaigns for electoral votes have regularly occurred but have received little attention. A brief examination of these campaigns is helpful.

In 1960, several electors mounted a campaign to alter the votes of their colleagues. The Democrats' slate of electors in Alabama included five electors who were pledged to the Democratic candidate and six who were unpledged. The latter group comprised Southern Democrats who did not support Kennedy. Nine days prior to the final vote, the six unpledged Alabama electors stated that they would cast their votes "for an outstanding Southern Democrat who sympathizes with our peculiar problems in the South" (Peirce, 1968, 106). This announcement sparked an intense lobbying campaign *within* the Electoral College. The six Alabama electors joined with eight Mississippi electors and cast 14 electoral votes for Senator Harry F. Byrd. The Southern Democrats soon realized that if they could persuade 35 more electors to defect, they could throw the presidential election into the House of Representatives.

Ultimately the only other elector the Southern Democrats convinced was Oklahoman Henry Irwin. Irwin, dismayed that more fellow Democrats did not follow his lead, lobbied Republican electors to support the Southern Democrats' candidate. Irwin wrote to Republican electors and asked them to cast a vote for Byrd as president and Barry Goldwater as vice president. He also told Republicans that he was open to other candidates. Peirce (1968, 107) reports that Irwin received nearly 40 replies to his entreaties. Although many Republicans expressed sympathy with Irwin's position, most noted that they had a moral obligation to support Nixon. Undaunted, Irwin then contacted Republican National Committee members and Republican state chairmen, asking them to release Republican electors from their obligation to vote for Nixon. A party chair from New Mexico stated that while he found considerable support for the plan, most Republican officials believed that such a plan should not be "sponsored by the Republican organization" (Peirce, 1968, 107). In the end, Irwin's plan failed and Kennedy became president.

In 1976, Carter won the presidential election with 297 votes to Ford's 240. The election was so close that a change of 5,559 votes in Ohio and 3,687 in Hawaii would have given the election to Ford with 270 electoral votes. In another scenario, if 11,950 votes in Delaware and Ohio had shifted to Ford, the election would have resulted in an electoral tie—269 votes each. These scenarios are significant when examining the testimony of the 1976 Republican vice presidential nominee, Robert Dole. He stated that temptation may persuade electors in a tight race to change their vote for glory or for a monetary incentive, and the Republican Party was very aware of that in 1976 (Edwards, 2004, 71–72). Dole testified "we were shopping— not shopping, excuse me. Looking around for electors. Some took a look at Missouri, some were looking at Louisiana, some in Mississippi, because their laws are a little bit different. And we might have picked up one or two in Louisiana" (Edwards, 2004, 72). Clearly, such efforts to lobby electors are real and are in part affected by legislative statues seeking to control the vote of electors. A much more public campaign to induce faithless electors occurred in 2000.

The 2000 election spurred a very public campaign to induce faithless electors. In the days following the November 7 election, supporters of both candidates launched concerted efforts to persuade electors to change their votes. Recognizing the independence of electors, citizens bombarded electors with emails, telephone calls, and letters. Although these lobbying efforts have received little scholarly attention, they were surprisingly substantial. Perhaps the most noteworthy lobbying effort was a grassroots campaign initiated by two college students that targeted Republican electors from 18 states. The organization, Citizens for True Democracy, claimed to be a nonpartisan group seeking to improve political participation through election reform. The group provided interested citizens with the email addresses, home telephone numbers, and mailing addresses for 172 Republican electors in states with no legal penalties for renegade electors. The group provided sample scripts that citizens could use to email, telephone, or mail the electors. To support their claim of nonpartisanship, leaders of the group told media outlets that before the election they had compiled a similar list of Democratic electors that they would have used if the outcome had been different (i.e., if George W. Bush had won the popular vote and lost the electoral vote). The group leaders sought to democratize the Electoral College. In one of its sample letters, the group told electors that "patriotism should come before partisanship."

Citizens for True Democracy was not alone. A Democratic political consultant undertook a similar campaign in which he sent statistical analyses of the Florida vote to Republican electors in an effort to persuade them to change their votes (Walsh, November 20, 2016, A26). Meanwhile, Republican operatives were busy lobbying Republican electors to stay the course. Edwards (2004, 158) notes that prior to the November election, Republicans anticipated a split popular/electoral vote in the opposite direction (i.e., Gore as the electoral winner and Bush as the popular winner). As such, Republicans were busy crafting a media strategy to illustrate the undemocratic problems associated with the Electoral College. Finally, Republican electors who expressed concerns over the 2000 outcome were besieged with media requests for interviews.

At least a few Republican electors might have been receptive to these campaigns. In a survey of the 2000 Electoral College, when asked whether they thought George W. Bush was elected legitimately, two Republican electors responded negatively and two more conveyed that they were unsure (Alexander, 2012, 73). While this represents just 1 percent of all Republican electors in that body, it suggests that at least four of them were uneasy about the election's outcome. If three of these electors had abstained, the race would have been decided in the House of Representatives. Bush likely would have still won given the composition of the Congress at that time. While unlikely, if three had thrown their support to Al Gore, the abstention by Barbara Lett-Simmons would have denied Gore an Electoral College victory by one vote. Had all four electors decided to support Gore, then he would have emerged as the victor in the Electoral College. In any of these scenarios, it is highly likely the faithless votes would have been challenged during the joint session of Congress to count the electoral votes. The steadfastness of these few wavering Republican electors was critical to Bush's victory.

Assessing the effectiveness of elector lobbying campaigns is difficult. On the one hand, they have not resulted in election-swaying elector switching. On the other hand, they had a very real effect on electors. Surveys of electors since 2000 show that they receive substantial pressure from the citizenry. One elector noted that he would not serve again due to the immense pressure placed on him in 2000. Specifically, he said that he received over 35,000 emails and several computer viruses. Many electors reported similar experiences. On a more serious note, one elector reported she had received over 30 death threats. A great deal of pressure was placed on the "ceremonial" position of presidential elector. Though scholars have largely failed to recognize this "second campaign for the presidency," Electoral College lobbying campaigns are significant and potentially important. Despite Hamilton's claims, electors face a great deal of pressure to switch their votes.

Who Are Electors?

Thus far, we have seen how the office of elector has evolved over time, how electors are selected, and have learned a bit about those who have cast faithless votes in the institution. The remainder of this chapter uses data compiled from each of the past five Electoral College assemblages to gain a deeper understanding of those who serve in the body and what they think of it.[2]

Electors are generally much better educated and wealthier, are more likely to be male, are more likely to be white, and are far more active than the citizenry at large. In many ways, they resemble the demographics we might find in the US Congress. Table 6.3 conveys demographics for each of the last five Electoral Colleges. I also include a snapshot of the American citizenry in 2010, relying on US Census data from that year. While the demographics among the US citizenry have changed from 2000 to 2016, the 2010 Census data provide a sensible comparison between the citizenry and electors.

Members of the Electoral College are far more likely to have both a high school degree and a college degree. For instance, electors are nearly three times more likely to have a four-year college degree than are members of the citizenry. Further, while one in five American households earn more than $100,000 a year, about half of all elector households earn that amount. Many earn much more. About 10 percent of electors in each of the surveys report household incomes over $500,000 per year. We can also see that males are overrepresented in the body relative to the citizenry (approximately 60 percent to 49 percent), and the same goes for Caucasians (approximately 83 percent to 72 percent). The average age of electors tends to be around 60. During this time period, I found electors as young as 18 and more than a few in their nineties.

Not surprisingly, electors are extraordinarily active when it comes to politics. Although not reported in Table 6.3, nearly all electors work for a party

---

2. For an extensive examination of the characteristics and activities of presidential electors, see Alexander (2012).

Table 6.3 Demographics in the Electoral College

	2000	2004	2008	2012	2016	Citizenry
Males	61	60	59	59	58	49
Females	39	40	41	41	42	51
Age	56	59	58	61	64	37
Household income over $100K	41	48	54	56	52	20
White	83	86	81	83	83	72
African American	6	8	11	10	6	10
Latino	6	3	5	3	4	10
Asian American	2	1	1	3	2	5
Other ethnicity	2	2	2	1	5	3
High school degree or higher	99	99	99	99	99	89
College or postgraduate degree	72	74	74	82	75	28
Protestant	54	57	50	51	50	47[*]
Catholic	25	23	24	23	23	21[*]
Jewish	8	6	5	6	4	2[*]
Other religion	11	14	22	21	24	30

[*]Pew data; all other statistics for the citizenry are from 2010 Census data.

Data on electors created by author.

or a candidate, attend political meetings, try to influence others how to vote, and contact public officials. Few members of the electorate report engaging in these same activities. Much of electors' activity can be traced to their roles within their respective parties. Over 75 percent of electors from each of the surveys indicated that they had held an elective party position, and about half of all electors surveyed have held elective public office at some point in their lives.

The years under investigation are somewhat skewed toward the party that won the presidency in those years. For instance, the Electoral Colleges from 2000, 2004, and 2016 reflect more Republican membership in those bodies, while electors in 2008 and 2012 are composed of more Democrats. This is worth noting because some significant differences between Democrat and Republican electors exist. In many ways, these differences reflect the varying bases of support within the respective parties. For instance, among Republican electors in 2016, 71 percent were male, 58 percent made over $100,000 per year, 89 percent were Caucasian, and 64 percent were Protestant. Among Democratic electors in 2016, 54 percent were female, 43 percent made over $100,000 per year, 12 percent were African American, 6 percent were Latino,

31 percent were Protestant, 26 percent were Catholic, and 6 percent were Jewish. These patterns are consistent when looking at electors from the parties in each of the other elections in the study.

Most electors have not served in the body before, but some have served on multiple occasions. When asked why they chose to be an elector, most see it as a "once in a lifetime opportunity." Many also indicate that they wanted to be an elector as a means to express their civic duty. While many electors may be considered "fat cats," about half of all electors never contribute a dime to political causes. Rather than relying on surveys, I have gathered the financial contribution data for electors from each of the past five elections. Some do contribute extraordinary amounts, some contribute modest amounts, but many contribute nothing at all. Still, the financial contributions made by electors dwarf the financial giving of average citizens. However, it is not the case that electors are only chosen for their financial generosity. While some likely are, many are not. Instead, most are chosen for their significant political activity.

Given their attentiveness to politics and their close role in the presidential selection process, electors were asked a number of questions about the Electoral College. Doing so provides insights regarding the thoughts among the political elite as well as how electors actually view their responsibilities relative to representation. Table 6.4 provides information about how electors view different components of the Electoral College.

Several items are worth noting concerning electors' views about the Electoral College. First, we can see that one's partisanship reflects how they see the body. Differences between the parties is most stark when it comes to the adoption of a national vote for president. For instance, not one Republican from the 2016 body indicated they would support a move to a direct popular vote. While this may not be too surprising given Hillary Clinton's 3-million-vote margin across the country, at least 5 percent of Republicans from the 2000 assemblage indicated they would support a move to a national popular vote and nearly 10 percent more were unsure. In spite of their defeat in 2000, less than a majority of Democrat electors supported a move to a national popular vote. This number has steadily increased over time, culminating with 66 percent of all Democrat electors from the 2016 election indicating they would like to see the direct election of the president.

Far more ambiguity occurs when examining how electors feel about the winner-take-all process most states use. Republican electors are far less likely to support a change favoring proportional representation or district representation like that used in Maine and Nebraska. This is interesting because

Table 6.4 Electors' Thoughts on the Electoral College

	2000			2004			2008			2012			2016		
	All	Dems	Repubs	All	Dems	Repubs	All	Dems	Repubs	All	Dems	Repubs	All	Dems	Repubs
Support Change in Unit Rule															
% yes	24	43	5	18	36	3	29	35	16	17	8	30	24	38	13
% no	59	32	85	60	38	89	57	49	72	69	78	55	56	35	73
% unsure	16	23	9	11	26	8	14	15	12	14	14	15	20	27	14
Support Change to a National Popular Vote															
% yes				20	44	1	18	50	4	31	48	6	29	66	0
% no				64	30	93	64	32	91	51	29	85	60	8	99
% unsure				16	26	6	18	18	5	18	23	9	11	26	1
Support Automatic Tabulation of Electoral College Votes															
% yes				11	16	7	18	22	10	17	17	18	10	15	6
% no				68	55	78	65	60	75	59	56	64	73	60	82
% unsure				21	29	15	17	18	15	24	27	18	18	25	12

Created by author.

(1) many of the Republicans in these surveys come from smaller states that do not yield large electoral prizes and (2) a change to these systems would be more aligned with the small government principles many Republicans have used to defend the current Electoral College system. Democrat electors tend to be far more divided on the topic, failing to convey a consistent preference for one or the other. This, too, would seem to contradict many theories regarding the Democrats' advantage among larger, more populated states and the unit rule's capacity to provide the party with large numbers of electoral votes in a few key states (e.g., New York, California, and Illinois). It would be expected, then, that Democrats would be reluctant to move away from the unit rule. As with a move to a national popular vote, it is likely that electors are considering not only what they might believe would be in their party's interest but also what would be in the interest of their respective states. This dynamic embodies the complex nature of representation, as one is not only an individual living in a particular state but also a member of a larger entity that places ideology at the forefront.

The one area where the parties coalesce in their thoughts about the Electoral College is in regard to an elector's independence. In each of the years under examination, majorities of both Democrats and Republicans would not support efforts to make electoral votes automatic. It would appear, then, that a substantial number of electors continue to see their role as a trustee rather than a delegate. No more than 1 in 5 electors would support the automatic tabulation of votes in any of the last five elections, and just 1 in 10 electors in 2016 thought that should be the case. Although Republican electors are more likely to reject such efforts, Democrats also seem to support the right of electors to maintain their independence. Interestingly, 2016 marked the largest contingent of those who would like to make sure electors have the right to choose whom they wish. Chapter 7 examines the very-high-profile campaign to get electors from this election to vote contrary to the wishes of their respective parties.

Because I considered the possibility to be so remote, I failed to ask members of the 2000 Electoral College whether they had been lobbied or whether they had given any consideration to voting contrary to expectations. On receiving their surveys, however, it was abundantly clear that they were subjected to an intense lobbying campaign. Subsequent surveys have asked whether electors were lobbied. Table 6.5 reports those results.

Table 6.5 illustrates that Electoral College lobbying campaigns have occurred on a consistent basis in recent elections. This is a form of political activity that has generally not been in the public's view and about which scholars

Table 6.5 Lobbying the Electoral College

	2004	2008	2012	2016
Contacted (All)	29	83	55	85
Contacted (Democrats)	18	91	51	66
Contacted (Republicans)	38	68	61	100

Question: Did anyone contact you in an effort to influence your electoral vote?

Created by author.

know little. Electoral College lobbying has occurred in both closely contested elections (e.g., 2016) and those that were not particularly close (e.g., 2008). The 2016 campaign was very much in the public's eye, and Table 6.5 shows that *every single Republican elector surveyed reported being lobbied to change his or her votes.* Yet, the 2008 campaign occurred largely out of the public's eye. In that election, Barack Obama defeated John McCain by 10 million votes and nearly 100 Electoral College votes. Far from a misfire, there would seem to be little reason to appeal to electors to change the outcome of the general election. Still, 9 out of 10 Democrats were contacted to change their vote in 2008. These Electoral College lobbyists argued that Obama was unqualified to serve as president because he was not born in the United States. In addition to emails, phone calls, and handwritten letters, some electors were threatened with lawsuits if they chose to vote for Obama (Alexander, 2012, 141–142). The campaign was unsuccessful as no Democrats joined the ranks of the faithless in 2008.

After the 2016 election, a study of political activity in Ohio found that 13 percent of respondents lobbied the Electoral College (Copeland and Alexander, 2018). It is evident that many citizens believe that they can appeal to the Electoral College to change the results of the general election. This presents us with a bit of a paradox. On the one hand, it would appear that at least some Americans see electors as having the freedom to exercise their own judgment. Electoral College lobbying campaigns represent attempts to get electors to vote contrary to their party's wishes or those of the citizenry. On the other hand, most Americans have little understanding or expectation that electors will vote in any other fashion than that which the vote in their states would dictate. And while electors themselves express a preference to maintain their independence, very few actually vote contrary to expectations. The presence of Electoral College lobbying and the lack of support in making their votes automatic beg the question as to whether an attentive audience of potentially faithless electors exists within the body. The following section examines this issue in greater detail.

Wavering Electors in the Electoral College

In my first survey of presidential electors, I considered the possibility of elector defection to be so unlikely I did not even ask about it. That four Republican electors questioned Bush's legitimacy was surprising, as electors are considered to be the most partisan of partisans. Subsequent surveys have included a question probing an elector's consideration of defection. Specifically, I asked electors whether they gave any consideration to defecting by placing themselves on a 10-point scale from no consideration to strong consideration. To my surprise, a considerable number of electors in every election give some consideration to going rogue.

Table 6.6 identifies the relative frequencies with which electors from both parties have considered defecting. More than 10 percent of all electors in the past four elections have given some consideration to casting a faithless vote. This would suggest that approximately 50 electors in any given presidential election consider voting contrary to expectations. As a point of reference, this would be akin to the entire state of California's Electoral College delegation voting for someone other than the head of their party's ticket. Few imagine that such a thing can happen, yet a surprising number of electors consider doing so. In spite of these considerations, few actually follow through with the act.

Table 6.6 **Number of Electors Who Gave Some Consideration to Defecting**

	2004	2008	2012	2016
% giving some consideration (all)	9	12	7	21
% (Democrats)	13	8	4	23
% (Republicans)	5	18	10	20

Question wording: On a scale of 1 to 10 (1 being none and 10 being a great deal), please circle how much consideration you gave to casting your electoral vote for a candidate other than the one to which you were pledged.

Created by author.

Only one faithless vote occurred in 2004, and it was likely due to a mistake. An elector in Minnesota cast both a presidential and a vice presidential ballot for John Edwards (the vice presidential nominee). The vote was cast in secret and no elector owned up to the deed. No faithless votes were cast in 2008 or 2012. In each of those elections, several electors who expressed unease about their party's nominee were replaced prior to the general election. The same thing occurred in 2016. At least two Republican electors indicated that they would not vote for Trump. Both stepped down and were replaced. These electors were not alone in their ambivalence toward their party's nominee. Table 6.6 reveals that *one in five electors* considered casting a faithless vote in the 2016 election. This is the highest proportion reported among any of the Electoral College assemblages examined. These electors are explored in greater detail in the following chapter. That so many electors consider voting faithlessly suggests that a sizable number of electors do not wish to make electoral votes automatic but see their role to be more aligned with that of a trustee than a delegate.

I label those who give some consideration to defecting as "wavering electors." Research has shown that wavering electors share many characteristics with past faithless electors (Alexander, 2012). Individuals who have gone rogue have several things in common. They have sought to make a statement about (1) a public policy, (2) the electoral process, or (3) a particular candidate (Alexander, 2012, 46). Wavering electors from the past few elections generally fall into one of these categories. These electors differ from their more committed counterparts in several consistent ways (Alexander, 2012). Committed electors are more active within their political party and more likely to contribute large amounts of money than are wavering electors. Wavering electors also are less enthusiastic about their party's ticket than are committed electors. It is likely they consider defecting because the head of their party's ticket is not their favorite candidate within the party. Wavering electors are also less critical of the opposing party's ticket than are committed electors. Finally, several demographic characteristics stand out among wavering electors. Wavering electors are generally less educated, have lower household incomes, are more likely to be male, and are more likely to be a minority.

Table 6.6 illustrates that wavering electors are more likely to occur among members of the losing party. This is true in each of the elections for which data exist. Electors from the losing party have been two to three times more likely to consider defecting than those from the winning party. This could be due to several factors. It could reflect frustrations with the ticket or with the campaign itself. For instance, wavering Republican electors in 2008 were less enthusiastic about their party's standard-bearer, John McCain, than were committed Republican electors in that election. Similarly, wavering Republican electors in 2012 did not have very high evaluations of their party's nominee, Mitt Romney. A defection from the losing party would also not cost the party the presidency, while a defection from the winning party could potentially do so. Although the chances would be slim, the approbation incurred from costing one's party the election would not be worth the risk for most people.

Conclusion

The appearance of faithless electors is more than scholarly fodder. Real issues of representation emerge when the transmission of popular votes to electoral votes is disturbed through human action. Faithless electors can and sometimes do disenfranchise hundreds of thousands of voters with their actions. The incidence of these electors has not waned and in fact has increased over time. Although they are often seen as inconsequential to electoral outcomes, faithless electors have affected outcomes in the past (e.g., the election for vice president in 1836). Given the persistence of close electoral outcomes in recent elections, their independence is important to consider in such contests. Their ability to affect who wins the presidency is a real possibility.

Surveys of electors reveal that many of them are lobbied to change their votes and a significant number of them consider doing so. It is worth noting that one elector from the 2004 Electoral College wrote on his survey that he would have defected had he thought it would have "made a difference" (Alexander, 2012, 114). In response to this research, it has been argued that "the possibility of elector mischief is quite real and should be addressed before its potential is realized" (Alexander, 2012, 184). Although the conventional wisdom dictates that electors are to serve as delegates, simply acting as "rubber stamps" of the general election, many citizens and more importantly many electors continue to see their role as trustees. This is a disconnect deserving much more attention. An understanding of the "rules of the game" is essential for representation to occur. Confusion over the original and evolved expectations of electors is manifest in confusion over their role as a trustee or a delegate. This clouds the rules of the game relative to their representative function in selecting the president of the United States. This confusion must be addressed in order to fully understand representation in the presidential selection process.

That large numbers of electors consider voting for someone other than their pledged ticket has implications for presidential elections in particular and for democratic theory in general. The legitimacy of the presidential selection process relies on electors' remaining faithful to their party's ticket. The vast majority of the time, electors remain committed to their party. President Benjamin Harrison once suggested the decision to go rogue might make an elector "the object of execration and in times of high excitement might be the subject of a lynching" (Longley and Peirce, 1999, 111). Harrison's warning was put to the test in the wake of the 2016 election. We turn to this tumultuous contest in the next chapter.

7

Alexander Hamilton and the 2016 Election

THE PREVIOUS CHAPTER detailed the office of presidential elector, those who serve as electors, and how they view the Electoral College. While almost all electors faithfully follow the wishes of their political parties, some do not, and the results of the surveys suggest that many more consider voting contrary to expectations than previously thought. I have been writing about the prospect of faithless electors from the time I conducted the first survey of electors. While we had one faithless vote in 2000 and one more in 2004, no electors did the deed in the 2008 and 2012 elections. It is worth noting that several expressed an interest in doing so in advance of those elections and were replaced by their parties before they had a chance to act on their impulse.

In 2016, Hillary Clinton and Donald Trump held some of the lowest approval ratings of any candidates in a presidential election. In the week before the election, 42 percent of Americans viewed Clinton favorably, while 54 percent had an unfavorable view of her. Similarly, 40 percent of Americans held a favorable view of Trump, while 56 percent held an unfavorable view of him (RealClearPolitics, 2016). Clinton faced a very strong challenge during her primary race from Bernie Sanders, and many of his supporters never fully got behind Clinton's candidacy. Trump's surprising path to the Republican nomination involved a crowded field and was marked by a number of public spats with his rivals. Some Republicans labeled themselves "Never Trumpers," calling on party members to support some candidate other than Trump in the general election. It is fair to say that many activists in both parties were unhappy with their party's nominees.

Frustration with the candidates was not lost on members of the Electoral College. Nearly six months prior to the November election, I argued that their historically low approval would likely invite many electors to consider casting faithless votes (August 8th, 2016). Months prior to the general election, some electors indicated their dissatisfaction with their choices and suggested they might not support their party's nominee. This talk intensified in the days before the election and exploded with Trump's Electoral College victory.

The 2016 election witnessed the most rogue electoral votes in history, outside of those cast due to the death of a candidate. Ten electors from across the country attempted to cast faithless votes and seven ultimately were successful in doing so. This chapter examines the so-called Hamilton elector movement in the 2016 Electoral College.

The 2016 Election—Background

Throughout the general election, both Clinton and Trump polled at historically low levels among voters. Each faced bruising primaries, for different reasons. Clinton, the establishment candidate of the Democrats, received a surprising challenge from Bernie Sanders, an Independent septuagenarian senator from Vermont. Sanders unabashedly wore the label of a "Socialist" and challenged Clinton from the left. Sanders won 23 primaries and caucuses and finished with approximately 43 percent of the pledged delegates. Clinton had a difficult time combating the populism of Sanders, and many pundits saw the 2016 campaign as a year for political outsiders.

Trump capitalized on his outsider status along with his name recognition throughout the Republican primaries. His attacks on fellow Republicans were unorthodox. He often gave nicknames to his opponents and attacked them personally. From "Lying Ted Cruz" to "Little Marco" Rubio, Trump drew the ire of many in the Republican establishment. Yet, many grassroots supporters enjoyed his unconventional approach. When it became apparent that Trump would win the nomination, there was talk of a revolt at the Republican convention. A month before the convention, reports surfaced that dozens of Republican delegates were considering a plan to block Trump from the nomination. The *Washington Post* reported that "a growing group of anti-Trump delegates is convinced that enough like-minded Republicans will band together in the next month to change party rules and allow delegates to vote for whomever they want at the convention, regardless of who won state caucuses or primaries" (O'Keefe, June 17, 2016). Although some fireworks occurred, the uprising was quickly put down with little fanfare.

During the general election, Trump campaigned as he had in the primaries, continuing his populist message and indicating the potential of a rigged election process. Polling throughout most of the fall suggested that Clinton held an advantage over Trump. Given the antipathy toward the major party candidates, third-party candidates enjoyed increased attention throughout the fall. Libertarian nominee Gary Johnson, Green Party nominee Jill Stein, and Independent Evan McMullin received the bulk of the attention. Both Johnson and Stein had run under their respective party's banners in previous elections.

Johnson, who had been a governor of New Mexico, teamed up with William Weld, a former governor of Massachusetts. Throughout the summer and into the fall, Johnson polled around 10 percent, with a high nearing 15 percent in September (RealClearPolitics, 2016). Around that time, Johnson attracted a great deal of media attention and made the rounds on many talk shows. However, it was a moment on "Morning Joe" that likely doomed his candidacy for the remainder of the campaign. When asked about the Syrian city of Aleppo, he answered by asking, "What is Aleppo?" (Rappeport, September 8, 2016). The city was at the center of a refugee crisis in the midst of the Syrian civil war, and Johnson's quip did not go over well in the media. His apparent lack of knowledge or his glibness over the crisis gave the impression that he was not a truly serious candidate. Throughout the remainder of the campaign, he received much less coverage (never having the chance to debate Clinton or Trump as part of the nationally televised debates) and his poll numbers declined. Johnson ended up receiving roughly 3 percent of the national vote, which still managed to be the highest total for a third-party candidate in 20 years. Stein finished with just over 1 percent of the vote.

McMullin presented an interesting case. A lifelong Republican, McMullin personified the "Never Trump" sentiment in the party and ran as an Independent. He was a former CIA officer and earned an MBA from the Wharton School of Business at the University of Pennsylvania. His political experience consisted of volunteering for the Mitt Romney campaign in 2012 and serving as the chief policy director for the House Republican caucus in 2015. His late entry into the 2016 race prevented him from running a truly national campaign. He instead focused his energies in several key states, including his native Utah. Although he had little chance of winning in a national campaign, he sought to find an unconventional path to the presidency through the Electoral College. He pursued a "Hail Mary" strategy that relied on neither Clinton nor Trump securing a majority of votes in the Electoral College. If this were to happen, the race would be thrown into the House of

Representatives. From there, the logic was that McMullin would be viewed as a viable consensus candidate that the House could choose over both Clinton and Trump. Although unlikely, the historically bad polling numbers for both Clinton and Trump provided a glimmer of hope to those supporting this scenario. One McMullin supporter, Washington Secretary of State Sam Reed, stated that Trump "doesn't stand for most of the principles of the Republican Party" which was why he was supporting McMullin's candidacy (Camden, November 2, 2016). Indicating a preference for trustee-style representation, another McMullin supporter, Slate Gorton (a former US Senator), suggested that "Republican electors might be tempted to vote for someone they think is more qualified" and that there would be "a great maneuvering over who the electors vote for" (Camden, November 2, 2016). As we will see, although McMullin was not the target, electors did pursue a similar strategy during the interregnum period between the general election and the day the members of the Electoral College met to cast their votes.

On the day of the election, it was expected that Clinton would be triumphant. Josh Katz of the *New York Times* gave Clinton an 85 percent chance of winning the election (November 8, 2016). Betting site PredictIt similarly set the odds of Clinton winning at 82 percent (Light, November 8, 2016). Nate Silver put the odds of Clinton winning at 71 percent (November 8, 2016). While these models proved to be pretty reliable in predicting the final vote totals for the populace across the country, they did not accurately account for the razor-thin Trump victories in Michigan (by 0.23 percent), Pennsylvania (by 0.72 percent), Wisconsin (by 0.77 percent), and Florida (by 1.2 percent). Trump's performance, particularly in Michigan and Wisconsin, was especially surprising. In the days preceding the general election, most national polls coalesced around a Clinton victory. However, some noted that the "misfire" path was a legitimate road to the presidency for Trump. Silver put the odds of Trump winning the Electoral College but losing the popular vote at around 10 percent. Although unlikely, this is exactly what happened. At the time, it was argued that if a misfire were to happen, it would put the Electoral College under a spotlight and make Trump's talk of "rigged elections" somewhat awkward (Alexander, October 31, 2016).

As the evening unfolded, several interesting scenarios came to light. Each revealed that the 2016 election would result in another hairbreadth election (see Table 5.4). For instance, a shift in less than 40,000 votes in Pennsylvania, Wisconsin, and Michigan would have given Hillary Clinton 278 electoral votes, enough for her to claim the presidency. A shift in just over 60,000 votes in Florida and Michigan would have also been enough for Clinton to earn an

Electoral College majority. Similarly, a shift in 68,000 votes in Florida and Wisconsin would have also given Clinton an Electoral College victory.

Recall that most all states operate under a winner-take-all system; only Maine and Nebraska award their electoral votes on a district-by-district basis. This practice came extraordinary close to being the most-talked-about feature of the Electoral College in 2016. A shift in less than 17,000 votes in Michigan and Pennsylvania would have given Clinton 268 electoral votes to Trump's 270. Trump claimed Maine's second congressional district, which would have put him exactly at the 270-vote threshold to win the presidency. Had Maine used the winner-take-all method, the election would have ended in a tie, 269–269! The race would have then gone to the House of Representatives— provided all the presidential electors voted as anticipated. We have already seen that electors are frequently lobbied to change their votes, and the 2016 assemblage was besieged to do so. The incentives among electors to change their vote in such a close electoral contest would have been monumental.

This scenario is one that "Never Trumpers" had floated for months in an effort to prevent Trump from ascending to the presidency. As we saw with McMullin, the hope was to have the House select a compromise Republican candidate among the top three candidates receiving votes in the Electoral College. Since no third-party candidate won any electoral votes on November 8, this plan would have required at least one elector to cast a vote for someone other than Clinton or Trump. Although the election did not end in a tie, this Hail Mary plan remained in play throughout the interregnum period—all the way through the vote of the Electoral College.

With victories in Pennsylvania and Florida, it became clear that Trump would cross the 270-vote threshold to win an Electoral College majority. Even without Michigan, his electoral vote total stood at 290—20 more votes than he needed to win the presidency. Shortly before midnight, Hillary Clinton called Trump to concede the election. The following day, Clinton publicly accepted the results. However, many others did not. All eyes then turned to the Electoral College, which was seen as a last effort to prevent a Trump presidency.

Alexander Hamilton and the 2016 Election

Trump's victory not only was surprising but also catalyzed a plan that had been discussed months in advance on the chance Trump was able to win in the general election. Historian H. W. Brands claimed, "Donald Trump is the guy our fathers warned us about. Our Founding Fathers, that is" (March 31,

2016). Brands argued that "the drafters of the Constitution distrusted the opportunist who played on popular emotions in the quest for political power" (March 31, 2016). Seeing Trump as an opportunist, he notes that "the mere existence of the electors serves as a reminder of the founders' fear of emotion running away with the republic" (March 31, 2016). Whereas the *original* Electoral College removed the passions of the people by placing the selection of the president in the hands of a temporary, intermediary body of learned individuals, the *evolved* Electoral College is associated with the direct election by the citizenry. The original body was to be a republican institution, whereas the evolved body has become a democratic institution.

The original vision of the role of electors is drawn directly from Hamilton's words. In *Federalist 68*, he argued that the Electoral College would be composed of those individuals who would be "most capable of analyzing the qualities adapted to the station, and acting under circumstances favorable to deliberation, and to a judicial combination of all the reasons and inducements which were proper to govern their choice (Rossiter, 1961, 412). These individuals would be best able to evaluate candidates and make a decision in the interest of the country. For Hamilton, the opportunity for electoral mischief would be minimized by relying on a temporary body of individuals dispersed across the country. He states that such a system

> will be much less apt to convulse the community with any extraordinary or violent movements . . . And as the electors, chosen in each State, are to assemble and vote in the State in which they are chosen, this detached and divided situation will expose them much less to heats and ferments, which might be communicated from them to the people, than if they were all to be convened at one time, in one place. (Rossiter, 1961, 412)

Hamilton painted a picture of the elector as a trustee of the people rather than a delegate. As we have seen, this conceptualization changed with the rise of political parties and the adoption of the winner-take-all rule. However, the 2016 election was no ordinary contest, and the call to have electors exercise their discretion was made months before the election and went into overdrive in the month after the election.

Following the Republican convention, some questioned whether the Electoral College might prevent a Trump presidency (Silverstein, August 4, 2016). Such conjecture was prompted by Baoky Vu, a Republican elector from Georgia, who said that he would not be voting for Trump. Vu stated he was going to assert his independence because of his disdain for Trump's tactics and temperament. He wrote: "Donald Trump's antics and asinine behavior has cemented my belief that he lacks the judgment, temperament and gravitas to lead this Nation" (Silverstein, August 4, 2016). Vu further stated that:

> This is the Republican Party of Lincoln and Reagan and Romney and Ryan, not the Party of Donald Trump. As a 2016 Presidential Elector, I am forever grateful to our state Party and our Chairman for bestowing this once-in-a-lifetime honor on me. I take my role seriously and in the face of the difficult choice before us, I will always put America First over party and labels. (Silverstein, August 4, 2016)

Shortly after his announcement, he was asked to step down, and he obliged. Back then, I predicted that "quite a few electors will be testing their consciences when they assemble this December," and this is what indeed occurred (Alexander, August 8, 2016). Vu was not the only elector to suggest that he or she might go rogue and vote against the party's nominee.

In early October, a clip from "Access Hollywood" surfaced in which Trump was having a lewd, off-the-record conversation about women. At the time, Trump was trailing in the polls, and the tape had some in the Republican Party looking for ways to remove him from the ticket. A Republican elector from Virginia, Erich Reimer, stated that he prayed "for the good of the country that either Trump steps down as the GOP nominee or that the Republican Party finds a way to utilize the Electors who will be given the opportunity to vote in the Electoral College to still elect a Republican and conservative administration" (Cheney, October 9, 2016). South Dakota Governor (and presidential elector) Dennis Daugaard bluntly tweeted: "Enough is enough. Donald Trump should withdraw in favor of Mike Pence. This election is too important" (Cheney, October 9, 2016). These were not the only electors struggling with their nominee.

A Republican elector in Texas, Art Sisneros, created a stir when, after the election, he indicated that he might withhold his vote for Trump. He resigned his position as elector prior to the Electoral College's meeting but was compelled to explain his rationale in doing so. In a post titled "Conflicted Elector in a Corrupt College," Sisneros made the case that the role of an elector is that of a trustee rather than a delegate. He flatly stated that "there is no indication that Electors were ever to be directed by the population on how to vote. Their votes were to be their own, made in the best interest of those they represented" (Sisneros, November 26, 2016). Using Hamilton's vision,

Sisneros claimed that electors would "be trusted to act in the best interest of those they represented" (November 26, 2016). Yet, he acknowledged that the body has changed over time and that

> we no longer operate with the same wisdom and discernment as our forefathers. Where they warned of the evils they experienced which flow from the excess of democracy, we demand the voice of the people be heard. The difference between a republic and democracy is all but lost in public discourse by conservatives and progressives alike. (November 26, 2016)

He argued that the pledges electors sign are antithetical to the original intent of the Constitution. Thus, electors who voted for the people they believed were best suited for the office are being faithful rather than faithless to the Constitution. This is similar to the rationale offered by his fellow Texan, Bill Greene, who cast a rogue vote for Ron Paul rather than Donald Trump when the Texas delegation met. Recall Greene's logic in Chapter 6 that the election should be seen as a "straw poll" by electors. Similar to Sisneros, Greene argues that while election results should weigh in the electors' decision making, it is up to electors to ultimately determine who they think would be best suited to become president and vice president of the United States.

Sisneros's main concern with Trump was that he was not "biblically qualified to serve in the office of the Presidency" and that voting for Trump "would bring dishonor to God" (November 28, 2016). In noting his choice to resign rather than break his oath or to vote for Trump, he stated that he would be able to sleep well at night but would "also mourn the loss of our republic" (November 28, 2016).

Another Texan, Republican elector Chris Suprun, wrote an op-ed in the *New York Times* shortly after Sisneros announced his intention to resign, imploring fellow electors to coalesce around a compromise candidate rather than vote for Trump or Clinton. Pointing to Trump's character, Suprun argued that he was being asked to vote "for someone who shows daily he is not qualified for the office" (December 5, 2016). Referring to *Federalist 68*, he stated that the

> Electoral College should determine if candidates are qualified, not engaged in demagogy, and independent from foreign influence. Mr. Trump shows us again and again that he does not meet these standards. Given his own public statements, it isn't clear how the Electoral College can ignore these issues, and so it should reject him. (December 5, 2016)

His announcement came in the midst of a very public campaign by a group calling themselves "Hamilton electors" who were seeking to find an alternative candidate they could rally behind. Suprun's announcement made the Hamilton electors' campaign much more interesting.

Three days before the election, Robert Satiacum, a Democratic elector from Washington state, made headlines when he vowed he would not vote for Hillary Clinton if she carried the state. He said that he could not vote for Clinton "because she's a criminal, she doesn't do enough for American Indians, and she's done nothing but flip back and forth" (Hartmann, November 5, 2016). Satiacum followed through with his promise, voting for Faith Spotted Eagle when the Electoral College met on December 19.

It is apparent that many electors in 2016 subscribed to the Hamiltonian vision throughout the campaign. Buoyed by wavering electors such as Vu, Reimer, Daugaard, Sisneros, Suprun, and Satiacum, Electoral College lobbyists believed they had a receptive audience among both Democrat and Republican electors. It would take 37 Republican defections for them to be successful in throwing the selection of the next president to the House of Representatives. The hunt for 37 defections was in full swing from November 8 until the Electoral College met on December 19. It proved to be a very intense, public, and multifaceted campaign that few electors anticipated when they assumed their positions many months in advance of the election.

Lobbying the 2016 Assemblage

Electoral College lobbying is a practice that has occurred on a regular basis but has largely gone undetected by most political observers. As we saw in Chapter 6, a significant amount of Electoral College lobbying occurred in 2004, 2008, and 2012. Drawing from that research, I suggested that "Electoral College lobbyists may be able to take advantage of a specific election's context by tailoring their messages for maximum persuasiveness among wavering electors in any given contest (Alexander, 2012, 167). The 2016 election provided a perfect storm for those seeking to lobby the Electoral College. Recall that in Table 6.5, we observed that *all* the Republican electors in 2016 reported they were contacted in an effort to change their vote. Democrats were also besieged by Electoral College lobbyists. Based on my surveys of electors from 2000 to 2012, I argued that "elector lobbying may be a plausible tactic either in a close race or in a race with a combustible candidate" (Alexander, 2012, 182). Trump's unconventional campaign and bombastic style provided fertile ground for such an occurrence. Writing three months before the general election, I predicted that a Trump victory would undoubtedly trigger an Electoral College lobbying campaign (Alexander, August 8, 2016)—and this is exactly what occurred in the aftermath of the election.

Lobbying is a common tactic to influence government policies. Research on the practice reveals that lobbying takes place at virtually all levels of government and takes many forms. David Truman (1951) argues that lobbying activity is likely to proliferate based on the complexity of the society. The existence of multiple "access points" to government actors creates additional opportunities for lobbyists to influence government. Government structures, then, can either encourage or discourage lobbying activity. For instance, Frederick Boehmke (2002) finds the scope of direct democracy in a state has a positive effect relating to the number of interest groups in a state *ceteris paribus*. Lipsitz's finding that voters in swing states are more likely than voters in non-swing states to go to the ballot box in competitive campaign cycles (2009, 203) is relevant to the practice of Electoral College lobbying. The Electoral College is yet another access point to lobby. Elector lobbying represents a form of political behavior unique to the existence of the institution. Many citizens simply do not give up after the November election is held. Instead, they consider the Electoral College as an additional access point to influence the election outcome.

Both Trump and Clinton engendered discussions about faithless electors in advance of the November election, with Republican and Democrat electors alike threatening to join the ranks of the faithless. Trump's candidacy in particular generated a great deal of discussion about the role of the Electoral College in potentially stopping him from becoming president. Much of that discussion called on Hamilton's proposition in *Federalist 68* that the Electoral College process "affords a moral certainty, that the office of President will never fall to the lot of any man who is not in an eminent degree endowed with the requisite qualifications" (Rossiter, 1961, 414). Hamilton goes on to state that

> talents for low intrigue, and the little arts of popularity, may alone suffice to elevate a man to the first honors in a single State; but it will require other talents, and a different kind of merit, to establish him in the esteem and confidence of the whole Union, or of so considerable a portion of it as would be necessary to make him a successful candidate for the distinguished office of President of the United States. (Rossiter, 1961, 414)

Hamilton maintained that having a temporary body of electors would also work to protect the presidential selection process from "cabal, intrigue, and corruption." Yet, electors have hardly remained insulated from the pleas of citizens looking for any means to change the outcome of the general election. This has been true in close elections as well as those where the outcome was clear and convincing.

In the days after the 2016 election, nearly 5 million Americans signed a petition to have electors consider voting for Clinton rather than Trump. The campaign to "flip" presidential electors was very public and was tied to protest movements across the country in the wake of the election. Many celebrities also took part in the campaign, including Lady Gaga, Pink, and Sia. *Saturday Night Live* even had a skit with "Hillary Clinton" appealing to electors to vote for her. The Clinton character shows up on the doorstep of a Republican elector with a sign saying, "I know you're an elector." Members of the Electoral College were squarely in the sights of the public and other members of the body.

The widespread lobbying that occurred in 2016 was not unprecedented, as we saw in the previous chapter. While Electoral College lobbying appears to be a regular feature every four years, the 2016 campaign was exceptional. For instance, an elector from Michigan, 20-year-old college student Michael Banearian, reported that he had received death threats, with one angry individual saying he would put a "bullet in your mouth" (King, November 30, 2016). Other electors claimed they were being besieged by a barrage of letters, emails, Facebook messages, tweets, and phone calls. The survey responses are consistent with media reports of elector lobbying.

Many respondents indicated that they had received over 100,000 emails, hundreds to thousands of letters, and scores of phone calls. Some believed the communication they received was orchestrated by the Clinton campaign. Others noted that much of the communication consisted of form letters and therefore was not very effective. However, a number of electors stated that they read all of the information they received—indicating that they took their jobs seriously and believed they had an obligation to listen to their fellow Americans. Much of the Electoral College lobbying encouraged electors to vote for Clinton because (1) she won the popular vote or (2) Trump was unfit for office. Electors received information about the history of the Electoral College, past faithless electors, potential Russian involvement in the election, copies of the *Federalist Papers*, and the laws regarding their ability to vote their conscience. Several electors even reported that they received offers to have their fines paid if they were to vote faithlessly.

Two months after the Electoral College met, an elector stated that "the hateful emails are still being sent but now with the message that every bad thing that happens or bad decision Trump makes will be the fault of the electors. The language is vulgar and many have said we will go to hell for voting for President Trump" (Survey #150, 2017). One elector blithely stated: "I considered the thousands of emails sent to me, asking me to not vote for Trump, to be excessive, bothersome, obnoxious, and boring" (Survey #16, 2017). Another claimed that "the Electoral College saved the United States and World from the socialist global agenda" (Survey #255, 2017). Similarly, another Republican elector indicated that "Hillary would destroy America. Corruption abounds. We are not safe. Our children are ignorant, we must speak the same language. Borders should be secure, people are lazy, must have pride and work. God saved us this time. We must change back to God!" (Survey #283, 2017). It would appear that these Republican electors were firmly committed to their votes.

In addition to the avalanche of emails, letters, social media posts, and telephone conversations, many electors were personally contacted by fellow electors. These "Hamilton electors" were looking to capitalize on concerns Republicans had openly expressed about Trump. As one elector noted, "at their origin, electors were the last check on the popular will. 'Faithless' electors were part of the system. Political parties have misused the Electoral College for partisan purpose" (Survey #104, 2017). Yet, political parties are the gatekeepers to the institution. Consequently, the power of partisanship is extraordinarily strong in the Electoral College. Thus, the campaign to upend Trump by fellow electors faced an uphill climb.

The Hamilton Elector Movement

In addition to lobbying by citizens, members of the Electoral College made the case that they had a duty to vote their conscience over the wishes of the citizenry and their respective political parties. Relying on Hamilton's description of the role of electors, these individuals proclaimed themselves to be Hamilton electors. Adding hope to Electoral College lobbyists was the public campaign by the Hamilton electors. These electors (mostly Democrats) sought to find a compromise candidate who was neither Trump nor Clinton (O'Donnell, 2016). They stated they were relying on Hamilton's vision of the role of elector as articulated in *Federalist 68*. This is similar to the telegraph campaign by some electors in 1960 to get Republican and Democrat electors to support an alternative candidate to Kennedy or Nixon. However, the 2016 campaign was much more visible and coordinated.

Bret Chiafalo and Michael Baca were the co-founders of the Hamilton electors. Chiafalo, an elector from Washington state, and Baca, an elector from Colorado, stated that they were seeking to use electors as a "break in case of emergency fire hose that's gotten dusty over the last 200 years" (O'Donnell, November 21, 2016). Speaking of the 2016 election, Chiafalo proclaimed that "This is an emergency" (O'Donnell, November 21, 2016). Their stated goal was to find a compromise candidate whom electors could unite behind. They floated names such as former Massachusetts Governor Mitt Romney and Ohio Governor John Kasich as possible alternatives. Both Republican governors had been harsh critics of Trump during the campaign. However, both indicated that they hoped Republican electors would be the ones to ultimately determine whom electors should support as a compromise candidate. They noted that the biggest concern they heard from fellow electors was that '"the people have spoken, why don't you go with the people?' But if we did that, then Clinton would be the president" (O'Donnell, November 21, 2016). These electors, then, were not seeking to have the Electoral College unite behind the popular vote winner (Clinton) but instead sought to abide by the result that a Republican had fairly won the majority of Electoral College votes across the nation. They just did not want that Republican to be Trump.

A website dedicated to the Hamilton elector movement was created, and many of these individuals reached out to other electors. They gained the support of Larry Lessig and Richard Painter (a chief ethics counsel to George W. Bush). Days before the election, they believed that "as many as 30 Republicans were thinking of flipping their votes" (personal correspondence, December 9, 2016). They sought to create an appearance of momentum in an effort to convince Republican electors to publicly rebuke Trump. Such campaigning was antithetical to what Hamilton envisioned for the Electoral College. He had argued that the transitory nature of the body and the fact that electors would meet in each of their own states would help shield them from intense lobbying. In spite of Hamilton's claim, few electors were able to escape the "heats and ferments" communicated to them from the citizenry and even from within the body.

In the days following the November election, reports surfaced about Russian interference in the election. As a consequence, 80 electors signed a petition to receive a briefing by James Clapper, Director of National Intelligence, prior to the Electoral College vote on December 19 (Cheney and Debenedetti, December 12, 2016). Citing *Federalist 68*, they stated that a fundamental reason for the office of elector was to guard against attempts by foreign powers to influence elections in the United States. Hamilton writes about the danger of foreign influence:

> Nothing was more to be desired than that every practicable obstacle should be opposed to cabal, intrigue, and corruption. These most deadly adversaries of republican government might naturally have been expected to make their approaches from more than one querter [*sic*], but chiefly from the desire in foreign powers to gain an improper ascendant in our councils. How could they better gratify this, than by raising a creature of their own to the chief magistracy of the Union?

In spite of their efforts, electors were not briefed on the matter.

The Hamilton movement received some momentum from Suprun's op-ed in the *New York Times*. He was the first Republican to openly urge others to abandon Trump for an alternative Republican candidate. Recall that two other Republicans had conveyed their worries and resigned. The belief that other Republican electors had similar concerns was widespread among the Hamilton elector group. This was due to questions about Trump's character as well as fear among the Republican establishment over Trump's party reliability.

In response, the Trump campaign was hard at work to prevent mass defections. The Republican National Committee and state political parties were reportedly in touch with Republican electors multiple times in advance of the election (Cheney, December 13, 2016). Ronald Reagan similarly had reached out to electors prior to their meeting in 1980. It has become a common practice for the parties to maintain a close eye on their electors in advance of their votes. This suggests the very real concern among party officials that electors may go rogue. Several days before the 2016 election, one elector who had indicated that he would have preferred another candidate over Trump was asked whether he would maintain his pledge to vote for him. He responded: "Let's say that somehow the American people nominated a guy who had murdered 47 people, carved 'em all up and put 'em in a ditch and hadn't been caught yet, and he got nominated for president. Well, you know, then I might change my mind" (Cheney, December 13, 2016).

Taking issue with Hamilton, one elector stated: "I will state authoritatively . . . that Alexander Hamilton was incorrect in his projection in *Federalist 68* that the Electoral College would protect the Republic from a demagogue" (Survey #90, 2017). This elector stated that he had spoken to over 20 other electors "to assess and then persuade them to consider voting for another Republican" (Survey #90, 2017). He went on to say that after meeting with fellow electors in his state, they "decided that Donald Trump was unfit and possibly the election was compromised by a foreign adversary nation" (Survey #90, 2017). He noted that he believed over 20 Republican electors were considering switching their votes, but since so few had indicated doing so publicly, many were afraid to do so. He suggested that had a critical mass of Republican electors indicated their intention to vote for a Republican alternative, many others would have likely followed suit. Some evidence for this rationale exists as one Republican elector stated in her survey that had an elector or two on the East Coast voted faithlessly, she would have been much more likely to do so. The desire to conform among party members is not surprising. What is surprising is that so many considered voting against Trump.

As we have seen, 20 percent of Republican electors gave *some* consideration to voting for someone other than Trump. For some context, 27 Republican respondents considered voting faithlessly. This alone suggests the Hamilton electors were within reach of the 37 Republicans needed to block Trump in the Electoral College. Generalizing these results to the population of electors suggests that there were around 60 wavering Republican electors in the 2016 Electoral College![1] Although Electoral College lobbyists (both in the citizenry and among the Hamilton electors) fell well short of their goal to get 37 Republican electors to defect, a record number of electors did vote contrary to expectations. The following section examines faithless and wavering electors in the 2016 assemblage.

Faithless and Wavering Electors in the 2016 Electoral College

While electors have come to be chosen for their fidelity rather than their judgment, we saw in the previous chapter that many are not as committed to their party's tickets as typically thought. When the Electoral College met, 10 electors attempted to break ranks and vote for candidates to whom they were not pledged. Two electors were removed and replaced, one changed his vote in accordance with his state's popular vote, and seven cast faithless votes. Protestors were present at virtually every state's meeting of electors. Five

---

1. Nearly 50 percent of all electors responded to the survey. Responders and non-responders were virtually identical among known characteristics.

Democrat electors voted for the likes of Bernie Sanders, John Kasich, Colin Powell, and Faith Spotted Eagle. Two Republican electors voted for Ron Paul and John Kasich.

Early in the morning the day the Electoral College met, Maine elector David Bright released a statement explaining how and why he would cast his vote that day. He indicated that he would be voting for Bernie Sanders because he was a "Democratic elector" not a "Clinton elector." He was a Sanders supporter and cited the fact that Sanders had carried Maine in the Democratic primary. In casting his vote for Sanders, he hoped to inspire young, idealistic voters to stay involved with the political process. He added that if he thought enough Republican electors would defect from Trump in favor of Clinton, he would have cast his vote for Clinton. While his post explained what he planned to do, what actually happened is even more intriguing.

After Bright cast his vote for Sanders, the chair of the meeting ruled his vote was out of order because he violated his oath of office. Bright considered objecting to the ruling but did not do so after considering what likely would have occurred. He opined that had he objected, the lone Republican (as Trump won Maine's 2nd congressional district) would have abstained, leaving the remaining three Democrats to decide on his objection. Having already ruled that Bright violated his pledge, the chair would have been one vote against Bright. Another of the Democrat electors was a Sanders supporter, but Bright felt that she would have been put in an awkward position as a member of the Democratic National Committee if she were to support his faithless ballot. He further believed that had he pushed the issue further, he would be replaced and not permitted to voice his opinion at the close of the Electoral College ceremonies. Consequently, he agreed to vote for Clinton when the electors were asked to vote again. Although his ballot was not counted for Sanders, his actions apparently affected a fellow Democrat elector in Hawaii, David Mulinix.

Hours after Bright's attempted recalcitrance, Mulinix cast his vote for Sanders rather than for Clinton. He did so after reportedly being inspired by Bright's speech in support of Sanders. He saw his choice as one between a "corporate shill" (Clinton) and a "fascist" (Trump). Stating that he could not vote for either, he voted for Sanders, whom he believed was the real choice of the people. Mulinix conceded that he was happy that by the time he voted, his vote would not cost Clinton the election, so he could cast his vote with confidence. He added that "we shouldn't have electors . . . The Electoral College is outdated. Maybe it worked in 1789 when almost nobody could read or write.

Maybe it made sense then, but we are way past that" (Gonzales, December 20, 2016).

Two other electors, Muhammad Abdurrahman of Minnesota and Baca of Colorado, attempted to vote faithlessly but were instantly replaced by alternate electors. Abdurrahman's vote was unexpected as he had not made much news prior to the Electoral College meeting. He attempted to vote for Bernie Sanders but was immediately replaced. It is noteworthy that the law permitting his replacement came into effect after the 2004 faithless vote for John Edwards that continues to be a mystery. Baca, one of the founders of the Hamilton elector movement, wrote John Kasich's name in on the preprinted ballot in Colorado. The Colorado electors had been warned that they would be replaced if they sought to vote contrary to expectations. While several mulled doing so, Baca was the only one who followed through with the plan.

Four Washington state electors joined the ranks of the faithless, including Chiafalo, the other co-founder of the Hamilton elector movement. Although he sought to vote for Kasich, in a show of solidarity Chiafalo voted for former Secretary of State Colin Powell, who was the choice of fellow Washington electors Levi Guerra and Esther John. At 19, Guerra was one of the youngest to serve in the 2016 Electoral College. Chiafalo indicated that the entire delegation voted under protest because they had not been given access to a briefing on alleged Russian interference.

Satiacum was the final member of the Washington delegation to cast a faithless vote. Instead of a nationally known name, he chose to vote for Faith Spotted Eagle, a Native American environmentalist. Satiacum was a member of the Puyallup tribe and had supported Bernie Sanders during the primary. As a result of Mike Padden's faithless vote in 1976, the state of Washington passed a law criminalizing the act of faithless voting by attaching a $1,000 fine to anyone who violated the law. As a consequence, it is believed the Washington faithless electors are the first to be fined for voting contrary to expectations.

The two Republican faithless votes came from Greene and Suprun of Texas. While Suprun's vote was expected, Greene's was not. Because electors in Texas cast their votes in private, it was not immediately known who had cast the second faithless vote. Suprun voted for Kasich and Greene for Ron Paul. Even before the electors met, Texas Governor Greg Abbott had announced that a bill had been filed to bind electors to the popular vote in the state. This likely occurred due to the controversy surrounding Suprun and Sisneros's resignation.

In addition to these individuals, data from the surveys of electors show that the Hamilton movement had a more receptive audience than what materialized in the final tally of electoral votes. Recall that Table 6.6 revealed that 21 percent of all electors considered defecting, with more Democrats (23 percent) than Republicans (20 percent) considering rogue votes. That more electors from the losing side voted faithlessly and considered voting faithlessly is consistent with previous research on wavering electors. Yet, the number of electors from the winning side who considered defecting is very different from previous research on wavering electors. Still, only two Republicans failed to vote for Trump.

Recall that the Hamilton movement needed 35 more Republicans to break ranks and vote for an alternative candidate to deny Trump an Electoral College majority. Although few actually did, many more considered doing so. The 20 percent of Republican electors who could be considered as wavering electors in the 2016 campaign is a much higher proportion than that found in previous elections for the winning candidate. This suggests that the strategy of appealing directly to electors to change the outcome of the election was not as far-fetched as some thought.

Previous research on wavering electors suggests they are less tied to their party's candidates and are less likely to have contributed money or time to political campaigns than committed electors (Alexander, 2012). These same factors seem to be at play among wavering electors in the 2016 campaign. Table 7.1 details the bivariate correlations between these factors. Committed electors are those who gave no consideration to defection. Wavering electors

Table 7.1 Correlations Among Wavering Electors

	Wavering Democrats	Wavering Republicans
Trump Feeling Thermometer	0.034 (0.730)	−0.485** (0.000)
Clinton Feeling Thermometer	−0.398**(0.000)	−0.020 (0.822)
Contributed in 2016	−0.089 (0.369)	−0.247** (0.004)
Contacted to change vote	0.253** (0.008)	X***
Support automatic tabulation of Electoral College votes	−0.178 (0.066)	−0.175* (0.039)
Age	−0.151 (0.124)	−0.248** (0.004)

* Correlation significant at 0.05 level (two-tailed).

** Correlation significant at 0.01 level (two-tailed).

*** No correlation can be reported since every Republican elector was contacted.

are those who gave some consideration to voting contrary to expectations. An examination of the 2016 wavering electors finds that many were far more critical of their party's candidate than their more committed counterparts. Concern about their party's nominee appears to be the most impactful factor affecting electors' calculus to vote faithfully. This may not be too surprising given the public dissatisfaction with the Trump and Clinton candidacies.

Whether electors make a financial contribution is also related to their relative commitment to their party's nominee. Wavering electors were far less likely to have made a financial contribution during the 2016 election cycle than were committed electors. This was especially true among wavering Republican electors. Electoral College lobbying was positively related to one's consideration of defection among Democrats. We cannot know the extent of this effect for Republicans as all Republicans were contacted to change their votes. Wavering electors of both parties were strongly in favor of maintaining the independence of electors rather than making electoral votes automatic. Lastly, we can see that younger electors were more likely to consider defecting than were older electors. This is particularly the case for Republican electors. Some respondents indicated that they felt they needed to follow the party line if they were to have a future in the party. A concern over party ostracism is among the reasons that has been offered as to why we see so few faithless votes in American history, and the survey responses support this to some degree.

Table 7.2 details the candidate evaluations among committed electors and wavering electors regarding a number of political figures who were prominent in the 2016 campaign. Both Clinton and Trump were not even the most admired candidates among their respective electors, and the differences between committed electors and wavering electors in their evaluation of Trump and Clinton are noteworthy. Table 7.2 reveals that wavering Republicans placed Donald Trump as the fourth-highest-rated political figure among those they evaluated. Trump was not the highest-rated figure among committed Republicans as well, with Pence claiming the highest rating. Still, wavering Republicans rated Trump at just a 6.28 compared to the 8.68 among committed Republicans on the 10-point scale. Similarly, Hillary Clinton scored a 6.63 among wavering Democrats and 8.48 among committed Democrats. She actually fared worse than Trump among her partisans—placing as the fourth-highest-rated Democrat by committed electors and as the fifth-highest-rated Democrat among wavering electors.

Wavering Republicans gave Ted Cruz, Jeb Bush, Mitt Romney, John Kasich, and Ron Paul higher evaluations than did committed Republican electors. Only Pence, George W. Bush, and Paul Ryan received higher

Table 7.2 Wavering and Committed Electors Evaluate Candidates Differently

Candidate	Committed Republicans	Wavering Republicans	Difference	Committed Democrats	Wavering Democrats	Difference
Donald Trump	8.68	6.28	−2.4	1.19	1.25	0.06
Marco Rubio	6.88	5.96	−0.92	2.42	2.61	0.19
Mike Pence	9.18	8.36	−0.82	1.66	1.92	0.26
G. W. Bush	7.48	6.75	−0.73	3.33	2.8	−0.53
Chris Christie	5.6	4.96	−0.64	1.8	2.04	0.24
Paul Ryan	7.01	6.6	−0.41	2.11	2.33	0.22
Ted Cruz	6.15	6.2	0.05	1.68	1.7	0.02
Jeb Bush	5.17	5.32	0.15	3.31	3.08	−0.23
Mitt Romney	5.75	5.96	0.21	3.54	3.42	−0.12
John Kasich	4.45	4.88	0.43	4.48	4.38	−0.1
Ron Paul	4.91	5.6	0.69	2.5	2.88	0.38

	Committed Democrats	Wavering Democrats	Difference	Committed Republicans	Wavering Republicans	Difference
Tim Kaine	8.17	5.88	−2.29	2.08	2.48	0.4
Hillary Clinton	8.48	6.63	−1.85	1.6	1.52	−0.08
Bill Clinton	8.25	6.46	−1.79	2.6	3.36	0.76
Cory Booker	7.67	6.1	−1.57	2.06	2.52	0.46
Andrew Cuomo	6.54	5	−1.54	2.2	2.46	0.26
Barack Obama	9.41	8	−1.41	1.78	2.16	0.38
Joe Biden	9.21	8.17	−1.04	2.85	3.04	0.19
Elizabeth Warren	8.52	7.52	−1	1.4	1.96	0.56
Bernie Sanders	7.12	7.67	0.55	1.75	2.32	0.57

Created by author.

evaluations than Trump among wavering Republicans. It is likely that a variety of factors were at play among these individuals. Trump's candidacy gave pause to many in the party. The arguments presented by Vu, Daugaard, Sisneros, and Suprun likely were shared by many others.

For Democrats, wavering electors gave higher evaluations for Barack Obama, Joe Biden, Elizabeth Warren, and Bernie Sanders than they did for Hillary Clinton. Clinton did not fare well among committed Democrats either. Obama, Biden, and Warren all scored higher than Clinton among these individuals too. This suggests a lack of enthusiasm for Clinton among those who would be expected to be her most ardent supporters. Recall that most electors are selected at party conventions. Strong partisanship does not translate into candidate loyalty. This can be seen with several of the faithless electors. Neither Clinton nor Trump was the candidate of choice for these individuals. Many of Clinton's faithless votes were from supporters of Bernie Sanders. Concerns among Republican electors centered around Trump's personal characteristics and his party reliability.

Conclusion

Although the Electoral College always figures prominently in presidential campaigns, the many arguments surrounding the body were in sharp focus due to the events of the 2016 election. From the popular vote/electoral vote split, to the significance of the winner-take-all rule used in most states, to the independence and conceptualization of the role of electors, the rules of the presidential selection process were on full display. Days after the contest, some legislators sought to put an end to the Electoral College by requiring the president to receive the most votes cast from across the country. This effort gained little momentum and was not even referred to a committee. The record number of faithless electors also stimulated efforts to curb their independence. These efforts are commonplace *after* faithless votes have been cast in past elections.

The election marked the sixth misfire election and the 19th time a candidate was elected president with less than a majority of the vote. Certainly, both Clinton and Trump were historically unpopular candidates. The magnification effect discussed in Chapter 6 did little to boost Trump's popularity during his presidential honeymoon period: his approval rating hovered between 38 and 45 percent over his first three months in office (Gallup, April 2, 2018).

The Hamilton movement drew on the foundations of the institution. Seeing their responsibility to serve as trustees rather than delegates, many electors carefully undertook their duties. Some drew from another of the authors of the *Federalist Papers*, John Jay. In *Federalist 64*, Jay contended that voters may be "liable to be deceived by those brilliant appearances of genius and patriotism which like transient meteors, sometimes mislead as well as dazzle" (Rossiter, 1961, 391). Writing for *The Atlantic*, liberal pundit Peter Beinart reversed his thoughts on elector independence in light of the 2016 election. In a zealous argument recognizing many of the undemocratic features of American politics, Beinart concluded that he was wrong to argue against the Electoral College. He states: "Before this election, I supported abolishing the Electoral College. Now I think America needs electors, who, in times of national emergency, can prevent demagogues from taking power" (November 21, 2016). He concedes that it took a Trump president-elect for him to realize that the Framers were prescient and he was naïve when it came to the Electoral College.

Whether electors should exercise their authority to act independently provided additional drama to the interregnum period from November 8 to December 19. It required electors (and party leaders) to evaluate what the Electoral College was intended to do versus what it has become. It provided a clear reckoning of Korzi's distinction between the original body and the evolved body. Data from the surveys of electors indicate that they are often split between these conceptualizations of the role of electors. Most, in fact, believe they do have the right to consider their votes, but with deference to their party's (and the public's) wishes.

In 2016, millions of Americans called on electors to exercise independence and select someone other than Trump. Both Democrat and Republican electors broke ranks and voted for candidates to whom they were not pledged. Although this did not change the outcome of the election, their votes were recorded and the likes of Colin Powell, John Kasich, and Bernie Sanders received votes for president. Similarly, Elizabeth Warren, Carly Fiorina, Maria Cantwell, and Susan Collins received votes for vice president in the Electoral College, even though they did not appear on ballots to voters across the country. These figures did not campaign or spend a single dollar to earn those electoral votes. Over 125 million Americans cast votes for Trump or Clinton. Those who voted in the general election likely did not think very much, if at all, of the electors who were charged with translating those popular votes into electoral votes. In short, few citizens believed they were entrusting their votes to electors who should use their wisdom to select the president and vice president in lieu of the citizenry.

Just after the 2016 assemblage met, I argued that faithless electors should be curtailed, noting that the practice "produces unnecessary uncertainty in an already maligned process and runs counter to the expectations of the office of presidential elector" (Alexander, January 3, 2017). The disconnect between the original and evolved vision of the role of elector deserves far greater attention moving forward in presidential elections.

8

Reform Efforts and Thoughts on the Electoral College

THROUGHOUT THIS BOOK we have seen that the Electoral College has remained a very controversial feature of American politics. Advocates of the institution often cite its necessity in forcing candidates to run national campaigns. Chapter 4 provides ample evidence that this is not the case. Instead, a handful of states can be reliably counted on to receive campaign visits and subsequently determine the outcome of presidential races. We have also observed the existence of many hairbreadth elections, including six misfire contests. Concerns over the legitimacy of incoming administrations are consistently raised in the wake of these campaigns. Lastly, surveys of electors suggest that while we may think elections are determined on the second Tuesday in November, for many who serve in the Electoral College the race does not conclude until they have their say. Although faithless electors rarely occur, many electors mull their choices and some follow through by casting rogue votes in contradiction to those cast in the general election.

An assessment of the institution requires us to distinguish whether we are evaluating the original body or the evolved body. Significant differences exist between these two notions. Many of the issues the Framers grappled with at the Founding (legislative intrigue, presidential independence, voter parochialism, slavery, presidential power, the independent selection of the president, and the desire to produce a system that was able to obtain a consensus at the Convention) are now obsolete (Edwards, 2004, 80–89). The adoption of the 12th Amendment, the rise of political parties, and the move to select electors through popular election would be bemusing to those who crafted the original institution in Philadelphia. The Electoral College process has been described as "complex and unusual" (Whittington, 2017, 3). Robert

Dahl criticizes the institution thusly: "No part of the Constitution revealed the flaws in its design more fully than the provision for the Electoral College" (2003, 77). Still, the Electoral College determines our one nationally elected leader and ostensibly one of the most powerful individuals in the world. In this concluding chapter, I examine how the institution performs relative to norms of representation in mass democracies. I investigate why, in spite of the many criticisms of the Electoral College, it persists. I do this relative to an examination of reform efforts aimed at the institution.

Norms of Representation and the Electoral College

This book set out to examine the Electoral College in the context of norms of representation. Virtually all the controversies surrounding the body stem from arguments concerning who is or is not represented by the institution. Chapter 2 examined extant theories of representation that are applicable to the Electoral College. Hannah Pitkin (1967) argued that an understanding of representation requires an understanding of the context to which the term is applied. It matters whether we are trying to represent "people," "states," "political parties," "groups," or "the country." Arguments can be made that the Electoral College seeks to represent each of these entities. Yet, the degree to which each is represented varies considerably. Proponents and opponents of the institution tend to emphasize at least one of these dimensions of representation over others in their arguments.

Normative arguments can and should be made as to what ought to be represented through the presidential selection process. Arguments over the institution rarely acknowledge the complex dimensions of representation as they relate to what we hope the presidential selection process achieves. They tend to ignore or discount the importance of those elements of representation that run counter to their opinions. Perhaps more troubling is that many arguments over the body fail to work from a common understanding of the origin and evolution of the Electoral College. One's reliance on the original view of the Electoral College or the evolved one matters a great deal. Even then, different interpretations of the original or evolved body can reasonably be made.

There are good reasons to evaluate the body using the original intentions of the Framers. However, I argue it is more intellectually honest to evaluate the body relative to its evolution and actual practice. Muller (2007, 374) concludes that "despite the long history of presidential elections decided by the Electoral College, it is fairly clear that the College operates in a fashion wholly unrelated to its envisioned role." For good measure, he adds that "the defense of the Electoral College in the Federalist Papers reads almost comically in the present" (2007, 374).

From the outset, the Electoral College has never operated as intended. This can be seen in a variety of ways. The rise of political parties necessitated the first major change to the body—the passage of the 12th Amendment. The widespread adoption of the unit rule by states signified a preference that the popular vote should be used to select electors. Regarding electors, the notion they would be chosen for their independence faded quickly and was replaced by an expectation that they would be obedient to their respective political parties. Ironically, electors who go rogue today are referred to as "faithless," rather than being "faithful" to their duties. Further, recall that initially many Framers believed that the House of Representatives would likely be called on to select the president due to the likelihood that few candidates would be able to muster a majority in the Electoral College. Party tickets, coupled with the unit rule and elector fidelity, made this scenario far less likely.

While robust arguments exist as to how electoral votes ought to be awarded (district, proportional, or winner-take-all), few today would argue that state legislatures should actually choose electors. Even fewer would likely argue that electors should exercise their independent judgment in choosing the president and vice president over the wishes of those who selected them. And even fewer would likely want the decision of who the president should be to be determined by the House contingency procedure—a procedure that profoundly advantages less populated states, violates the principle of separation of powers, and could lead to a president and vice president of different parties. In fact, these artifacts of the original Electoral College are among the chief targets of proposals to reform the institution.

Many arguments in favor of maintaining the Electoral College point to the wisdom of the Framers of the Constitution. Yet those same Framers struggled mightily over the presidential selection process. Chapter 3 revealed that the Framers believed in many things, state sovereignty, popular sovereignty, and national unity among them. Conventional wisdom notes that the Framers opted for a body of electors because the citizenry either would not have the requisite information or would likely cast their votes for their "favorite sons." Neither rejects a citizen's *right* to select the president. In fact, several Framers vociferously made the case for a national popular vote. Seeking to balance concerns related to the potential dominance of densely populated states relative to less populated states (including slave-holding states), a body of electors was offered as a means to refine the views of the citizens of the respective states. This line of thinking, along with the emergence of the Connecticut Compromise, gave birth to the original Electoral College process.

This brief examination of the Framers' struggles over the Electoral College reveals many layers of representation. Seeking to balance matters ranging from state sovereignty to slavery to civic infrastructure, the Framers produced a *political* rather than a *normative* solution when it came to the selection of the chief executive. The Framers did not begin with normative principles of representation and seek to apply them to the selection of the nation's chief executive. Instead, much like the lawmaking process, they spent months cobbling together a system they could agree to rather than one they believed was optimal. It is worth remembering the primary purpose of the Convention was to remedy problems associated with the Articles of Confederation. Instead of amending the Articles, the Framers ditched them altogether. Their pragmatism and desire to create a system that worked took precedence over any pride they had in the Articles. Toward this point, Schumaker suggests that today's Electoral College could benefit from that same spirit. He states:

> While the Constitution remains a sacred text for most Americans, this understanding is based more on mythology than thoughtful analysis of the sorts of provisions that might enable American government to work more effectively in the twenty-first century and to avoid some of the crises and calamities that might occur but from which we receive little inoculation under our current Constitution—including the Electoral College. (2012, 205)

With the benefit of hindsight, we can evaluate the extent to which the system they created conforms to accepted norms of representation.

Chapter 2 detailed expectations regarding representation in mass democracies. Pitkin categorizes representation along the following dimensions: formalistic, descriptive, symbolic, and substantive. Each relates to the Electoral College in different ways. Given the many goals of the Electoral College, this makes sense, as Pitkin emphasizes that representation is a complicated subject requiring one to examine it from a variety of fronts.

Formalistic representation is of particular importance to understanding the Electoral College in the context of representation. While most Americans do not understand the mechanics of the institution, the process should be clear to presidential aspirants. The process has been in existence for over 200 years and is relatively straightforward. While one may disagree about the rules, they are well known and clear. One obstacle to reform is how new rules might change the process and potential outcomes. I revisit this concern below. Still, changes to the process at the state level occur on a regular basis. Currently, 11 states and the District of Columbia have joined the National Popular Vote (NPV) plan. States continue to consider elector "binding" laws as well as awarding their electoral votes through district or proportional representation rather than by the unit rule. Although not directly related to the Electoral College, state laws related to the franchise may have significant effects on Electoral College outcomes. State laws relating to the body can complicate formalistic representation for the institution because not all states play by the same rules.

Pitkin also discusses the roles of authorization and accountability when it comes to representation. Authorization refers to a representative's ability to act on behalf of others. Few question whether a president who has been selected through the Electoral College process has authority. The magnification effect of the Electoral College has been lauded as a great virtue of the institution in giving newly elected presidents authority. At the same time, misfire elections have generated great controversy and tumult. Additionally, the lack of competition in many states brings into question the degree to which citizens in many states feel represented by the winning candidate. This is closely related to accountability. Many presidents have won the presidency with pluralities of the popular vote. Moreover, almost all presidents simply write off significant swaths of the country and campaign primarily in battleground states. This feature of presidential elections (occurring due to the Electoral College) renders votes as essentially meaningless in a vast majority of states across the country. Unless one lives in a swing state, it is difficult to make the case that the Electoral College allows voters to hold the president accountable for his or her actions. Concerns over accountability represent a significant weakness of the Electoral College

Another component of representation is how, once they are in office, representatives see their role in making public policy. Nearly 400 years ago, Edmund Burke distinguished trustee governance from delegate governance. In the former, representatives are entrusted to make policy independent of their constituency, using their best judgment to come to decisions. In the latter, representatives should make policy in consultation with their constituency, making decisions based on citizen input. Once elected, presidents confront the degree to which they make decisions along the trustee–delegate spectrum. However, the Electoral College process also grapples with the degree to which representatives (i.e., presidential electors) assert their independence or their obedience to the electorate. Electors have largely come to be seen as vestigial organs in the presidential selection process. Originally envisioned to serve as trustees who would use their independent judgment to determine the person best suited to serve as the nation's chief executive, the rise of political parties and the appearance of party tickets changed the expectation of the office considerably. In tandem with the universal practice of electors being chosen by the electorate (rather than by state legislatures), the role of elector changed to that of a rubber stamp. Although states have passed laws to bind electors and remove their independence, many electors appreciate their freedom and some continue to exercise it. The case of elector independence highlights the disconnect between the original Electoral College and the evolved body.

As we have seen, the Electoral College has been the subject of much consternation. After the 2000 election, Burdett Loomis and Paul Schumaker (2002a) brought together nearly 40 political scientists to evaluate how well the Electoral College aligned with American political ideals and practices. Several years later, Gary Bugh (2010b) conducted a similar exercise, bringing together over a dozen scholars who weighed in on the subject. The collective research from these works is instructive. In Bugh's treatment, Schumaker contributed a chapter where he developed nine criteria associated with norms of representation to assess the Electoral College: simplicity, equality, sincerity, neutrality, participation, legitimacy, governance, inclusiveness, and feasibility. He uses these criteria to evaluate the Electoral College as well as commonly proposed alternatives to the status quo. Schumaker contends that these criteria are useful because arguments purporting to use "popular sovereignty" as a basis for maintenance or change are flawed. He states that because "the will of the people can only be determined by counting votes, and different voting procedures yield different outcomes," it is next to impossible to determine what constitutes popular sovereignty (2010, 205).

Simplicity refers to the clarity or complexity of the electoral system. The degree to which the citizenry understands the electoral process determines whether it is viewed as simple or complex. Ideally, an electoral system should be widely understood by its citizenry.

Equality consists of each citizen having an equal value when voting. Political equality is a bedrock principle for democratic regimes.

Sincerity occurs when voters "can readily locate candidates who represent their principles and interests" and are encouraged to vote for such candidates (Schumaker, 2010, 209). Linking voter preference to candidate preference is an important element of Schumaker's notion of sincerity. Voting strategically rather than for one's preferred candidate in an effort not to waste one's vote suggests insincerity in the electoral system. Linking voter preferences to candidate preferences is an important cue elected representatives must draw from in order to effectively make decisions once in office.

For Schumaker, voting systems should not contain advantages favoring particular candidates, voters, groups, or geographic locales over others. Thus, electoral systems should strive for *neutrality*—where no particular candidate, group, voter, or geographic locale is advantaged relative to others.

Regarding *participation*, Schumaker contends that electoral systems should be evaluated relative to their ability to encourage or discourage voter turnout. Democratic republics require citizen participation, and a system that may discourage participation would be undesirable.

Legitimacy has been discussed at length elsewhere in this book and is another criterion Schumaker uses to evaluate electoral systems. Legitimacy occurs when citizens willingly accept that those in power have a right to their positions. Legitimacy is intimately connected to *governance*. Governance is the ability for leaders to "enact and implement policies that address social and economic problems" (Schumaker, 2010, 215). The ability to make and implement public policies is the *raison d'être* of government.

Inclusiveness represents the "diversity of interests and ideals included within electoral and governing organizations" (Schumaker, 2012, p. 217). The Electoral College represents the Framers' attempt to create a system that would lead to broad-based campaigns with wide appeal. The institution is the result of the Framers' struggle over how to create a presidential electoral system that would be inclusive of as many interests as possible in the nascent republic. They recognized that regional candidates or factions supported by narrowly confined interests would fail to engender wide support and would likely lead to great conflict across the nation.

Lastly, recognizing the *feasibility* of any change to the current system is an important element reformers must consider if they wish to change the current Electoral College process. Understanding whether change is possible is an important consideration in any discussion of Electoral College reform proposals.

With these criteria in mind, it is worth recalling the admonition that no electoral system is perfect and flaws are likely to exist in any process used to aggregate votes. Yet, establishing criteria and evaluating systems based on these criteria allow observers to examine the degree to which the criteria are satisfied, emphasized, or deemphasized. These criteria are related to those discussed by Pitkin and Burke. They also have the benefit of directly relating to issues surrounding the Electoral College.

Schumaker concludes that the Electoral College performs poorly in regard to simplicity, equality, neutrality, and participation. Regarding simplicity, he suggests that few citizens understand the process. This is especially the case when it comes to the office of presidential elector. As discussed throughout this book, the Electoral College does not represent all citizens equally. Less populated states are overrepresented in the body. Both sparsely populated and densely populated states are largely neglected on the campaign trail. This fact works against norms of equality and neutrality. Lastly, we have observed that the Electoral College appears to affect voter participation across the states. All things being equal, swing states observe higher participation levels than non-swing states. That so few states fall into the swing state category makes this observation more concerning. Even in the areas in which he finds the Electoral College to be supportive of norms of representation (legitimacy, in-clusiveness, and feasibility), he attributes this to historical virtue rather than actual practice. He argues that because the Electoral College has been intact for over 200 years, it is viewed as legitimate and inclusive, requiring candidates to build coalitions across the country. However, he questions whether the latter occurs, as campaigns largely take place in battleground states and ignore large portions of the country. As for the former, the body has come under scrutiny on a number of occasions due to misfire elections, rogue electors, and disproportionate popular/electoral vote margins. It could be argued that the Electoral College has remained a legitimate institution in spite of its flaws rather than because of its merits. As Schumaker points out, "legitimacy can be undermined when people question the fairness of the results because of the complexities and potential irregularities of the electoral process" (2010, 213).

One particular concern many critics have regarding the Electoral College is the contingency election procedure. Although it has not been used since 1836 (caused by faithless electors), its possibility persists. The contingency procedure favors federal over national interests by giving one vote to each state's delegation in the House. The least populated states have the same voice as the most populated states. This magnifies disparities in population relative to a state's power to select the president. Because the House selects the pres-ident and the Senate selects the vice president, it is possible that the House could select a president of one party while the Senate selects a vice president of the opposing party. This scenario was considered as recently as 2012. In that election, Republicans firmly controlled the House and Democrats controlled the Senate (with the tie-breaking vote of sitting vice president and vice pres-idential candidate Joseph Biden). Had a contingency election occurred, the prospect of a Mitt Romney/Joseph Biden outcome would have created an awkward political spectacle. The contingency procedure fails on most all dimensions regarding norms associated with representation.

In sum, the Electoral College does not perform well in light of the criteria developed to evaluate electoral systems. A number of concerns emerge beyond the typical criticisms that it treats citizens unequally and exhibits significant malapportionment among the states. It is a complex system, fails to generate sincere voting, likely discourages turnout across the country, and is exposed to concerns regarding legitimacy. Keeping in mind that no system of aggregating votes is perfect, Schumaker applied these same criteria to common reform proposals for the Electoral College. These proposals are discussed below.

Proposals to Reform the Electoral College

Robert Bennett estimates that nearly 10 percent of all constitutional amendments have been aimed at reforming or abolishing the Electoral College (2006, 48). These efforts generally consist of three varieties. Not surprisingly, each reform addresses concerns about how the Electoral College distorts representation. First, some have sought to remove the risks associated with rogue electors by making electoral votes "automatic." Second, reformers have sought to address concerns over "wasted votes" precipitated by the existence of the winner-take-all feature most states employ. Third, opponents of the institution have maintained that the system should be abolished in favor of a national popular vote. I discuss each of these reforms below.

The automatic plan is among the more benign reforms to alter the Electoral College. Although faithless votes rarely occur, they have occurred with some frequency over the past 70 years, culminating with the 2016 Hamilton elector movement. While few electors choose to go rogue, an alarming number consider doing so. Their independence is not lost on political parties and concerned citizens throughout the states. A majority of states have taken actions to prevent faithless electors, and the most aggressive statutes exist in states that witnessed faithless votes. Chapters 6 and 7 made clear that members of the Electoral College are routinely lobbied to change their votes. Yet, the automatic plan has never gained much traction. This is likely because (1) few see electors changing the outcome of an election and (2) it represents a Band-Aid for larger concerns over representation regarding the Electoral College.

Over the course of American history, less than 1 percent of all electors have voted contrary to expectations. And while faithless electors did force the Senate to choose the vice president in 1836, they have never changed the outcome of a presidential race. In spite of changes in the expectation that electors will follow their party's wishes, the Constitution has not changed on the matter, and therefore it is widely accepted that electors continue to be free agents. At the state level, statutes to punish faithless electors have mainly been enacted *after* an elector has voted faithlessly. Consequently, a move to adopt the automatic plan is unlikely until a presidential election is thrown into chaos as a result of faithless votes. If that were to happen, a constitutional crisis would likely ensue during the joint tabulation of electoral votes as the Congress has the responsibility of adjudicating disputed ballots. Wholesale change to the Electoral College would be far more likely than a tweak to the system in the wake of such an occurrence.

Short of inertia, the main other rationale to maintain elector independence is that the Constitution is silent as to what happens if a nominee dies from the time of the election to the time the Electoral College meets. Technically, electors would be able to vote for whomever they please if such a situation were to occur. Yet, the notion that mostly anonymous electors would have the best claim to make such a decision is dubious. It would seem, perhaps, that party leadership might have a stronger claim to fill a vacancy. Perhaps even more concerning is that using the same logic, electors could band together to substitute candidates of their own choosing over those offered by the major parties. This is exactly what was attempted as part of the 2016 Hamilton elector campaign. As we saw in Chapter 5, electors from multiple elections have considered such strategies. In spite of the expectation by most citizens that electors serve as delegates, most electors believe they are trustees—just as the original Constitution envisioned them.

A second, more contentious reform is to award electoral votes within a state either proportionally or by congressional district. The impetus behind this category of reform is to make votes more meaningful in states that are generally written off by presidential campaigns. There are key differences between the proportional scheme and the district scheme. In theory, the proportional plan provides a more accurate reflection of the will of the voting populace. For instance, in a state like Ohio, which has 18 electoral votes, it might be relatively easy to determine how to proportionally award electoral votes. A 51–49 outcome would likely yield a 10–8 electoral vote split between the candidates. While this case may be relatively easy to determine, deciding how to award votes proportionally can create great difficulty in many other situations. For instance, in a state with three electoral votes, awarding two electoral votes to the winner and one electoral vote to the loser in a closely contested election (e.g., 51–49) does not accurately reflect the voters' wishes in that state. A 1.53–1.47 split would be truly proportional. Therefore, some have maintained that under the proportional scheme, electoral votes should be awarded based on fractions. Yet, few believe such a change is likely (at best) or constitutional (at worst). As a consequence, much more attention has been devoted to reforms using the district plan.

Proponents claim that the adoption of district representation would have the added virtue of encouraging a more local approach to campaigning. Advocates of state and local power should be in favor of awarding votes in this fashion. Competitive congressional districts have been targeted in states that are uncompetitive in recent elections. In 2008, Barack Obama won the 2nd congressional district in Nebraska while losing the statewide popular vote 57 percent to 42 percent. Similarly, Donald Trump earned an electoral vote from Maine's 2nd district but lost the statewide popular vote in the state 48 percent to 45 percent. Obama and Trump dedicated campaign dollars to these districts that they would not otherwise have done if they did not award their electoral votes based on the district method.

Critics charge that awarding votes using this method would make the redistricting process more polarizing, would replace swing states with swing districts, and would increase the likelihood of "spoiler" candidates receiving electoral votes and depriving any candidate of receiving an Electoral College majority. Edwards warns that the district plan would "dramatically increase the significance of redistricting and even create more incentives for creative gerrymandering than there are now because presidential electors would be at stake" (2004, 153). He notes that "redistricting has made approximately 90 percent of House districts noncompetitive and distorted the translation of votes into seats" (2004, 153). He contends that a move to the district plan would likely worsen this phenomenon. Korzi argues that due to gerrymandering, the winners in the overwhelming majority of congressional districts would be pretty easy to predict in a presidential contest. Consequently, candidates would "target only that relatively small number of competitive districts—they would likely come to be termed 'battleground districts'—avoiding 'safe' districts. We would still be in a situation where large swaths of the United States would not receive attention from the presidential campaigns" (2010, 56).

Lastly, district representation may encourage the presence of regional candidates who may lack national appeal. The rise of Southern Dixiecrats in the 1940s, 1950s, and 1960s was among the reasons the Electoral College came under great scrutiny in the legislature. In 1948, Strom Thurmond captured 39 electoral votes, or 7 percent of all electoral votes, in spite of receiving less than 3 percent of the national popular vote. George Wallace's strong third-party showing in the 1968 election prompted the Bayh-Celler amendment, which represents the last serious proposal to abolish the Electoral College by the US Congress. Although it was endorsed by President Richard Nixon and enjoyed widespread public opinion, the amendment failed to receive a full vote in the House or Senate. The district plan would give citizens the opportunity to vote for their favorite "sons" or "daughters" in highly gerrymandered districts and could lead to multiple candidates receiving electoral votes across the country. If this were to happen, securing an Electoral College majority would likely be more difficult to achieve.

In the wake of the 2016 election, several studies examined what the electoral vote landscape would have looked like if votes had been determined by congressional district rather than by the unit rule. Derek Muller (February 24, 2017) finds that Trump would have won 230 congressional districts to Clinton's 205. Once the popular vote from each state was accounted for, the final tally would have given Trump 290 electoral votes to 248 for Clinton. Under district representation, Trump would still have won the presidency, albeit with a smaller margin of victory. Harry Enten (January 31, 2017) postulates that under such a system, Clinton could have won the national popular vote by as much as 5 percent and still lost the White House due to the ways congressional districts are drawn.

The most radical reform is to discard the system altogether in favor of a national popular vote. Whereas the move to proportional or district representation would be up to each state to decide, the move to a national popular vote would seem to require a constitutional amendment—which most see as a very tall order. It is useful to consider what would be the best means to achieve a popular vote as there are multiple ways of doing so. To do this, I examine the benefits and problems associated with plurality and majority elections.

A plurality election occurs when the candidate receiving the most votes is selected, while a majority requires a candidate to receive 50 percent + 1 of the total votes in order to win an election. This is an important distinction not only for its normative dimensions but because it affects how direct election should be implemented. A primary criticism of the current Electoral College process is the possibility that the "wrong winner" can be selected due to its rules. Subsequent concerns over legitimacy are used to support abolishing the institution in favor of a popular vote. However, candidates selected by a plurality of voters cannot easily claim a mandate to lead when they were not the preference for a majority of voters. Moreover, many observers suggest that the move to a popular vote may introduce more third-party candidates, which would likely thin electoral margins in the national vote. Nearly 40 percent of all presidents came to the office receiving a plurality rather than a majority of the national popular vote. Receiving a majority of the vote has been difficult to achieve and would likely be even more difficult if the Electoral College did not exist. Consequently, many reformers have argued for "instant runoff voting" (IRV) for the direct election of the president.

In contrast to a traditional runoff election between two candidates after an election where no candidate among a group of candidates receives a majority of the vote, IRV asks voters to rank order their preferred candidates. The results are then tabulated by reallocating votes based on voters' rankings. Amy (May 30, 2018) summarizes the process:

> In IRV, voters mark their preferences on the ballot by putting a 1 next to their first choice, a 2 next to their second choice, and so on. A candidate who receives over 50% of the first preference votes is declared the winner. Otherwise, the weakest candidate is eliminated and his or her votes are reallocated to the voters' second choices. This reallocation process continues until one candidate receives a majority of the votes.

It is argued that this process (1) ensures that the candidate chosen has majority support in the electorate, (2) encourages participation among those voters who favor a third-party candidate, (3) decreases the likelihood of a spoiler candidate affecting the outcome of the election, and (4) eliminates the costly process of running a separate runoff election between the top two candidates in a general election. IRV is used in a number of countries and has gained popularity in several cities throughout the United States in recent years. Voters in Maine approved a ballot initiative in 2016 to adopt IRV for statewide races, including those for the governorship, US House, and US Senate.

Discussing the possibility of amending the Constitution in favor of a national popular vote, Schumaker points out that "the obstacles to amending our Constitution have been the graveyard of other reform proposals" (2010, 205). The institution has remained remarkably resilient. Much of this is due to the amendment process. Nonetheless, the direct election of the president has been the favored reform plan among those seeking to alter (or abolish) the Electoral College (Bugh, 2010a, 88). Bugh finds that floor debates, votes, or approvals relating to the Electoral College declined considerably over the past century, with none occurring since 1979 (2010a, 80). He attributes this inertia, in part, to disinterest among Republicans to engage the matter. Just 10 percent of all legislation introduced to reform the body from 1981 to 2010 was introduced by Republican members of Congress (Bugh, 2010a, 90). While the ideology of smaller government and states' rights may account for much of this reluctance, it is also worth recognizing that less populated states are disproportionally represented by Republicans. The alleged benefits of the Electoral College for small state representation likely plays a role in Republicans' lack of interest in reforming the body. In his analysis of reform proposals associated with the Electoral College, Mark McKenzie finds that for "all votes since 1950 on direct election in the Senate, being a small-state senator increases the probability one will oppose direct election by over 20 percent" (2010, 109). While one's political party may affect how one view's the Electoral College, the size of one's state also matters considerably. Sixteen states have five or fewer Electoral College votes and 32 states enjoy a disproportionate Electoral College vote share relative to their populations (recall Table 4.1). This makes amending the Constitution in favor of a direct popular vote especially difficult.

Given the inertia behind a constitutional amendment, another means to achieve a national popular vote has materialized. As mentioned above, the NPV plan seeks to create a compact among states that would go into effect once participating states maintain at least 270 Electoral College votes. States in the compact agree to award all of their electoral votes to the winner of the national popular vote in an effort to ensure the candidate receiving the most votes nationwide ascends to the presidency. Advocates contend that it would make all votes across the country equal, would increase voter turnout (especially in states that are "not in play" due to the unit rule), and would provide a means to avoid misfire elections. Given the many hurdles and the prospective difficulty involved in amending the Constitution, the NPV plan has gained traction among reformers of the Electoral College. Eleven states and the District of Columbia have enacted the plan, representing 172 electoral votes. Connecticut is the most recent state to pass the legislation, enacting it in May 2018.

The NPV plan is not without its critics. Some consider it too clever for its own good, suggesting that it may not pass constitutional muster, could lead to constitutional crises in the selection of electors at the state level, or may be a shortsighted (and potentially illegitimate) means to achieve its purpose. While proponents claim that the compact emphasizes the power of states, opponents contend that the compact infringes on the rights of non-compacting states. They also argue that the compact could not go into effect without congressional approval (Muller, 2007, 393). Muller contends that the NPV plan violates the rights of non-compacting states as they may lose "political influence under the Presidential Electors Clause at the expense of compacting states" (2007, 392). The compact would require congressional approval; absent that approval, he contends it would be unconstitutional. This is an issue that would surely find its way to the courts if the situation presented itself.

Likewise, one can imagine the problems created if a compact state voted for a ticket that lost the national vote but won the Electoral College vote. State election officials would undoubtedly face great pressure to renege on the compact and electors would be besieged to either stand firm or change their vote. Confusion among the citizenry would likely ensue. Such a scenario would be especially thorny for a compact state that voted for the winner of the Electoral College who failed to secure the national popular vote. For instance, had the NPV plan been in effect in 2004 and John Kerry was able to squeak past George W. Bush in Ohio, he would have won the Electoral College vote but would have trailed Bush by 3 million votes across the country. Implementation of the compact would have meant election officials in states such as California, New York, New Jersey, Massachusetts, and Vermont would have had to select Republican electors in spite of their losing by large margins in those states. An uproar over such a process is not difficult to imagine.

Although instructive, this hypothetical scenario is somewhat unfair. Had the NPV plan been in effect, we would expect that the campaigns would have adapted accordingly. They likely would have campaigned very differently, leading to different electoral vote tallies. Still, it reveals potential complexities to the implementation of the NPV plan.

Lastly, because the NPV plan does not occur through the amendment process, it would be open to change from one election to another. The failure to establish a long-term resolution to the presidential selection process is viewed as a significant weakness. This concern is often coupled with the charge that the plan is an "end run" around the Constitution. One of the objectives of the NPV plan is to increase legitimacy in the presidential selection process. However, changing the Electoral College process through a compact among a minority of states would run counter to this aim. The promise of court battles, elector lobbying, and confusion among voters would represent significant hurdles for advocates of the NPV plan.

Evaluating the Electoral College Relative to Norms of Representation

Summarizing research evaluating the merits and deficiencies of the Electoral College, Schumaker indicates that scholars have accepted "that no perfect voting system" exists and that "all methods of aggregating votes have strengths and weaknesses" (2010, 205). The legitimacy of a voting system comes under great scrutiny in close contests. Lutz, Abbott, Allen, and Hanson astutely observe that "no one is happy with the outcome of close elections, but they will occur occasionally no matter which electoral system we use" (2002, 51). The magnification effect due to the unit rule has frequently served to imprint greater legitimacy on those winning close Electoral College contests. Yet, misfire elections have turned close elections into constitutional crises. While no voting system is perfect, it is worth examining how well the Electoral College fares in comparison to alternatives that have been proposed in its place. Attention is focused on the current Electoral College system, reforms centered on the "automatic plan," and reforms directed at popular vote plans.

To examine reform proposals, it is worth recalling the criteria Schumaker offered earlier: simplicity, equality, sincerity, neutrality, participation, legitimacy, governance, inclusiveness, and feasibility. The automatic plan is relatively straightforward, essentially eliminating the office of elector in favor of the automatic tabulation of electoral votes. This would remove concerns of a faithless elector negating hundreds of thousands of votes or, worse, changing the expected outcome of an election.

Many states already have "binding laws" that seek to make electoral votes automatic by removing electors who choose to vote contrary to expectations. Throughout history, most of these statutes were put into place immediately after the appearance of a rogue elector. Short of removal, some states have penalized electors by levying fines for faithless votes. Texas considered several bills to bind electors after experiencing two faithless votes among their electors in the 2016 Electoral College. However, those bills failed to make it out of committee and electors in the state continue to have discretion as to how they cast their ballots.

Removing discretion from electors and making all votes automatic is a relatively modest proposal. It satisfies many of the criteria set forth by Schumaker. It is simple to understand, does not favor one party over another, and could marginally increase voter participation. Further, it would reduce uncertainty, which should benefit legitimacy and sincerity. Removing the office of elector would do little in regard to treating voters across the country equally, nor would it make the process any more or less inclusive. Given the scenarios proposed by the Hamilton elector movement, it may ease concerns regarding governance by limiting deal making by electors made outside of the electoral process.

The potential for mischief among electors has not caused enough alarm for a constitutional amendment. Short of an amendment, the Uniform Faithful Presidential Electors Act has been proposed as an alternative means to curtail faithless votes. Completed by the Uniform Law Commission in 2010 and adopted by five states, the act would provide a uniform means to bind electors for all states who adopt it. Any violation of an elector's pledge would constitute the elector's resignation from office. Wholesale adoption of this act failed to materialize, suggesting that efforts to bind electors will likely continue to occur at the state level.

Whereas proposals to make electoral votes automatic may be seen as minor, proposals to move to a popular vote would abandon the Electoral College process altogether. These proposals generally take two forms: popular plurality or instant runoff elections. In a popular plurality election, the potential to have presidents elected with very low pluralities is strong. This would especially be the case with the emergence of strong third-party or regional campaigns. This concern is among the reasons why instant runoff elections are often proposed if the nation were to select its leader by a nationwide popular vote. As discussed above, the single biggest advantage for IRV is that it ensures that a majority of voters convey a preference for the winning candidate.

Either of these formats could be achieved by two methods: constitutional amendment or the NPV plan. Prospects for a constitutional amendment have been shown to be quite dim. There has been little appetite for wholesale reform in Congress, and the likelihood of rallying three-quarters of the states to support such a change is small—in spite of the fact that presidential elections largely take place in just a handful of states. The NPV plan, which would require considerably fewer states to ensure its passage, has gained momentum as the more likely means to achieve a national popular vote. Yet, under the NPV plan, popular plurality rather than IRV would control who would become the next president. This is an important fact to consider when evaluating reforms to change the Electoral College. If an appetite for change did occur, it is worth considering how these two modes of selection fare compared to one another relative to norms surrounding representation. Schumaker (2010, 204) argues that "there are theoretical and analytical reasons for believing that instant runoff voting may be better than either the current Electoral College or the popular vote system sought by proponents of the interstate compact." He adds that "instant runoff voting may better satisfy widely accepted criteria for evaluating electoral systems than the current or the popular plurality systems" (2010, 204–205).

Schumaker finds that both popular plurality and IRV perform admirably relative to the current Electoral College process. In comparison to the Electoral College, popular plurality is simpler, treats every vote equally, reduces insincere voting, is more neutral, may increase voter turnout, may benefit governance, and is feasible through the NPV plan. Under popular plurality, the candidate with the most votes is declared the winner. This is simple to understand and ostensibly gives voters from across the country an equal voice in the outcome. A common criticism to a national popular vote is that campaigns would focus their attention on the coasts, or at least urban areas. This may or may not be true. It is likely that campaigns will devote resources to turning out their supporters, wherever they reside. This would probably lead campaigns to visit areas that traditionally receive little attention. Democrats would likely spend more time in places with large urban populations, such as New York, Massachusetts, and California. Republicans would likewise visit urban centers in states like Tennessee, Texas, and Georgia. At the same time, both parties would campaign for votes in many areas across the country they have previously ignored. This could increase the cost of campaigns, but it would also likely increase participation. States would no longer be "in or out" of play, which would encourage sincere voting and support neutrality in the presidential selection process (i.e., not favoring certain types of voters).

Whether popular plurality would make governance easier relative to the Electoral College is debatable. This would depend on the size of one's victory as well as how an "expanded" presidential contest might affect congressional races. *If* a national popular vote leads to longer coattails for the incumbent president, then we could expect he or she would have an advantage once assuming office. However, popular plurality runs the risk of selecting leaders who have marginal support from across the country. A president coming to office with less than 40 percent of the vote may have a difficult time with his or her agenda. This is a very real possibility in popular plurality contests.

Additional concerns with popular plurality elections center on legitimacy, inclusiveness, and feasibility. Leaders elected in close contests or with small pluralities would face the greatest risks to legitimacy for popular plurality elections. Allegations of fraud, poor election administration, or an insufficiently broad coalition would likely be raised after a close contest or one where a candidate failed to muster a significant portion of the national vote. Similarly, it is uncertain that popular plurality elections would yield candidates with national appeal. This is especially true in a multiparty contest. Multiparty contests increase the likelihood that a candidate with regional appeal or an ideological extremist could gain a plurality of the vote. This is among the reasons runoff elections are often mandated in multi-candidate races and why IRV is seen as a beneficial alternative to popular plurality elections.

Lastly, although the NPV plan provides a means to achieve a national popular plurality election short of a constitutional amendment, it is not without its faults. Apart from concerns over its constitutionality or practicability, the prospect that enough states will join the compact in the near future seems remote. If serious debate were to occur regarding the implementation of a direct popular vote as a result of the NPV, it is likely to arouse opposition due to concerns over not just whether we should move to a national popular vote, but also the benefits and problems associated with popular plurality elections. IRV retains many of the virtues of popular plurality elections while limiting the problems associated with the practice.

Schumaker suggests IRV may perform best relative to norms associated with representation. Although somewhat complex to understand, it retains high marks regarding equality, sincerity, neutrality, participation, legitimacy, governance, and inclusiveness. Unlike popular plurality elections, it ensures the president and vice president will receive majority support from the electorate. It is far more inclusive, not limiting third-party participation, yet requiring broad support across the electorate. The lack of a "wasted vote" is expected to increase participation for voters across the country. IRV would also reduce biases in favor of the two-party system (increasing sincere voting) as well as biases favoring voters in swing states (treating all voters equally). Lastly, majority support would suggest that incumbent presidents may more easily claim a mandate to pursue their agenda once in office.

The fact that a constitutional amendment (or perhaps a constitutional convention) would be needed for it to occur significantly decreases its feasibility. A pronounced and broad increase in enthusiasm for change would need to occur to make IRV a real possibility to replace the current Electoral College process. The 2016 election was one where many of the faults of the institution came to the surface: a misfire election, faithless electors, and Electoral College lobbying. Yet, public support for the Electoral College *increased* after the 2016 contest, and changes to the body have been a nonstarter in Congress. It would appear unlikely then, that wholesale change to the body is on the immediate horizon.

Parting Thoughts

In the days before the 1976 election, Neal Peirce opined "the nation may face the greatest threat in this century that the antiquated electoral college system will elect the President who lost the popular vote" (Peirce, 1976, 8). Although it came to pass in that election, that outcome has happened twice since, in 2000 and in 2016. Protests and lawsuits accompanied both of those contests, but in each case the losing ticket conceded the election and constitutional crises were averted. Interestingly, support for the Electoral College actually peaked after the 2016 election, with 47 percent of Americans wanting to keep the system (Gallup News Service, December 2, 2016). When Peirce was voicing his concerns, a Gallup survey in 1977 found that a remarkable 73 percent of Americans approved of an amendment to do away with the Electoral College (Gallup News Service, November 16, 2000). Although support for the institution was at its highest after the 2016 election, it is worth noting that 49 percent of Americans in that same survey indicated they would support an amendment to select the president through a popular vote. In 2010, Gary Bugh wrote that "recent elections that have come close to wreaking havoc on the U. S. political system . . . have preceded little, if any, increases in proposed electoral amendments" (Bugh, 2010a, 87). Since the controversial 2016 election, the NPV movement has added an additional state (Connecticut) to the compact, several states have considered laws to bind electors, and several lawsuits have been filed to challenge the winner-take-all feature most states use to award their electoral votes. Perhaps most notably, a president who ascended to the office through a misfire election expressed a preference for a national popular vote. Still, a major overhaul of the Electoral College seems unlikely in the near future.

Douglas Chalmers argues that the rise of "gross inequality, executive recklessness, corruption, and stalemate" suggests that democratic institutions are not operating as they should and are in need of reexamination (2013, 14). Edwards (2004) has vigorously argued that the Electoral College violates the principle of "one person, one vote" and therefore violates political equality. He contends that the Electoral College should be abandoned in favor of a direct popular vote. For Edwards, making every vote equal is the best means to represent the citizens of the entire country. This rationale is consistent with many of the reform proposals aimed at the Electoral College. It emphasizes democracy over republicanism and can be witnessed in many institutional changes in American politics over time. Cynthia Culver Prescott sums up the push toward democratization in the United States:

Over the past two hundred years, our nation has expanded the privileges of citizenship to more and more Americans. African Americans gained citizenship in 1868 and Native Americans in 1924. Women gained the right to vote in 1920. African American suffrage was enshrined in the Constitution in 1870; nearly a century later, the Voting Rights Act of 1965 removed legal barriers against Blacks exercising the franchise. We have made our representative democracy more direct over the past two centuries, particularly through the direct election of senators (1913). Initiative, referendum and recall powers were also introduced in many states during the early twentieth century. Viewed in this context of expanding political rights and greater power for American voters, the Electoral College system appears anachronistic. (2017, 27–28)

Dahl points out a number of demerits relating to the Constitution. He argues that citizens should not hold the document as sacrosanct. He acknowledges that while the Framers were exceptional, eminent, and thoughtful, they were not omniscient. Dahl suggests that the Framers' devotion to pragmatism was more important than their creating a document based on normative principles devoted to ideals. He concludes that the Electoral College process envisioned by the Framers "was almost immediately cast into the dustbin of history by leaders sympathetic with the growing democratic impulses of the American people, among them James Madison himself" (Dahl, 2003, 17). He goes on to note that the Electoral College is perhaps the most obvious example of the Framers' "inability to foresee the shape that politics would assume in a democratic republic" (2003, 17).

The panic Peirce envisioned with the prospect of a misfire election in 1976 largely failed to materialize with the misfire elections in 2000 and in 2016. Still, a great deal of attention was devoted to the integrity of the presidential selection process. In both instances, the winning president's party controlled the House of Representatives and a majority of state legislatures. This likely created little impetus to change the institution. After the 2016 election, this was the case in spite of Trump's insistence that he would prefer to move to a popular vote (Nelson, April 26, 2018).

Concerns over the popular/electoral vote split are likely to persist. Griffin, Teixeira, and Frey (2018) suggest that changing demographics in the United States may make misfire elections even more common. They find that the electorate is becoming older, less White, and more educated. These changes will have different effects for the two major parties. The rising non-White population will likely benefit Democrats, while the aging of America will likely favor

Republicans. However, the changing demographics in the United States will not be evenly distributed across the states, which will likely affect Electoral College strategies and outcomes. New states may emerge as battlegrounds (e.g., Wisconsin, Texas, and Arizona), and some states may lose their precious standing as battlegrounds (e.g., Florida, Michigan, and Pennsylvania). They find "quite a few future scenarios could mimic the result of the 2016 election—a Democratic win in the popular vote with a Republican win in the Electoral College" (2018, 1). It would be hard to imagine that tumult would not occur if one party systematically loses in this fashion. Herron, Francisco, and Yap (2010, 143) note that "there is little protest against elections anywhere in the world. Unless there is a suspicion of fraud or other subversion of the public will, open dissidence rarely occurs."

Morris Fiorina argues that "Americans are closely divided, but we are not deeply divided" (2006, xiii). He attributes this to the binary choices parties often provide. Opinions on many issues are not well defined, creating uncertainty and ambivalence for many citizens. He contends that while a polarized minority exists, most Americans are far less strident in their beliefs. This is important because it provides some credibility to arguments suggesting a national popular vote would be a better means of aggregating votes than the current Electoral College system.

The Electoral College provides few incentives for candidates to run broad campaigns that appeal to voters across the states. Rather than forcing candidates to pay attention to them, the least populated states in the country rarely, if ever, are wooed by presidential aspirants. The same is true among many of the most populated states. Advocates for a national popular vote contend that candidates would campaign across the country—in urban, suburban, and rural areas. It could invigorate state parties and force campaigns to advertise and visit many more places than they do under the Electoral College system. What *exactly* this would look like is uncertain, which is one reason why lawmakers are reluctant to move toward such a change.

Pitkin contends that

> Democratic representation means that the actions of these policy makers are supposed to be responsive to the wishes of the people. Moreover, simple correspondence between what citizens want and what policy makers do is not enough. A benevolent dictatorship is not a representative democracy. The latter depends not only on correspondence or responsiveness but also on institutionalized arrangements that reliably create such connections. The most essential and irreplaceable

of these institutions is the free and competitive national election in which all citizens can participate equally. (1967, 232–234)

Whittington astutely observes that "while the American state constitutions share many similarities with the U. S. Constitution, no state after 1787 decided to follow the federal example and adopt a version of the Electoral College for themselves" (2017, 3). It would be unlikely that such a system would be palatable for most citizens within the American states today. Nonetheless, the Electoral College has persisted at the federal level in spite of hundreds of attempts to amend or abolish it. Edwards has suggested that much of the inertia toward changing the Electoral College is due to its long existence. In arguing in favor of the American Revolution, Thomas Paine began his wildly popular *Common Sense* (1776) by stating that "A long habit of not thinking a thing wrong, gives it a superficial appearance of being right, and raises at first a formidable outcry in defense of custom. But the tumult soon subsides. Time makes more converts than reason."

This study has examined the Electoral College based on its intended purposes and its eventual application. We have seen that the original Electoral College is very different than the evolved Electoral College. The institution has never acted as intended. Political parties have dominated the institution and the acceptance of broad citizen participation changed the body considerably in a very short time. Arguments that draw on the original intent of the Electoral College ignore what the institution has become. Yet, some components of the Electoral College continue to be in limbo. While most citizens would not expect presidential electors to use their own judgment in selecting the president and vice president of the United States, electors continue to believe that they have the right to do so. The steady appearance of faithless electors over the past 70 years illustrates that many are willing to follow through with the act. Recognizing and acknowledging the differences between the original and evolved body is necessary in order to have an informed discourse over the institution's merits and demerits.

When examined relative to expected norms of electoral systems, several prominent weaknesses emerge in the Electoral College. First, it fails to treat all citizens equally. This is a paramount principle in American politics. Proponents rightly point out that the Senate also violates political equality and the Electoral College was born of the same compromise that brought the country the House and Senate structures. Yet, the push toward democratization in the United States has been steady and robust. The operation of the Electoral College itself very quickly moved from one where state legislatures were expected to select electors to one where the citizenry was tasked with the choice. Second, the Electoral College is a complex process that few Americans understand. Electoral systems should be relatively straightforward. Unnecessary complexity discourages turnout and weakens linkages between institutions and the citizenry. Similarly, the Electoral College's attention to swing states discourages turnout and asks citizens to vote for candidates who have no chance of winning any votes in their state. This feature severely hampers accountability. Additionally, misfire elections and the prospect of contingent elections pose a great risk to the legitimacy of incoming presidents. Misfire presidents have tended to have few successes in office and are not rated well by historians. Risks associated with misfire elections far outweigh the alleged benefits of the magnification effect, which we have seen is largely overblown. Lastly, the potential for chicanery posed by faithless electors needlessly exposes the Electoral College to issues of uncertainty. While few electors use their discretion, most believe they have the ability to vote as they please—and a record number did so in 2016.

Just as the original Electoral College was a result of political compromise, any change to the evolved Electoral College will be the result of political dealings. While appealing to empirical data and normative values should be controlling, ultimately policymakers must come to agreement on what best serves the American people. Jeremy Bentham argues that for the representative, "paramount to his duty to a party is, in every occasion, his duty to the whole" (quoted in Fairlie, 1940, 242). It is expected that the representative must sacrifice the desires of the party to the desires of the country when the occasion requires it. Yet, uncertainty as to how changes to the body will affect politicians' own political fortunes will continue to stymie efforts to amend or abolish the Electoral College. Until large numbers of citizens from both parties grow weary of the institution or policymakers believe changes to the body will not hurt their party's fortunes, it is unlikely wholesale change to the Electoral College will occur—in spite of the fact that the body fails to accomplish many of the claims its advocates maintain.

References

Abadi, Mark. November 9, 2016. Donald Trump blasted the Electoral College in 2012, before it gave him the presidency. BusinessInsider.com. http://www.businessinsider.com/donald-trump-electoral-college-popular-vote-2016-11?r=UK&IR=T

Abbott, David, and James Levine. 1991. *Wrong Winner: The Coming Debacle in the Electoral College.* New York: Praeger.

Abby, Phillip, and Michael Debonis. January 23, 2017. Without evidence, Trump tells lawmakers 3 million to 5 million illegal ballots cost him the popular vote. *Washington Post.* https://www.washingtonpost.com/news/post-politics/wp/2017/01/23/at-white-house-trump-tells-congressional-leders-3-5-million-illegal-ballots-cost-him-the-popular-vote/?utm_term=.f38940d75ac9

Alexander, Robert. 2012. *Presidential Electors and the Electoral College: An Examination of Lobbying, Wavering Electors, and Campaigns for Faithless Votes.* Amherst, NY: Cambria Press.

Alexander, Robert. August 8, 2016. Unease in the Electoral College. TheHill.com. http://thehill.com/blogs/pundits-blog/presidential-campaign/290751-unease-in-the-electoral-college

Alexander, Robert. October 31, 2016. Talk of a rigged election could get awkward, fast. TheHill.com. http://thehill.com/blogs/congress-blog/presidential-campaign/303600-talk-of-a-rigged-election-could-get-awkward-fast

Alexander, Robert. January 3, 2017. "Faithless electors"—Not Electoral College—Cause voter suppression. TheHill.com. http://thehill.com/blogs/pundits-blog/presidential-campaign/312549-faithless-electors-not-the-electoral-college-are

Alexander, Robert, David Brown, and Jason Kaseman. 2004. Pinning a face on the Electoral College: A survey of the class of 2000. *PS: Political Science and Politics* 37(4):833–838.

Amy, Douglas. May 30, 2018. Instant runoff voting: No substitute for proportional representation. Fairvote.com. http://www.fairvote.org/instant_runoff_voting_no_substitute_for_pr

Anonymous. March 25, 2017. Personal correspondence, Surveys #16, 90, 104, 150, 255, 283.

Anonymous. April 29, 2017. Personal correspondence, Survey #314.

Anonymous. December 9, 2016. Personal correspondence. Member of Hamilton electors.

Banzhaf, John. 1968 (Winter). One man, 3.312 votes: A mathematical analysis of the Electoral College. *Villanova Law Review* 13(2):304–346.

Barreto, Matt, Mara Cohen-Marks, and Nathan Woods. 2009. Are all precincts created equal? The prevalence of low-quality precincts in low-income and minority communities. *Political Research Quarterly* 62(3):445–458.

BBC News. November 7, 2016. US election 2016: Could vote-swapping help Clinton? BBC.com. https://www.bbc.com/news/blogs-trending-37901022

Beinart, Peter. November 21, 2016. The Electoral College was meant to stop men like Trump from being president. TheAtlantic.com. https://www.theatlantic.com/politics/archive/2016/11/the-electoral-college-was-meant-to-stop-men-like-trump-from-being-president/508310/

Bennett, Robert. 2006. *Taming the Electoral College*. Stanford, CA: Stanford University Press.

Bennett, Robert. 2010. Current Electoral College reform efforts among the states. In *Electoral College Reform: Challenges and Possibilities*, ed. Gary Bugh. Burlington, VT: Ashgate Press, 187–201.

Berman, Ari. May 9, 2017. Wisconsin's voter-ID law suppressed 200,000 votes in 2016 (Trump won by 22,748). *The Nation*. https://www.thenation.com/article/wisconsins-voter-id-law-suppressed-200000-votes-trump-won-by-23000/

Best, Judith. 1975. *The Case Against Direct Election of the President*. Ithaca, NY: Cornell University Press.

Blais, Andre. 2004. How many voters change their minds in the month preceding an election? *PS: Political Science and Politics* 37(4):801–803.

Blais, Andre, Louis Massicotte, and Agnieszka Dobrzynska. 1997. Direct presidential elections: A world summary. *Electoral Studies* 16:441–455.

Blake, Aaron. November 14, 2016. Trump lost the popular vote: That doesn't mean he would have lost a popular vote election. *Washington Post*. https://www.washingtonpost.com/news/the-fix/wp/2016/11/14/trump-lost-the-popular-vote-that-doesnt-mean-he-would-have-lost-a-popular-vote-election/?utm_term=.b17efc038083

Boehmke, Frederick J. 2002. The effect of direct democracy on the size and diversity of state interest group populations. *Journal of Politics* 64:827–844.

Box, Brian, and Joseph Giammo. 2009–2010 (Winter). Late deciders in U.S. presidential elections. *American Review of Politics* 30:333–355.

Brands, H. W. March 31, 2016. How Trump has proved the Founders right. Politico.com. https://www.politico.com/magazine/story/2016/03/trump-founding-fathers-electoral-college-213777

Briffault, Richard. November 16, 2016. The "faithless" elector. Medium.com. https:// medium.com/equal-citizens/richard-briffault-the-faithless-elector-ba7b50fc8ba1

Bruncken, Ernest. 1914. Some neglected factors in law-making. *American Political Science Review* 8(2):222–237.

Bryce, James. 1995. *The American Commonwealth*. Vol. 2, with an introduction by Gary McDowell. Indianapolis, IN: Liberty Fund. http://oll.libertyfund.org/titles/ bryce-the-american-commonwealth-2-vols

Bugh, Gary. 2010a. The challenge of contemporary Electoral College reform. In *Electoral College Reform: Challenges and Possibilities*, ed. Gary Bugh. Burlington, VT: Ashgate Publishing, 77–93.

Bugh, Gary, ed. 2010b. *Electoral College Reform: Challenges and Possibilities*. Burlington, VT: Ashgate Publishing.

Burke, Edmund. 2012. Miscellaneous writings. Indianapolis: Liberty Fund. Retrieved October 27, 2018, from Project MUSE database.

Camden, Jim. November 2, 2016. Evan McMullin supporters pursue "Hail Mary" Electoral College gambit. *Spokesman Review*. http://www.spokesman.com/stories/ 2016/nov/02/evan-mcmullin-supporters-pursue-hail-mary-electora/

Chalmers, Douglas. 2013. *Reforming Democracies: Six Facts About Politics That Demand a New Agenda*. New York: Columbia University Press.

Change.com. Electoral College: Make Hillary Clinton president. https://www. change.org/p/electoral-college-make-hillary-clinton-president-on-december-19- 4a78160a-023c-4ff0-9069-53cee2a095a8; retrieved March 25, 2017.

Cheney, Kyle. October 9, 2016. Will the Electoral College turn on Trump? Politico.com. https://www.politico.com/story/2016/10/electoral-college-trump-clinton-229406

Cheney, Kyle. December 13, 2016. RNC keeps close tabs on the Electoral College vote. Politico.com. https://www.politico.com/story/2016/12/rnc-trump-electoral- college-232537

Cheney, Kyle, and Debenedetti, Gabriel. December 12, 2016. Electors demand intelli- gence briefing before Electoral College vote. Politico.com. https://www.politico. com/story/2016/12/electors-intelligence-briefing-trump-russia-232498

Citrin, Jack, Donald P. Green, and Morris Levy. 2014. The effects of voter ID notifica- tion on voter turnout. *Election Law Journal* 13(2):228–242.

Collinson, Stephen. October 19, 2016. Why Trump's talk of a rigged vote is so dan- gerous. CNN.com. https://www.cnn.com/2016/10/18/politics/donald-trump- rigged-election/index.html

Copeland, Lauren, and Robert Alexander. 2018. It's not over until it's over: Electoral college lobbying after the 2016 presidential election. Manuscript in preparation.

Crezo, Adrienne. December 6, 2016. The first (and last) serious challenge to the Electoral College system. MentalFloss.com. http://cms.mentalfloss.com/node/ 13012/first-and-last-serious-challenge-electoral-college-system

Cronin, Thomas, and Michael Genovese. 2010. *The Paradoxes of the American Presidency*, 4th ed. New York: Oxford University Press.

Culver Prescott, Cynthia. 2017. Citizenship, civil rights, and electoral politics. In *Picking the President: Understanding the Electoral College*, ed. Eric Burin. Grand Forks: Digital Press at the University of North Dakota, 27–30.

Cummings, William. February 17, 2017. Trump falsely claims biggest electoral win since Reagan. *USA Today*. https://www.usatoday.com/story/news/politics/onpolitics/2017/02/16/trump-falsely-claims-biggest-electoral-win-since-reagan/98002648/

Dahl, Robert. 1990 (Autumn). Myth of the presidential mandate. *Political Science Quarterly* 105(3):355–372.

Dahl, Robert A. 2003. *How Democratic Is the American Constitution?* New Haven, CT: Yale University Press.

Donovan, Todd, and Shaun Bowler. 2004. *Reforming the Republic: Democratic Institutions for the New America*. Upper Saddle River, NJ: Prentice Hall.

Duverger, Maurice. 1954. *Political Parties: Their Organization and Activity in the Modern State*. New York: Wiley.

Edwards, George. 2004. *Why the Electoral College Is Bad for America*. New Haven, CT: Yale University Press.

Ely, John H. 1999. The apparent inevitability of mixed government. *Constitutional Commentary* 16:283–292.

Enten, Harry. January 31, 2017. Under a new system, Clinton could have won the popular vote by 5 points and still lost. FiveThirtyEight.com. http://fivethirtyeight.com/features/under-a-new-system-clinton-could-have-won-the-popular-vote-by-5-points-and-still-lost/

Eulau, Heinz, John Wahlke, William Buchanan, and Leroy Ferguson. 1959. The role of the representative: Some empirical observations on the theory of Edmund Burke. *American Political Science Review* 53(3):742–756.

Fairlie, John. 1940. The nature of political representation II. *American Political Science Review* 39:456–466.

FairVote. April 29, 2018. Faithless electors. http://www.fairvote.org/faithless_electors.

Farrand, Max. 1913. *The Framing of the Constitution of the United States*. New Haven, CT: Yale University Press.

Feerick, David. 1968. The Electoral College: Why it ought to be abolished. *Fordham Law Review* 37(1):26–27.

Fiorina, Morris P., with Samuel J. Abrams and Jeremy C. Pope. 2006. *Culture War? The Myth of a Polarized America*, 2nd ed. New York: Pearson Longman.

Gaines, Brian. 2001. Popular myths about popular vote/Electoral College splits. *PS: Political Science and Politics* 34:71–75.

Gallup News Service. November 16, 2000. Americans have long questioned the Electoral College. http://news.gallup.com/poll/2305/americans-long-questioned-electoral-college.aspx

Gallup News Service. December 2, 2016. Americans' support for Electoral College rises sharply. http://news.gallup.com/poll/198917/americans-support-electoral-college-rises-sharply.aspx

Gallup Poll. Trump job approval. http://news.gallup.com/poll/203207/trump-job-approval-weekly.aspx, retrieved April 2, 2018.

Gimple, James, Karen Kauffman, and Shanna Pearson-Merkowitz. 2007. Battleground states versus blackout states: The behavioral implications of modern presidential campaigns. *Journal of Politics* 69(3):786–797.

Golder, Matt. 2005. Democratic electoral systems around the world, 1946–2000. *Electoral Studies* 24:103–121.

Gonzales, Sara. December 20, 2016. Here is a complete list of faithless electors. https://www.theblaze.com/news/2016/12/20/here-is-a-complete-list-of-faithless-electors

Gossett, William. 1970. Direct popular election of the president. *American Bar Association Journal* 56:225–231.

Green, John, John Jackson, and Nancy Clayton. 1999. Issue networks and party elites in 1996. In *The State of the Parties: The Changing Role of Contemporary American Parties*, ed. John Green and Daniel Shea. Lanham, MD: Rowman and Littlefield, 105–119.

Greene, William. January 7, 2017. Bad education, not "faithless electors" causes voter suppression. TheHill.com. http://thehill.com/blogs/pundits-blog/presidential-campaign/313266-bad-education-not-faithless-electors-causes-voter

Griffin, Robert, Ruy Teixeira, and William Frey. April 2018. America's electoral future: Demographic shifts and the future of the Trump coalition. *States of Change*. Center for American Progress, Brookings Institution.

Haider-Markel, Donald, Melvin Dubnick, Richard Elling, David Niven, and Paul Schumaker. 2002. The role of federalism in presidential elections. In *Choosing a President: The Electoral College and Beyond*, ed. Paul D. Schumaker and Burdett A. Loomis. New York: Chatham House, 53–73.

Hajnal, Zoltan, Nazita Lajevardi, and Lindsay Nielson. 2017. Voter identification laws and the suppression of minority votes. *Journal of Politics* 79(2):363–379.

Hardaway, Robert. 1994. *The Electoral College and the Constitution: The Case for Preserving Federalism*. Westport, CT: Praeger.

Hartmann, Margaret. November 5, 2016. Rogue Electoral College voter announces campaign to be most hated person in America. *New York Magazine*. http://nymag.com/daily/intelligencer/2016/11/rouge-electoral-college-voter-refuses-to-vote-for-hillary.html

Heidotting Conley, Patricia. 2001. *Presidential Mandates: How Elections Shape the National Agenda*. Chicago, IL: University of Chicago Press.

Henry, Patrick. June 5, 1788. Anti-Federalist Papers. http://www.let.rug.nl/usa/documents/1786-1800/the-anti-federalist-papers/speech-of-patrick-henry-(june-5-1788).php

Herron, Erik, Ronald Francisco, and Fiona Yap. 2010. Election results and social stability. In *Choosing a President: The Electoral College and Beyond*, ed. Paul D. Schumaker and Burdett A. Loomis. New York: Chatham House, 143–160.

Hill, David, and Seth McKee. 2005. The Electoral College, mobilization, and turnout in the 2000 presidential election. *American Politics Research* 33(5):700–725.

INS v. Chadha. (1983). *Oyez*. https://www.oyez.org/cases/1981/80-1832?page=23&order=title&sort=asc#! Retrieved June 18, 2018.

Jaffe, Sarah. November 15, 2016. Why anti-Trump protests matter. *Rolling Stone*. https://www.rollingstone.com/culture/culture-news/why-anti-trump-protests-matter-113934/

Jones, Jeffrey. January 22, 2018. Trump's first-year job approval worst by 10 points. *Gallup News*. https://news.gallup.com/poll/226154/trump-first-year-job-approval-worst-points.aspx

Judson, Margaret. October 21, 2016. What is the automatic plan? It could be the answer to Electoral College concerns. *Bustle.com*. https://www.bustle.com/articles/190377-what-is-the-automatic-plan-it-could-be-the-answer-to-electoral-college-concerns

Kaminski, John, and Gaspare Saladino, eds. 1988–2009a. Ratification by the states: New York. Vols. 4–7. In *The Documentary History of the Ratification of the Constitution*, ed. John Kaminski, Gaspare Saladino, Richard Leffler, Charles Schoenleber, and Margaret Hogan. Madison, WI: Wisconsin Historical Society.

Kaminski, John, and Gaspare Saladino, eds. 1988–2009b. Ratification by the states: Massachusetts. Vols. 4–7. In *The Documentary History of the Ratification of the Constitution*, ed. John Kaminski, Gaspare Saladino, Richard Leffler, Charles Schoenleber, and Margaret Hogan. Madison, WI: Wisconsin Historical Society.

Katz, Josh. November 8, 2016. Who will be president? *New York Times: The Upshot*. https://www.nytimes.com/interactive/2016/upshot/presidential-polls-forecast.html

Kerbel, Matthew, Michael Cornfield, Marjorie Randon Hershey, and Richard Merelman. 2002. Electoral college reform and media coverage of presidential elections. In *Choosing a President: The Electoral College and Beyond*, ed. Paul D. Schumaker and Burdett A. Loomis. New York: Chatham House, 113–124.

Ketcham, Ralph, ed. 1986. *The Anti-Federalist Papers and the Constitutional Debates*. New York: Mentor.

Kimberling, William. 1992. "The Electoral College." *Essays in Elections 1*. National Clearinghouse on Election Administration, Federal Election Commission. Washington, DC.

King, Alexandra. November 30, 2016. Electoral college voter: I'm getting death threats. CNN. https://www.cnn.com/2016/11/30/politics/banerian-death-threats-cnntv/index.html

Korzi, Michael. 2010. "If the manner of it be not perfect": Thinking through Electoral College reform. In *Electoral College Reform: Challenges and Possibilities*, ed. Gary Bugh. Burlington, VT: Ashgate Publishing, 43–62.

Kurland, Phillip, and Ralph Lerner, eds. 1987. *The Founders' Constitution*. 5 vols. Indianapolis, IN: Liberty Fund.

Liebelson, Dana. January 31, 2013. The GOP's plan to rig the Electoral College, explained: how the GOP could win by losing. *Mother Jones*. https://www.motherjones.com/politics/2013/01/gops-election-rigging-plan-explained/

Light, Larry. November 8, 2016. Markets predict Clinton will beat Trump. CBS News. https://www.cbsnews.com/news/markets-predict-hillary-clinton-will-beat-donald-trump/

Lima, Christiano. February 17, 2017. Survey: Historians rank Obama 12th best president. Politico.com. https://www.politico.com/story/2017/02/all-time-best-president-united-states-rankings-235149

Lineberry, Robert, Darren Davis, Robert Erikson, Richard Herrera, and Priscilla Southwell. 2002. The Electoral College and social cleavages: Ethnicity, class, and geography. In *Choosing a President: The Electoral College and Beyond*, ed. Paul D. Schumaker and Burdett A. Loomis. New York: Chatham House, 161–175.

Lipsitz, Keena. 2009. The consequences of battleground and spectator state residency for political participation. *Political Behavior 31*(2):187–209.

Longley, Lawrence, and Neal Peirce. 1999. *The Electoral College Primer 2000*. New Haven, CT: Yale University Press.

Loomis, Burdett A., Jeffrey Cohen, Bruce Oppenheimer, and James Pfiffner. Electoral college reform, the presidency, and Congress. In *Choosing a President: The Electoral College and Beyond*, ed. Paul D. Schumaker and Burdett A. Loomis. New York: Chatham House, 74–86.

Lutz, Donald, Philip Abbott, Barbara Allen, and Russell Hansen. 2002. The Electoral College in historical and philosophical perspective. In *Choosing a President: The Electoral College and Beyond*, ed. Paul D. Schumaker and Burdett A. Loomis. New York: Chatham House, 31–52.

Madison, James. 1966. *Notes of Debates in the Federal Convention of 1787*. New York: W.W. Norton.

Mainsbridge, Jane. 2003. Rethinking representation. *American Political Science Review 97*(4):515–528.

McCarthy, Justin. September 25, 2015. Majority in U.S. maintain need for third major party. Gallup News. http://news.gallup.com/poll/185891/majority-maintain-need-third-major-party.aspx

McCrone, Donald, and James Kuklinksi. 1979. The delegate theory of representation. *American Journal of Political Science 23*(2):278–300.

McKenzie, Mark. 2010. Systemic biases affecting congressional voting on Electoral College reform. In *Electoral College Reform: Challenges and Possibilities*, ed. Gary Bugh. Burlington, VT: Ashgate Publishing, 95–112.

Muller, Derek. 2007. The compact clause and the national popular vote interstate compact. *Election Law Journal 6*:372.

Muller, Derek. February 24, 2017. Five fictional Electoral College outcomes from the 2016 presidential election. *Excess of Democracy*. http://excessofdemocracy.com/blog/?month=february-2017&view=calendar

National Election Studies. 1995–2002. *The NES Guide to Public Opinion and Electoral Behavior*. http://www.umich.edu/~nes/nesguide/nesguide.htm; retrieved April 30, 2004.

Nelson, Louis. April 26, 2018. Trump pushes to swap Electoral College for popular vote. Politico.com. https://www.politico.com/story/2018/04/26/trump-electoral-college-popular-vote-555148

Norris, Pippa. 1997. Choosing electoral systems: Proportional, majoritarian, and mixed systems. *International Political Science Review* 18(3):297–312.

O'Donnell, Lilly. November 21, 2016. Meet the "Hamilton electors" hoping for an Electoral College revolt." *The Atlantic.* https://www.theatlantic.com/politics/archive/2016/11/meet-the-hamilton-electors-hoping-for-an-electoral-college-revolt/508433/

O'Keefe, Ed. June 17, 2016. Dozens of GOP delegates launch new push to halt Donald Trump. *Washington Post.* https://www.washingtonpost.com/politics/dozens-of-gop-delegates-launch-new-push-to-halt-donald-trump/2016/06/17/e8dcf74e-3491-11e6-8758-d58e76e11b12_story.html?utm_term=.99afocab0f6c

Paine, Thomas. 1776. *Common Sense.* https://www.gutenberg.org/files/147/147-h/147-h.htm

Peirce, Neal. 1968. *The People's President: The Electoral College in American History and the Direct-Vote Alterative.* New York: Simon & Schuster.

Peirce, Neal. October 13, 1976. The Electoral College: The loaded pistol. *Pittsburgh Post-Gazette.* https://news.google.com/newspapers?nid=1129&dat=19761013&id=pqZRAAAAIBAJ&sjid=jGoDAAAAIBAJ&pg=3083,1279333

Peirce, Neal, and Lawrence Longley. 1981. *The People's President, The Electoral College in American History and the Direct Vote Alternative,* rev. ed. New Haven, CT: Yale University Press.

Pew Research Center. November 23, 2015. Beyond distrust: How Americans view their government. http://www.people-press.org/2015/11/23/1-trust-in-government-1958-2015/; retrieved June 8, 2018.

Pitkin, Hannah. 1967. *The Concept of Representation.* Berkeley: University of California Press.

Powell, Bingham G. 2004. Political representation in comparative politics. *Annual Review of Political Science* 7:273–296.

Raju, Manu, Dylan Byers, and Dana Bash. October 4, 2017. Exclusive: Russian-linked Facebook ads targeted Michigan and Wisconsin. CNN.com. http://www.cnn.com/2017/10/03/politics/russian-facebook-ads-michigan-wisconsin/index.html

Rakove, Jack. December 19, 2000. The accidental electors. *New York Times.*

Rappeport, Alan. September 8, 2016. "What is Aleppo?" Gary Johnson asks, in an interview stumble. *New York Times.* https://www.nytimes.com/2016/09/09/us/politics/gary-johnson-aleppo.html

Raskin, Jamin. September 2008. Neither the red states nor the blue states but the United States: the national popular vote and American political democracy. *Election Law Journal* 7(3):188–195.

RealClearPolitics. 2016. General election: Trump vs. Clinton vs. Johnson vs. Stein. RealClearPolitics.com. https://www.realclearpolitics.com/epolls/2016/president/us/general_election_trump_vs_clinton_vs_johnson_vs_stein-5952.html

RealDonaldTrump. November 7, 2012. The Electoral College is a disaster for a democracy. https://twitter.com/realdonaldtrump/status/266038556504494082?lang=en

RealDonaldTrump. November 15, 2016. The Electoral College is actually genius in that it brings all states, including the smaller ones, into play. Campaigning is much different! https://twitter.com/realdonaldtrump/status/798521053551140864?lang=en

Rehfelt, Andrew. 2009. Representation rethought: On trustees, delegates, and gyroscopes in the study of political representation and democracy. *American Political Science Review* 103(2):214–230.

Reynolds v. Sims. (n.d.). *Oyez.* https://www.oyez.org/cases/1963/23; retrieved June 18, 2018.

Riker, William. 1982. *Liberalism Against Populism: A Confrontation Between the Theory of Democracy and the Theory of Social Choice.* San Francisco: W.H. Freeman.

Roche, John. 1961. The Founding Fathers: A reform caucus in action. *American Political Science Review* 55:811.

Rogers, Michael. 2010. A mere deception—a mere *ignis fatuus* on the people of America: Lifting the veil on the Electoral College. In *Electoral College Reform: Challenges and Possibilities*, ed. Gary Bugh. Burlington, VT: Ashgate Publishing, 19–41.

Rosenstone, Steven, and Mark Hansen. 1993. *Mobilization, Participation, and Democracy in America.* New York: Macmillan.

Ross, Tara. 2004. *Enlightened Democracy: The Case for the Electoral College.* Dallas, TX: Colonial Press.

Ross, Tara. November 1, 2004. The Electoral College: Enlightened democracy. Heritage Foundation. https://www.heritage.org/the-constitution/report/the-electoral-college-enlightened-democracy

Rossiter, Clinton. 1960. *Party Politics and America.* Ithaca, NY: Cornell University Press.

Rossiter, Clinton, ed. 1961. Federalist Paper No. 68. In *The Federalist Papers.* New York: Penguin.

Rotskoff, Al. April 16, 2004. Personal interview.

Sabine, George, and Thomas Thorson. 1973. *A History of Political Theory*, 4th ed. Hinsdale, IL: Dryden Press.

Schattschneider, E. E. 1942. *Party Government.* New York: Farrar and Rinehart, Inc.

Schumaker, Paul D. 2002a. Bush, Gore, and the issues of electoral reform. In *Choosing a President: The Electoral College and Beyond*, ed. Paul D. Schumaker and Burdett A. Loomis. New York: Chatham House, 1–9.

Schumaker, Paul D. 2002b. Analyzing the Electoral College and its alternatives. In *Choosing a President: The Electoral College and Beyond*, ed. Paul D. Schumaker and Burdett A. Loomis. New York: Chatham House, 10–30.

Schumaker, Paul D. 2010. The good, the better, the best: Improving on the "acceptable" Electoral College. In *Electoral College Reform: Challenges and Possibilities*, ed. Gary Bugh. Burlington, VT: Ashgate Publishing, 203–222.

Schumaker, Paul D., and Burdett A. Loomis, eds. 2002a. *Choosing a President: The Electoral College and Beyond*. New York: Chatham House.

Schumaker, Paul D., and Burdett A. Loomis. 2002b. Reaching a collective judgment. In *Choosing a President: The Electoral College and Beyond*, ed. Paul D. Schumaker and Burdett A. Loomis. New York: Chatham House, 176–208.

Seipel, Brooke. January 27, 2017. Trump brought up ending Electoral College, but McConnell talked him down: Report. TheHill.com. http://thehill.com/blogs/blog-briefing-room/news/316570-trump-wanted-to-get-rid-of-the-electoral-college-but-mcconnell

Shankman, Andrew. 2017. What the Founders were thinking: Why we have the Electoral College. In *Picking the President: Understanding the Electoral College*, ed. Eric Burin. Grand Forks: The Digital Press at the University of North Dakota, 17–20.

Shaw, Daron. 1999. The methods behind the madness: Presidential Electoral College strategies, 1988–1996. *Journal of Politics* 61(4):893–913.

Shaw, Daron. 2006. *The Race to 270: The Electoral College and the Campaign Strategies of 2000 and 2004*. Chicago, IL: University of Chicago Press.

Shepard, Steven. July 26, 2017. Poll: Half of Trump voters say Trump won popular vote. Politico.com. https://www.politico.com/story/2017/07/26/trump-clinton-popular-vote-240966

Siemers, David. 2002. *Ratifying the Republic: Antifederalists and Federalists in Constitutional Time*. Stanford, CA: Stanford University Press.

Silver, Nate. November 8, 2016. Who will win the presidency? https://projects.fivethirtyeight.com/2016-election-forecast/

Silverstein, Jason. August 4, 2016. Here's how the Electoral College could prevent a President Trump. *New York Daily News*. http://www.nydailynews.com/news/politics/electoral-college-prevent-president-trump-article-1.2738571

Sisneros, Art. November 26, 2016. A conflicted elector in a corrupt college. *The Blessed Path*. https://theblessedpath.com/2016/11/26/conflicted-elector-in-a-corrupt-college/

Slonim, Shlomo. 1986. The Electoral College at Philadelphia: The evolution of an ad hoc Congress for the selection of a president. *Journal of American History* 73(1):35–58.

Stanwood, Edward. 1898. *A History of the Presidency from 1788–1897*. Boston: Houghton Mifflin Company.

Stein, Robert, Paul Johnson, Daron Shaw, and Robert Weissberg. 2002. Citizen participation and Electoral College Reform. In *Choosing a President: The Electoral College and Beyond*, ed. Paul D. Schumaker and Burdett A. Loomis. New York: Chatham House, 125–142.

Stevenson, Richard. November 5, 2004. Confident Bush outlines ambitious plan for 2nd term. *New York Times*. https://www.nytimes.com/2004/11/05/politics/campaign/confident-bush-outlines-ambitious-plan-for-2nd-term.html

Stoke, Harold. 1940. "Who Makes the Laws." Cited in Fairlie, John. 1940. The Nature of Political Representation II. *American Political Science Review* 39:456–466.

Streb, Matthew. 2016. *Rethinking American Electoral Democracy*, 3rd ed. New York: Routledge.

Suprun, Christopher. December 5, 2016. Why I will not cast my electoral vote for Donald Trump. *New York Times*. https://www.nytimes.com/2016/12/05/opinion/why-i-will-not-cast-my-electoral-vote-for-donald-trump.html

Troy, Gil. November 20, 2016. When the Electoral College took down a winner. Thedailybeast.com. https://www.thedailybeast.com/when-the-electoral-college-took-down-a-winner?ref=scroll

Truman, David. 1951. *The Governmental Process*. New York: Alfred A. Knopf.

Two-thirds of presidential campaign is in just 6 states. National Popular Vote. http://www.nationalpopularvote.com/campaign-events-2016

Verba, S., K. L. Schlozman, and H. E. Brady. 1995. *Voice and Equality: Civic Voluntarism in American Politics*. Cambridge, MA: Harvard University Press.

Walsh, Edward. November 17, 2000. A quixotic effort to rally the "faithless"? Electors almost never defect. *Washington Post*, A26.

Weller, Chris, Gus Lubin, and Skye Gould. February 3, 2016. HAMILTON! The amazing true story of America's coolest founding father. BusinessInsider.com. http://www.businessinsider.com/the-true-story-of-alexander-hamilton-2016-1

Whittington, Keith. 2017. Originalism, constitutional construction, and the problem of faithless electors. *Arizona Law Review* 59(4):903–945.

Wilmerding, Lucius. 1958. *The Electoral College*. New Brunswick, NJ: Rutgers University Press.

Wire, Sarah. November 15, 2016. California Sen. Barbara Boxer files long-shot bill to scrap the Electoral College system. *Los Angeles Times*. http://www.latimes.com/politics/essential/la-pol-ca-essential-politics-updates-boxer-files-longshot-bill-to-scrap-the-1479234745-htmlstory.html

Wolak, Jennifer. 2006. The consequences of presidential battleground strategies for citizen engagement. *Political Research Quarterly* 59(3):353–361.

Index

Tables and figures are indicated by an italic *t* and *f* following the page number

Lightning Source UK Ltd.
Milton Keynes UK
UKHW011814031019
350952UK00004B/475/P

9 780190 939434